Toward Socialism

Toward Socialism

William Kashtan
General Secretary, Communist Party of Canada

Selected Writings 1966-1976

Progress Books Toronto 1976

PAPERBACK: ISBN 0-919396-32-1
CLOTHBOUND: ISBN 0-919396-33-X

Cover and book design: DAN HAMMOND
Typesetting: PROMPT GRAPHICS, TORONTO
Printing: EVEREADY PRINTERS, TORONTO

Published by Progress Books
487 Adelaide Street West
Toronto, Canada, M5V 1T4

CANADIAN CATALOGUING IN PUBLICATION DATA

Kashtan, William, 1909-
Toward socialism

1. Communist Party of Canada — Addresses, essays,
lectures. 2. Communism — Canada — Addresses, essays,
lectures. 3. Canada — Politics and government —
1963-   — Addresses, essays, lectures.* I. Title.

JL197.C5K38   329.9'71   C76-017200-5

Contents

Foreword

This selection of writings and speeches by the general secretary of the Communist Party of Canada is a book to be read by every forward-looking Canadian.

The selection chosen represents a comprehensive view of the policies, aims and principles of the Communist Party. Taken together they present the Communist alternative to the bankrupt policies of crisis-ridden state-monopoly capitalism.

The fast-moving events of the past decade — 1966 to 1976 — which the book covers, have produced new conditions of struggle favorable to the working class and democratic movements. They have been stormy years as the monopolists strove, with some success, to fasten the costs of recurring crises and high chronic inflation onto the backs of the working people. On the positive side they were, education-wise, vitally important years as the working people struggled in their own ways for new social and economic policies serving their needs.

The past decade of democratic struggle gave a marked impetus to unity in action of the working class and progressive forces. This higher degree of unity strengthened the fighting capacity of the working people, the trade union movement, progressive social and political organizations. Consequently the whole anti-monopoly movement has achieved a higher appreciation of the social and economic power which resides in the ranks of the working class and its democratic allies.

Significantly influencing the course of events in Canada are the victories won by the international working class and democratic forces over the past ten years. These victories, such as the historic defeat inflicted upon the forces of U.S.

imperialism in Vietnam, Laos and Cambodia; the ending, in Angola and other countries of Africa, of the last colonial empire; and the successful conclusion of the Helsinki Conference on Security and Co-operation in Europe, greatly strengthen the struggle of all the anti-imperialist forces.

The stirring events of the past ten years have served to sharply deepen the crisis of world imperialism, the principal enemy of the forces of peace, national liberation and social progress. Conversely, the past decade witnessed a steady strengthening of the economic and social base of the Soviet Union and the other socialist countries that stand as the bulwark of peace, national liberation and social progress in the world.

The economic, social and political developments of the past ten years, based as they are on the shift in the balance of forces in the world in favor of peace, democracy and socialism, have laid a sound basis for new forward advances for the working class and democratic forces in Canada. What is needed at this time, above all else, are sound working class policies skilfully combining economic and political struggle, unity and solidarity, and militant leadership capable of directing the main blows of the mass movement against monopoly and the governments which pursue policies serving monopoly interests.

What needs to be done now to move the whole anti-monopoly movement forward is what this book is all about. In its pages the events of the past decade are subjected to clear Marxist-Leninist analysis of all facets of Canadian and international developments in order to enrich the whole movement with practical and scientifically sound proposals.

A noteworthy aspect of the book is that in its pages William Kashtan, the outstanding spokesman of the Communist Party of Canada, speaks to the working people of our country.

In these selected works, the author explains the positions of the Communist Party on the vital questions facing Canada and Canadians. He exposes the political and ideological roadblocks that retard forward social development both on the home front and on the front of international working-class and democratic struggle — roadblocks that must be overcome if historical moments are not to be lost.

These questions and the immediate and long-term answers of the Communist Party are dealt with in the pages of this book in live and creative Marxism-Leninism.

Alfred Dewhurst, member,
Central Executive Committee,
Communist Party of Canada.

I

A new course for Canada

Comrade Chairman, fellow delegates, fraternal delegates and guests:

Our Party has just concluded a three month pre-convention discussion in which various aspects of Party policy have been critically examined on the basis of the NEC* policy statement and other resolutions published in *Viewpoint*.

Our Convention is called upon to sum up the discussion and set Party policy for the period ahead.

This period promises to be a stormy and crucial one.

We can already see its embryo in the upsurge of peace action throughout the country in reply to criminal U.S. aggression in Vietnam. We can see it in the ever-growing struggles of workers and the trade union movement for job security, democratic rights and rising living standards. We can see it in the protest actions of farmers particularly in Quebec and Ontario who are entering the fray against monopoly exploitation. We see it in the growing activities of students and young people for peace, civil liberties, democratic reform of education and for social change. We see it in the ferment among intellectuals and in the faculties. We see it too, in the growing number of white-collar and professional groups who are entering the trade union movement and taking the path of strike action in defence of their interests.

The picket line has become a normal part of the Canadian

*National Executive Committee, Communist Party of Canada. By decision of the 19th Convention, the names of this committee and of the National Committee were changed to Central Executive Committee and Central Committee. ED.

scene. Even the provincial police have the urge to picket as could be seen in Quebec recently.

These are but part of an ever-growing opposition to monopoly and its policies which reaches out to the most varied sections of the Canadian people. The results of the federal election reflected this process. In its own way the return of a minority Liberal government expressed dissatisfaction with and lack of confidence in the old parties. On the other hand the increased support given the NDP showed that an ever-growing body of Canadians are seeking new policies and new paths for democratic advance.

What is most typical today is the widespread questioning and criticism of parties and policies, including our own. Never were so many Canadians involved in discussing Canada's prospects in a changing world. Never were so many Canadians involved in re-examining moral and social values.

What these developments show is that conditions are ripening for significant changes in Canadian political life. The prospects are opening up for new alignments, with some sections of monopoly working for a turn to the right while the growing movements of the people are turning against monopoly and to the left. We are now at the beginning of this process which will be accelerated by developments in our country and in the world.

How true this is can be see in the appeal of Walter Gordon recently that the Liberal Party turn to the "left". Whether that party can in fact make such a turn is highly questionable to say the least, tied as it is to monopoly and its policies. However, the fact that Gordon was compelled to propose such a course for the Liberal Party suggests that at the grass roots of Canadian life there is a deep striving and quest for new policies and for parties which express them. This is being further stimulated by growing disillusionment and disgust with the old-line parties which the public airing of filth and corruption around the Gerda Munsinger case has helped to accentuate.

The way the capitalist press has dealt with it, one would think the Munsinger case is the most important matter of security confronting the country today. But the real problem — that of the security of the Canadian people and of

2

Canada itself — is being ignored. So is the role of the RCMP as a state within a state, with no apparent parliamentary or public controls over its activities.

The Canadian people have a right to ask — what is Parliament doing to look after the people's business? What has happened to the war on poverty? What about national medicare and the crisis in education? What about the Freedman report on technological change? What is Parliament doing to cope with rising prices? Not least, if the government is really concerned about a threat to the security of our country, what is being done to prevent the complete takeover of our country by the USA?

From what the Canadian people can see, the old-line politicians are more interested in washing each other's dirty linen in public than in dealing with these vital problems.

It is time that Parliament got on with the job it was elected to do.

Our Party and this Convention must take all these trends and developments fully into account. We must not allow ourselves to be dragged off into blind corners or be dismayed by temporary difficulties. On the contrary, the rising movements of the people, not only here but on a world scale should give us confidence that we are on the right road.

1. THE PATH TO PEACE

It goes without saying that this Convention has much to do.

First and foremost is the extension of the movement for peace which includes within it the struggle for a truly independent and democratic Canadian foreign policy.

We cannot close our eyes to the fact that the international situation has worsened and that U.S. imperialism has embarked on a course which makes the danger of world nuclear war more serious than ever.

Will there be peace or will there be an extension of the war? This question which is of direct concern to Canada is today being determined in Vietnam where the U.S. government has torn the 1954 Geneva Agreements to shreds and has undertaken a criminal war of aggression against the people of Vietnam. Poison gas, napalm bombs, defoliation, destruction of villages and hospitals, the slaughter of civilians — these and much more have been unleashed by the Johnson administration in a vain effort to destroy the will to resist of the Vietnamese people and prevent them from achieving their independence, sovereignty and territorial unity.

U.S. imperialism thought it could drive right through Vietnam like a hot knife through butter. Instead, faced with the heroism and self-sacrifice of a people fighting for its independence, backed by the growing solidarity of peoples everywhere, by the Soviet Union and by the mighty world socialist system, *U.S. imperialism is sinking deeper and deeper into the mire, in a war it cannot win.*

The U.S. government is today virtually isolated. All of progressive mankind, including an ever-growing body of the American people, stands opposed to Washington's criminal and insane policies. And in South Vietnam, despite the puppet Ky regime, backed by U.S. arms and money, a growing political crisis expresses itself in the demand that the U.S. "liberator" go home.

Go home, Yankee! This cry is ringing the world today!

Instead of drawing conclusions from its setbacks and bankrupt policies, the U.S. government is calculatingly escalating the war while pretending it wants to negotiate a settlement. It continues to send more and more armed forces to South Vietnam and has stepped up its air attacks on the Democratic Republic of Vietnam. President Johnson cynically rejected the proposal of the People's Republic of China for a mutual pledge that neither country will be the first to use nuclear arms against the other. Is it not clear that while talking about a "limited" war its real aim is to spread the war to all of Indochina and to China itself?

This is not a matter of indifference for the Canadian people. Canada is deeply involved and will be seriously affected because of the extent to which the government has integrated our country in U.S. war plans.

The road to escalation is the road to incalculable danger for all mankind.

There is only one sensible way out. If the U.S. government seriously wants to negotiate, let it stop its air attacks on the Democratic Republic of Vietnam. Let it withdraw its troops from South Vietnam. Let it state to the world that it will abide strictly by the 1954 Geneva Agreements. Let it negotiate with the National Liberation Front as the representative of the people of South Vietnam.

This is the path to peace. It corresponds with the struggle for peaceful co-existence and with the inalienable right of all peoples to their national independence and freedom. *In fact peace and national freedom are inseparable today.*

This ought to be the policy of our government. Instead it has publicly associated itself with the aims of U.S. policy, aims which jeopardize world peace and the security of our country. The Pearson government claims it is for a peaceful solution of the conflict. Yet at the same time it sells arms to the USA, arms which are used to kill, maim and destroy innocent people in Vietnam.

What kind of neutrality is this? Is this not shameless hypocrisy? Are U.S. dollars for arms more important than world peace? Is this the reason why the government refuses to publicly dissociate itself from U.S. aggression?

Paul Martin, Minister of External Affairs, recently declared he is on a "delicate mission" with the aim of seeking a solution to the present conflict. Such a mission, however, cannot possibly succeed if it is merely a cover and an apology for U.S. policy. It can succeed only if it is based on strict adherence to the 1954 Geneva Agreements, the withdrawal of U.S. troops and a recognition of the right of the Vietnamese people to determine their own destiny free of outside control.

Any other basis is sheer deception of the Canadian people, disservice to the cause of peace and to the security of our own country.

Our Party solidarizes itself fully with the four- and five-point programs of the Democratic Republic of Vietnam and the National Liberation Front of South Vietnam which are a concrete expression of the 1954 Agreements. We salute the heroic people of Vietnam whose epic struggle for freedom and independence will go down in history. We pledge to do all in our power to unite all Canadians to bring an end to U.S. aggression. *And we will not rest until this is achieved.*

It was with this in mind that we sent a Party delegation to Hanoi. We did so not only to solidarize ourselves with their just cause but also to strengthen the Canada-wide movement of support to that cause with the aim of making every Canadian conscious of the need to bring U.S. aggression to an end.

We are now at a decisive turning point in the struggle for peace. U.S. aggression in Vietnam, in Santo Domingo, in the Congo, its continued economic blockade and acts of military provocation against Cuba, the events in Indonesia, Ghana and Rhodesia, no less than the efforts of U.S. imperialism to make nuclear arms available to the West German militarists — all these are part of the drive of U.S. imperialism, backed by other imperialist powers, to reverse the course of history and prevent the inexorable advance of the peoples to national freedom, independence and socialism.

These events have led some people to ask: Has the balance of forces on a world scale shifted in favor of imperialism? Has the struggle for peaceful co-existence of different social systems been invalidated by events?

The answer is no on both counts! We live in a revolutionary age and no counter-revolutionary force can change it. The winds of change have spread to all continents. In Latin America, Africa and Asia profound movements of the people for national and social emancipation are growing in scope and depth. No temporary setbacks and defeats can stop this process. The guarantee for this lies in the growing economic and military strength of the Soviet Union and the world socialist system and the profound impact that system has on world affairs, as it lies in the worldwide movements for peace and freedom. Moreover, imperialism itself is in a deepening crisis and the contradictions within the imperialist system become more acute daily. The crisis in NATO illustrates that process.

Yes, the forces of peace, democracy and socialism are superior to those of imperialism. They are strong enough to curb the imperialist aggressors and prevent them from dragging the world toward atomic disaster. This is why we say that world war is *not* inevitable and that peaceful co-existence *can* be won. But peace and peaceful co-existence of different social systems will not come on a platter. They can only be won by the ceaseless and united efforts of the people.

The strength of the people would be multiplied a thousandfold were the world communist movement united. U.S. imperialism has taken advantage of the divisions in the world movement to step up its aggressive actions. Nowhere is the danger of division as evident as in Vietnam and nowhere would unity of action be as decisive in compelling U.S. imperialism to retreat.

No matter how revolutionary they may sound, those who oppose unity of action against imperialism, those who oppose unity of action in defence of the people of Vietnam are doing a disservice to the cause of peace, national liberation and socialism. History will never forgive them for rejecting a course which could make the struggle against imperialism a more effective one. In saying this it must also be said that the objective conditions for achieving unity of action are bound to have their effects.

Our Party will continue to work perseveringly for such unity of action on the basis of the principles of Marxism-Leninism and proletarian internationalism. We will strengthen in every way our solidarity with all the anti-imperialist forces in the world, be it in Latin America, Africa or Asia. We will strengthen co-operation with Communist and Workers' Parties on the basis of respect for each other's independence and the common struggle against imperialism and for socialism.

2. FOR AN INDEPENDENT CANADIAN FOREIGN POLICY

The sharpened international situation and the increased threat of nuclear war emphasize not only the need for a truly independent and democratic Canadian foreign policy but equally the need to build a powerful movement of the Canadian people to achieve it.

Canada cannot afford the present course taken by the

government which is subordinating the true interests of our country to the aggressive aims of U.S. imperialism. Canada needs a foreign policy which could make her a vital force for peace in the world. The best place to begin is by the government publicly dissociating Canada from U.S. aggression in Vietnam and demanding U.S. withdrawal from that country. Canada should oppose joining the OAS which is a cover for U.S. imperialism and instead extend the hand of friendship to the peoples of Latin America and demand that U.S. troops leave the Dominican Republic.

The interests of our country lie in opposing U.S. interference in the affairs of other countries, and in supporting the efforts of peoples to achieve their national independence and freedom, not in acquiescing in their suppression. *In fact, their victory will strengthen the ability of Canada to maintain its own independence.* The interests of our country lie in achieving genuine disarmament and unalterably opposing the proliferation of nuclear arms. This is why Canada should make it unmistakably clear that it is opposed to West German acquisition of nuclear arms in any way, shape or form. The government should stop acting as front man for the U.S. State Department and recognize the People's Republic of China and the German Democratic Republic and thereby help make the United Nations truly universal. It should extend two-way trade with all the socialist and newly-liberated countries on a mutually satisfactory basis, making credits available where necessary to develop such trade.

The time has also arrived for Canada to re-examine its relationship to NATO and to NORAD. NATO is in a deep crisis, dramatized by France's withdrawal from its military structure. The crisis arises from the fact that the widely-publicized pretence of a threat of Soviet aggression has been exposed as a malicious lie — and from the efforts of the U.S. government to commit NATO to its military adventures in the Far East. It arises from growing opposition to U.S. domination. Not least, it arises from the efforts of the U.S. government to make nuclear arms available to West Germany. In these conditions, Canada's security and peace in Europe lie not in NATO and its military entanglements, but in working for a European Security Pact and the eventual elimination of the NATO and Warsaw Pacts. Similarly with NORAD. The Bomarc missile bases do not enhance the security of our country, they endanger it. Canada's security would best be safeguarded by making it a nuclear-free zone. We join with all those who demand that these bases be closed down.

It is measures like these that can make our country a truly effective force for peace in the world. This is what we advocate. This is what we will press for everywhere we can. This is why this Convention needs to give particular attention to what our Party can do to help strengthen the peace actions of the people, to widen and extend them so that they can embrace millions of Canadians. This is also why every member of our Party, no matter where he or she may be, must become an active fighter for peace.

3. THE STRUGGLE AGAINST FOREIGN CONTROL
AND FOR CANADIAN INDEPENDENCE

The struggle for an independent and democratic foreign policy goes hand in hand with the need for a new direction in domestic policy. At the very center of this problem is the fact of increasing U.S. domination of the Canadian economy, the danger this holds for the sovereignty and independence of our country and its ability to pursue an independent course in foreign affairs, in trade and in independent economic development.

Our country is a victim of U.S. aggression. It is not the kind of aggression the peoples of Vietnam or Santo Domingo suffer from. But it is aggression nevertheless, a more subtle, all-pervasive kind of aggression whose end result would be no different to what the results of U.S. aggression in Vietnam would be if it was not effectively opposed — complete control of our country by a foreign power.

U.S. control and domination over the Canadian economy have already reached a stage which, unless checked and reversed, will lead to the complete loss of our independence and sovereignty. In fact, it is now suggested in some monopoly circles that it is already too late and that no other course is open to Canada except more and more integration with the USA. These Canadian monopoly groups and their press that take this position are striving to redirect the Canadian economy from east-west to north-south. The end result of such a redirection would give U.S. monopoly increasing control over Canada's resources, its power and water as well as its industries. It would close the door to Canada trading with the world. Not least, it would undermine, not raise living standards.

How far Canada has gone down this road can be seen in the economic guidelines imposed on U.S. subsidiaries in Canada by the U.S. government which are themselves a reflection of the growing difficulties of U.S. imperialism. This U.S. move brought to public light what had been apparent for some time — the fact that these subsidiaries are "Trojan horses" in Canada, operating in the interests of the foreign policy of the U.S. government, irrespective of its effect on the Canadian economy. But most important, what it exposed was the fact that these subsidiaries are above Canadian law, that the only laws they subscribe to are the laws of another country. What this means in practice was spelled out in the guidelines themselves which showed that the U.S. government has no compunction about exporting its problems and trying to solve them at other people's expense. It can also be seen in the arrogant way in which the FBI and CIA operate in our country, as if we were already conquered territory. "Operation Camelot" is but one of the more flagrant expressions of this — but not the only one.

This situation did not just happen. It followed directly from the policies of integration pursued by Liberal governments and the dominant monopoly interests in Canada. What before was described as integration is now being called continentalism. But essentially it is the same thing. And again it was the Liberal government, and more particularly Prime Minister Pearson, who advanced this policy as the answer to Canada's future.

It was in the name of continentalism that the auto pact was adopted which, while appearing to give some temporary advantages to the workers in the industry, at the same time is changing the character of the industry and closing the door to the production of Canadian cars.

Continentalism strengthens U.S. domination over an important sector of the economy and would, if extended to other industries, all but eliminate what remains of Canadian independence. It is already leading to the shut-down of some Canadian auto part plants and layoffs for workers.

In the name of continentalism a campaign is now underway to divert Canadian waters to the USA. The campaign emanates from the USA but its supporters are to be found in the old-line parties and in some monopoly circles whose patriotism runs only as far as the dollar sign. This question of water is of crucial importance to Canada and is directly tied up with whether Canadian waters are to be used for independent economic development and the needs of a growing population, for agriculture and power development, or to be used to develop the USA at Canada's expense.

Our Party has long warned of the danger to Canada's sovereignty and independence implicit in growing U.S. domination and control of almost every aspect of Canadian life, including the determination of our foreign policy. We long ago proclaimed there is another path which could and must be taken to ensure genuine national independence for our country. We pointed out the complicity of governments and Canadian monopoly in this sell-out and the need for policies of Canadian control, including nationalization, as a means of re-asserting Canada's sovereignty.

We welcomed the fact that the NDP began to recognize the threat to Canadian independence and developed a public position on this crucial issue.

We likewise welcome Walter Gordon coming forward on this issue and, in a book entitled *A Choice for Canada,* warning of the dangers to Canada that arise from increasing foreign control.

The fact that Mr. Gordon wrote his book at the present time may not be unrelated to the possibility of changes in the leadership of the Liberal Party. It also suggests that Mr. Gordon did not resign from the Cabinet only because of

11

wrong advice he gave on the elections but also because of policy differences having to do with the course Canada should take. Neither is it excluded that Mr. Gordon, in advancing his position and appealing for the Liberal Party to move to the "left", is trying to undermine the base of support of the NDP.

Irrespective of these motivations, what is important is the fact that his book gives expression to a rising Canadian consciousness and to growing opposition to U.S. domination of our country, coinciding with rising opposition and criticism of U.S. aggression in Vietnam and elsewhere. It indicates that forces are emerging among the non-monopolist Canadian capitalists and some sections of monopoly itself who want to weaken U.S. monopoly control, even though they are not yet prepared to give public support to action that is required to save Canada's independence.

This shows again that our Party was correct in saying that the capitalist class is not united and that sharp differences exist among them over the path Canada should take. There are differences between those who base themselves on the home market and those who are based on export trade, between small and medium business and big monopoly, between sections of Canadian monopoly and U.S. monopoly itself.

The working-class movement and our Party need to take these differences and real contradictions fully into account in developing policies and tactics. They are directly related to the question of what forces there are that can be united to weaken and eventually eliminate foreign control, curb monopoly and open the door to independent economic and political development and the march to socialism in our country.

Our Party would commit a sectarian mistake were we to ignore or minimize the significance of the position taken by Mr. Gordon *and fail to see the possibilities of a powerful movement being unleashed among broad sections of the Canadian people for a new direction in domestic policy.* We would be equally short-sighted if we failed to see the possibilities of new alignments and a powerful national and democratic movement shaping up around the central issues of foreign control and a Canadian peace policy that could well become key questions of another federal election within the next few years. Such a prospect could open the door to the achievement of a genuine democratic majority in Parliament.

Nor do we propose to trail behind this or that individual, this or that party. Our position is clear and forthright. We call for democratic public control and public ownership as the way to decisively curb and end U.S. domination of our country. At the same time we will support all intermediary measures and steps which lead to greater measures of democratic Canadian control over our resources and industry. These include the establishment of a Canadian Development Fund directed to stimulate publicly-controlled and independent economic development, as well as measures to produce parts and components for finished products — a policy that would not only mean more employment, but would also be an important step toward helping reduce the enormous international balance of payments problem and lessen our dependence upon the USA.

Democratic Canadian control should include measures to prevent further takeovers by U.S. interests and for the establishment of Crown Corporations to ensure it. It includes measures to compel U.S. subsidiaries to abide by Canadian laws and to be free to trade with all countries. It includes measures to develop a publicly-operated all-Canadian power grid and the adoption of a truly Canadian water policy.

Those who claim that such measures, including public ownership, would lower Canadian living standards are peddling false propaganda. It is simply not true. Such people are acting as apologists for a U.S. takeover of Canada. Nor is it true to say that an independent course for Canada is not possible. This possibility exists precisely because the world is not dominated by the USA, and because of a growing world socialist system and rising movements of the peoples in Asia, Africa and Latin America striving for their freedom. Genuine Canadian independence is directly tied up with the prospects of curbing U.S. aggression and achieving peaceful

13

co-existence. *This is why the fight to end foreign control cannot be separated from Canadian foreign policy — in fact is part of the fight for world peace and the prevention of nuclear war.*

We see no advantage in the solution of the problem of U.S. economic domination by handing over the control and ownership of Canada's resources to Canadian monopoly interests. Such a course would be like jumping from the frying pan into the fire. To regain control of our economy from foreign control requires the public ownership of the large corporations.

We welcome the public debate now opening up on the issue of foreign control. We see the curbing of U.S. control as an extension, an important part of the struggle the Canadian people are engaged in against the policies of monopoly in Canada.

4. FRENCH CANADA AND A NEW CONSTITUTION

Inseparably linked with the issue of independence from U.S. domination is that of the survival of Canada as one country, as a democratically united binational state. In the last few years the whole question of French-English Canadian relationships, of self-determination for French Canada, of a new made-in-Canada Constitution to replace the outmoded, colonialist BNA Act — all this has come to occupy a central place in our public life. The posing in a historically new way of the terms of union of French- and English-speaking Canada is a momentous challenge to all Canadians. While in English Canada there has been taking place a considerable heart-searching and intensive debate (stimulated by the Bi-Bi Commission hearings), in Quebec the "quiet revolution" has entered a new phase in its development.

What best characterizes the situation in French Canada today is the widespread and militant actions of the working class in defence of its interests, as well as the growing numbers of white-collar and professional people who have entered the ranks of the trade union movement and are likewise undertaking militant action for their demands. Students too have gone on strike.

14

What is evident is that growing numbers of the French-Canadian people are striving to get the benefits of the "quiet revolution" from which they have been excluded so far. *What is equally clear is that they are determined to push the "quiet revolution" forward despite the resistance of government and of monopoly interests who want to maintain the status quo.*

These growing struggles are part of and reflect the overwhelming demand for national and economic equality. This is what adds to their significance and, in this sense, is a contribution to the demand for a voluntary, equal union of the two nations and for the adoption of a new Canadian Constitution.

What is lacking, as yet, is the unfolding of a powerful enough national democratic movement in English and French Canada to compel adoption of such a Constitution. *What could accelerate such developments is the merging of the struggle for a new Constitution with the movement for an end to foreign control over the Canadian economy.* In any case, it should be clear by now that long overdue democratic reform measures including changes in tax structure, the reallocation of taxes and a more efficient and workable federal-provincial relationship are adversely affected by the failure to adopt a new Canadian Constitution. This harms the people of English and French Canada alike.

The democratic solution of the constitutional crisis is thus in the interests of both nations, opening up as it would the door to social and economic advance for the Canadian people.

As is already known the Communist Party of Quebec was established last year as a distinct entity. This action was an integral part of the struggle of our Party for a voluntary equal partnership of English and French Canada and the adoption of a new Canadian Constitution.

We are confident that this decision, with which the National Committee concurred, will be warmly greeted by the Convention and will find reflection in the adoption of proposed amendments to the Party Constitution.

The formation of the Communist Party of Quebec should undoubtedly help to extend its influence in the labor and democratic movement and among the genuinely national forces in Quebec. The Communist Party of Quebec can be assured that the entire Party will assist it in every way possible to become that vital force in Quebec political life. Communists all over the country can be equally certain that the Communist Party of Quebec will firmly uphold the banner of proletarian internationalism and the unity of the communist movement in this country.

5. FOR DEMOCRATIC ADVANCE

The recent dips in the stock market have shown how unstable the capitalist economy really is. All General Motors had to do was announce curtailing of production and it was enough to send shivers down the backs of Wall Street, Bay Street and St. James Street. This is not to suggest we are on the eve of an economic slump. What it emphasizes is that when a huge corporation like General Motors sneezes, this immediately affects the state of health of the economy and brings to light its inherent instability.

Let us have no illusions. Notwithstanding the glowing statements of many capitalist economists that the cycle is now under control and the crisis has been licked, this is far from the truth. *There is no capitalism without crisis, nor can there be.*

The basic contradiction between capital and labor continues as can be seen in the widespread strikes of this period. Anarchy of production arising from the essential nature of capitalism likewise continues. So does the problem of the market which arises from the contradiction between expanding production and the limited consumption of the people. Competition between monopolies on an international scale continues, in fact has sharpened in the recent period, and this in turn has resulted in intensified speed-up and increased exploitation of working people here as in all capitalist countries.

Not least, monopoly concentration continues and squeezes out medium and small business as it squeezes growing numbers of farmers off the land.

In saying this it must also be said that state-monopoly

16

capitalism has striven by a combination of measures, above all government intervention in the economy, not only to modify the operation of the cycle but to pursue policies of economic growth. This is a new feature in the situation that we must note.

But policies of economic growth under state-monopoly capitalism also create their own contradictions. In addition to those already mentioned, they tend to "overheat" the economy. They create a growing demand for workers, men and women alike, which in turn strengthens the working class numerically and gives it confidence to fight for a larger share of the values it creates. State-monopoly's policies of economic growth also lead to rising prices and accentuate inflationary tendencies.

Now, in the sixth year of the boom, the government, under pressure of monopoly interests, has begun to pursue a policy of restraint — that is, it has curtailed government expenditures and increased the interest rate, ostensibly with the aim of combatting inflation. But what it is striving for is the weakening of labor's bargaining position and imposing some form of wage restraint on the working class. That this is so can be seen in the proposal that compulsory arbitration replace collective bargaining.

Inflation and rising prices, or deflation and mass unemployment, these are the alternatives monopoly places before working people today. In these alternating policies one can see the inability of state-monopoly capitalism to guarantee ever-rising standards and useful work for a growing labor force.

Is there in fact a danger of inflation in Canada today? Are there too many dollars chasing too few goods? No, this is not the case at all. Even the Economic Council of Canada was compelled to admit there was still a "slack in the economy" and that the economy needed to expand to make work available for an ever-growing labor force, particularly of young people.

But even if inflation were an immediate danger, does it make sense to cut into people's purchasing power by raising prices and taxes and curtailing production? Does not the solution lie in further expanding production and overcoming the international balance of payments crisis by producing parts and components in Canada presently imported from the USA? Would this not help to stop the brain drain to the USA?

The problem confronting Canada is not old-time inflation but monopoly-rigged prices through which huge profits are amassed at the people's expense. Here is where the problem lies and it is here that action is necessary, and in two ways. First, by increasing taxes on the big corporations. Secondly, by providing the means by which consumers can resist monopoly gouging, can get the facts concerning prices and place demands for a public review of price increases, namely, a price review board which could to some degree act as pressure on monopoly-rigged prices.

In the present situation the working class is not confronted so much with the immediate problem of mass unemployment, although this could develop, as with speed-up and with rising prices that eat into purchasing power. This explains why growing numbers of working men and women are fighting so hard and in such militant fashion for substantial wage increases and for other improvements in their living standards, and reject those leaders who refuse to give them effective leadership.

What the workers are saying by their actions is that they want a life of security and dignity. What they are saying is that they should have a voice on how technological change and automation are to be carried through, that workers should have the right to strike during the contract — that they should have a voice on all aspects of economic development in this country.

This is the essence of the strike of the oil workers backed by a threat of a general strike in B.C., of the sick leave of railway workers in northwestern Ontario, and of the battles waged by Oshawa and Peterborough workers against the use of injunctions.

We are not among those who lecture the workers about "keeping their place" and "not rocking the boat". We leave that to the monopoly press. As for us, we take pride in our class, its rising militancy, solidarity and growing unity, all evidence of a growing conscious-

ness of the need for action against monopoly. We support the workers and trade union movement unreservedly in all their struggles to improve their living standards and extend their democratic rights. These struggles are a necessary part of the battle to curb the power of monopoly.

The significance of the growing country-wide struggles of the working class today lies not only in the workers' efforts to win a greater portion of the values they produce. It lies likewise in their efforts to protect themselves against the social and economic consequences of automation. Their fight for job security expresses their determination not to be the victims of automation. Conversely, the increasing use of injunctions by management throughout the country is related to the efforts of monopoly to impose technological change at the expense of the working class and prevent workers from using the strike weapon to defend their jobs and living standards. The threat of imposing compulsory arbitration has the same aim in mind.

The struggle against injunctions and compulsory arbitration is therefore a life and death matter for workers, and not only for workers. At bottom the question is: Shall society permit management to make decisions irrespective of their adverse affects on whole communities as well as working people, or through democratic public controls ensure that the technological revolution can lead to ever-higher living standards for working people and the entire population?

The struggle to limit management rights and put an end to injunctions; the defence of the right to strike, including during the period of the contract; the demand for legislation federally and provincially to make it mandatory for all companies to consult with the union before installing new machinery; the demand for the right of workers to be consulted on production norms as part of the battle for worker control over production and for participation in factory management — these are not only concrete expressions of the struggle for democratic public control and for an extension of the democratic rights of the trade union movement. They are vital if labor is to progress today.

The workers understand that such a struggle must be

waged and won now, not when automation is already in full bloom. Then it will be too late. *This is why the workers and the trade union movement need to unite their efforts on the economic, political and legislative fronts.* Only by so doing can they win their just demands and ensure that the fruits of automation and the technological revolution will benefit the entire population.

Involved here is also the need to enlarge the scope of collective bargaining to include questions hitherto the sole prerogative of management. This is a battle around which the entire trade union movement should unite, as it should unite around the drive to organize the unorganized, particularly the white-collar professions and service industries, and for government action for national medicare and increased pensions.

The technological revolution has likewise placed to the fore the necessity of a united trade union movement and of a trade union structure which will strengthen it through unification of unions in each industry. Not least, recent developments have emphasized anew how urgent it is to strengthen the autonomy and independence of the trade union movement so that it can play an increasingly effective role against foreign control of the Canadian economy. *In fact, as the trade union movement involves itself in the struggle against foreign control, for independent economic development and public ownership, it will create the conditions for strengthening its autonomy, its unity and its independence.*

Now is the time to wage a country-wide campaign for public ownership of the CPR as part of the effort to bring about a publicly operated and fully integrated transportation system.

The technological revolution, which has really only begun and will require a fundamental change in society (including genuine planning based on public ownership) if its benefits are to accrue to the people, places some demands sharply to the fore. In addition to the struggle for job security and for full employment, based on continuous and independent economic development, the labor movement ought to step up its fight for a guaranteed annual wage and a guaranteed annual income, not only for workers but for farmers as well, including the demand for wage parity with U.S. workers.

Moreover, automation raises in sharp relief the entire problem of leisure time based on the necessity of reducing hours of work as productivity rises, with no reduction in take-home pay. Culture and the arts are not something only for the rich and for the middle classes, with the workers finding their culture in the pubs. They are the democratic heritage of all the people and should be made available to them.

The scientific revolution likewise requires a virtual revolution in education.

Universities and all other post-secondary education must be free, coupled with provision for adequate living allowances, to enable all students to complete their training.

In fact, unless this is done at all levels of education our country will be unable to cope adequately with the technological revolution and will therefore fall behind. This applies equally to the extension of vocational training and retraining of workers to give them new skills. These workers ought to receive at least 90 per cent of their earnings while in training.

The workers and the trade union movement have the strength to cope with these new challenges providing they stand united in firm opposition to the policies of monopoly. Unity of workers in every industry, unity of all sections of the trade union movement — this is the key to advance today.

The growing actions of labor have their counterpart in the widening of the democratic and anti-monopoly movements and struggles of the people. All around us we see new demands being raised reflecting the changes taking place in the country and in the economy.

One of the most glaring expressions of these changes is the urban explosion. Growing cities are a charactertistic of this day and age. And they will continue to grow. Out of this arise movements for town planning, better housing, the elimination of slums, improved transportation, elimination of air pollution and countless other issues. These reflect the desire of working people to live as human beings, in clean surroundings and in dignity. New problems likewise arise from the emergence of the "cliff dweller" in the high-rise apartments which now cover many parts of the country.

Slums, poverty, ill health, inadequate education and pensions — these running sores of capitalism stand in sharp contrast to the life of abundance which ought to be the right of every Canadian, if the interests of the people were placed ahead of the profits of monopoly.

These big social issues, including rising taxes, must be our concern as they are the concern of growing numbers of democratic Canadians. To meet these new problems, we need to formulate effective programs. They should be related at the same time to the demand for a reallocation of taxes that would enable the municipalities to deal with such questions, including that of costs of education.

While many of these demands can be won now through united democratic pressures, in the final analysis the new policies Canada must have to become a vital force for peace, to strengthen its independence and make the technological revolution serve society, can only be realized if a democratic majority replaces the old-line parties in Parliament and embarks on far-reaching measures of democratic reform, including public ownership.

All the work of our Party should be directed to help bring this about. In our conditions it is the path through which we will advance to socialism.

Such a democratic majority will not necessarily be limited to the NDP. Other currents reacting to the anti-national pressures and policies of monopoly in French as well as in English Canada may emerge and become part of such a democratic majority. Nor can we exclude the possibility of further fragmentation and realignments shaping up within the old-line parties out of which progressive currents may arise and play their part in the achievement of a democratic majority.

This emphasizes the need for flexibility and close study of the processes at work today that are forcing realignments in Canadian political life. In this connection we need to study more carefully the motives causing many people to support Social Credit as a means of opposing the old-line parties and the forces which back them.

While the formation or crystallization of a genuinely democratic majority is a long-term process, the coming federal election could be an important step to its achievement.

The speed with which such a democratic majority could be attained depends on the role of the working class and particularly on that of the trade union movement, which has yet to play its full part in independent political action.

Here too our Party should make a deeper study of how to merge economic and political issues in ways that can help the workers break away from their support of the old-line parties and *en masse* take the path to independent labor political action. This includes continued and systematic efforts to win the affiliation of trade unions to the NDP.

No less urgent is the need to strengthen labor-farmer cooperation which has seriously declined in the past period. *The basis of such co-operation is mutual self-interest of workers and farmers in the common struggle against monopoly and its policies.* Such common action can and should be taken in the fight to nationalize the CPR and in support of the farmers' demand for a fair share of the national income.

Such action, as well as the development of the most varied movements in French and English Canada alike, merging with the national and democratic struggle to resolve the constitutional crisis, end U.S. domination of the economy and for an independent foreign policy is part of the conditions out of which a democratic majority can eventually be forged.

6. FOR CO-OPERATION OF THE LEFT

This process will be speeded up to the extent that all the forces of the left unite for common aims. This is now crucial.

Our Party cannot do the job alone. The NDP cannot do it alone. Neither can the trade union movement, the farm movements, the women's and peace groups. Nor can the new left among the students and intellectuals, nor the national and democratic forces in Quebec. *Separately they cannot break the power of monopoly. Together they can create the conditions for so doing.*

This is why from this Convention we call for such co-operation. *Our proposal is not a gimmick, a tactic, a manoeuvre. We seek co-operation on a long-term basis to achieve democratic progress today, to achieve a democratic majority tomorrow and eventually to achieve socialism in Canada.*

The basis for such co-operation is here, arising out of the need for new policies of peace, a new direction in economic policy, strengthening the independence of our country, curbing monopoly and extending democracy.

Nor do Communists have to wait for such agreement. We need to strengthen co-operation now with all progressive forces in the trade union movement and facilitate the emergence of a powerful militant movement that can defeat right-wing policy and bring about a truly united trade union movement. We need such co-operation in all peoples' organizations, in the movements for peace, among the women, the farm organizations, in the student movement, everywhere in fact that the battle for progress has to be waged.

We need co-operation and dialogue at the same time. Actually one leads to the other. Growing numbers of people are showing concern, not only with events today, but with the future and how it is to be realized. Interest in socialism is growing. This explains why our Party is often asked by working people and particularly by students: What kind of democratic guarantees will there be under socialism?

We have already declared in our Party Program that we seek and work for a peaceful transition to socialism. We wish to say further that with the achievement of socialism in our country all the democratic rights and institutions of the people will not only be protected but extended. *Socialism will in fact give them a far richer content than capitalism ever can.* Moreover, in our conditions in Canada, distinct from what occurred elsewhere because of different historical circumstances, we reject the idea of a one-party government as a necessary condition for the transition from capitalism to socialism, and work for the formation of a multi-party government whose aim will be the building of socialism. And we see the possibility of opposition parties continuing to function providing they respect the laws of the government building a socialist society.

Such a government would not undertake wholesale nationalization. It would nationalize the key sectors of the economy, in the first place those that are foreign-owned, the banks and credit system. There would be room in a socialist economy for medium and small business to operate until the conditions which made them necessary to society disappear.

Precisely because this is what we strive for, do we emphasize the need for unity and co-operation with those socialist-minded workers who seek a fundamental transformation of capitalist society. We need this co-operation to achieve a socialist society, as we need it today to resolve the problems confronting the working people. *However, it is not enough to want socialism. One must find the path to it and know what forces can bring it about. This is why we work for the unity of the working class and its allies as the foundation upon which a socialist society can be achieved.*

This is not yet fully understood in the new left, many of whom consider that individual and non-class action can achieve fundamental social change and reject all political parties, including our Party. We need to organize a friendly dialogue with the members of the new left, out of which it may be possible not only to clarify positions but also create the conditions for some of them to join the ranks of the fighters for socialism in our country.

In this connection, it used to be said at one time, "Go west young man." More recently this was changed to "Go north young man." We say to these young people and adults too: "Go LEFT young man." Join the Communist Party. This is the road to a bright and happy future.

A dialogue is necessary not only with the new left but with others as well, in the first place with religious-minded Canadians.

The Marxist Quarterly has done a fine job in dealing with this question. The British Columbia committee of our Party is likewise to be commended for arranging discussions with the United Church in that province. Many of our members have rich experience in this regard that needs to become the property of the entire Party.

What we want is not only a dialogue but that out of it conditions are created for broadening united action on all the vital issues of the day. To talk together is important. What we must also learn to do is act together.

We realize that such co-operation has to be worked for. It requires overcoming the prejudice of anti-communism in the labor and democratic movements, and sectarian tendencies among Communists.

Our Party will strive patiently and perseveringly to bring such co-operation about.

7. THE PARTY

How do we see the Party in this situation with a left turn in the making? What should its role be today? These questions have been uppermost in the thinking of members of our Party across the country for some time.

We are not the only ones who have given thought to the Party. After the last Convention the *Toronto Star* wrote an editorial entitled "Why the Reds Fail" in which it drew the conclusion that the source of our failure was that we "continued to talk of Marxism-Leninism."

What the *Toronto Star* sees as the source of our difficulties, we see as the source of our strength. Marxism-Leninism, because it is a science, gives us an ability to relate the present to the future, to see and understand the real processes and contradictions at work in capitalist society, and to make our contribution to the advance of the working class and democratic movements in their struggle against monopoly rule and eventually for the socialist transformation of society.

All aspects of life have to be guided by science and those parties and people who refuse to recognize this, will sooner or later be passed by. Our Party is guided by a science, the science of the laws of social change and this gives us the ability to see beyond temporary difficulties and setbacks.

No, Marxism-Leninism is not a source of weakness but of strength — for our Party and the working class — as the changing world today testifies. It is not Marxism-Leninism but imperialism and its ideology that are in deep-going crisis and on the defensive on a world scale.

We recognize, however, that we work in new conditions in our country and it is our slowness to grasp this fact that is the source of some of our weaknesses today.

These new conditions are expressed in the growing and varied movements of labor and the people reacting to the anti-national policies of monopoly and governments. All of these movements are profoundly democratic in character, all of them in one form or another beginning to challenge monopoly rule.

Our entire Party has not yet given sufficient thought to the significance of these movements. Some comrades still look somewhat narrowly at these developments mainly because we are not directly leading them. If I may say so, some of these comrades are looking at the world of today through sectarian glasses *when what is needed is for the Party to get into all these movements with both feet. Not in order to take them over,* but so as to make our specific and distinct contribution to the winning of the objectives set by these movements and to help them see further ahead.

Actually these developments are a very good thing. They show how much further the working class and democratic movements have advanced since the 20s and 30s, *and that we are not alone,* single-handedly fighting monopoly. *Nor do we want to be alone.* We want to be part of a growing and widening movement of labor and the people, playing our role and winning our spurs on the basis of what we do to help labor and the people win their objectives.

This is the challenge before us.

To the question of what is our specific role today I would say: it is to help unite all the democratic forces and the labor movement in a mighty coalition against monopoly, foreign and Canadian, and to create understanding of the leading role of the working class in such a democratic coalition. *Saying this also determines and underscores our relationship to these forces and the necessity for patient, persevering work to unite them around a common program of action.*

It goes without saying that the Party will not be able to move forward and play an effective role nationally, provincially or locally, by sitting on the sidelines or by remaining a propaganda organization. It will play an effective role if it reacts in timely fashion to all the pressing problems confronting labor and the people and advances constructive alternatives to the policies of monopoly. Not only that. It will play an effective role to the extent that we master the art of integrating and leading various movements of labor and the people and vigorously campaign on those issues which help the labor and democratic movements to advance.

Neither can the Party be effective if it adopts a defensive mentality, is uncertain, indecisive and indefinite in its proposals and almost seems to apologize for its existence. The working class will never turn to such a party and have confidence in it. It will however listen to a party which knows where it is going, has clear-cut answers corresponding with the situation and is willing and able to fight for its policies wherever people are to be found.

It is time, comrades, that some of us stopped apologizing for being alive. It is time a lot of us stopped being on the defensive. It is time we re-established confidence in our Party, in the truth of our policies and the science of Marxism-Leninism upon which it is based! *It is also time we stopped looking inwards for answers when they are to be found in organized work among the people.* And this is not to suggest that Party organization does not need improving.

Confidence based on conviction — this is our most vital and important asset. With such confidence and sound policies reflecting the reality around us, we can begin to move mountains.

The first question for us therefore is not how big or small the Party is, but whether it is *alive* and *doing* things.

We can take pride in the fact that our Party was among the first to warn the Canadian people of the danger of U.S. domination of our country and to point out the way to meet it. We were among the first to advance a coherent program of action to meet the challenge of automation. We were among the first to advance a program to resolve the crisis of Confederation. We were among the first to develop a rounded-out program to challenge monopoly rule. And we were among the first to warn of the dangers of U.S. aggression in Vietnam and elsewhere.

Our Party has participated in election campaigns municipally, provincially and federally, and has been active on various fronts. More and more workers in the unions and other progressive movements are turning to our members for guidance and leadership.

We say this not to boast but to establish the fact that size is not the only criterion — that, above all, it is the ability of a party such as ours to advance correct programs, policies and slogans that can unite labor and the people in action against monopoly and lead to a strengthening of all the forces of democracy and of the working class.

This is not to suggest that we can be satisfied with the size of our present membership. Not at all. We want a larger membership so that our Party can play an ever more effective role in the life of the country. The working class needs a strong Communist Party today to help it find its way forward in the complex conditions of its struggle against monopoly.

This is why we place so much emphasis on building our Party and the press. This is now the biggest challenge before us. We believe a basis for modest growth exists today arising from a growing questioning of the establishment and mounting criticism of monopoly. This can be seen in the growing militancy among workers and sharpening criticism of right-wing policy in the trade union movement, in the emergence of a new left among young people, in the universities and among intellectuals, the growing discrediting of the old-line parties, the increasing understanding of imperialism as the source of war danger, and of socialism as the force for peace. All these are part of the material out of which our Party and press can be built.

The question arises where to build our Party, our youth movement and our press? The answer is: *Everywhere we can!* But above all we should build it among the rising mass movements, be it in industry, among youth, the peace groups, women, the developing farm movements, the upsurge in French Canada. It is here that the most active and vital forces of progress are to be found.

Part of the process of building our Party is to make it known wherever a Party organization exists. The Party however, is known through individuals and what they do, in industry, the community, neighborhood or anywhere else. A Party club that is not alive and a center of activity is not likely to grow. A Party member who keeps to himself or herself is not likely to build the Party or press. A Party member who is not active in his trade union local, in a peace group or people's mass organization is not playing the role he or she should in uniting labor and the people for democratic advance. It is this we need to change in face of a changing and increasingly favorable political climate.

We are not yet fully conscious of the changing attitude toward us, the doors that are opening up in increasing numbers, only requiring that we learn how to walk in. Where we have done so, the atmosphere has invariably been a friendly one. What is most interesting in this connection is that people now seek answers from Communists — not anti-communists — about what we stand for.

Part of the change needs to be reflected in the conscious promotion of a growing number of Party public spokesmen. Our aim should be to have a public spokesman wherever a Party club exists. *The effort to achieve this in all its concreteness and with due regard to the circumstances is part of the struggle to build our Party and make it known to working people throughout the country.*

Equally important is the concentrated attention we need to give to further improve and extend the circulation of our press — the *Canadian Tribune, Pacific Tribune, Combat* and *Scan. We need to help make these papers militant expressions of our Party's views within the growing left in our country,* and as part of it, seek to bring them to shop stewards and militant workers generally, to left and socialist-minded people wherever they are.

We need an effective machinery to undertake such an effort. By itself, the press will not get to those we want to reach. It cannot walk. It can only be carried. Where this is done, as with *Combat* in Quebec, the results are significant. Where comrades have shown sufficient interest to use the press in the struggles of workers, in peace marches and elsewhere the results are salutary, showing what can be done. Is there not a lesson here? Is not the lesson the simple one of having at least one member in each club a press builder and making the entire Party conscious of and responsible for extending the press?

We are proud, and deservedly so, of the appearance of *Scan* which has begun to make an impact among sections of young people. Here too we have a responsibility of helping to build it among those young people who are beginning to move against the establishment and seeking social change. *Scan* can play an important role in our effort to build a socialist-oriented youth movement.

Our experience shows that recruiting young people into the Party is essential if the Party is to be revitalized. At the same time young people need to have an organization of their own. There are differences of opinion among our young comrades on what kind of organization to build. The panel on youth should help the Convention to come to a conclusion on this question.

The representation at this Convention shows that we are beginning to break through on the youth front, that far from having only "aging followers" as the *Toronto Star* characterized our Party editorially following the last Convention, we are slowly beginning to attract young people to our ranks. This is as it should be. *We need the restlessness, the élan, the urge to do things of the young people as much as we need the experience of older members of the Party.* And while the youth versus age approach has no room in our ranks, this should not make us close our eyes to the need for a bold promotion of young people into various areas of responsibility in our Party. This should be reflected in the election of the National Committee and in all Party committees.

Emphasizing the need of directing our main attention to labor and youth is not to suggest that other areas are unimportant. Not at all. All aspects of work are important but some, at a particular stage, have a special importance.

31

The battle of ideas is one of these, particularly today when Marxism has ceased to be a dirty word in Canadian political life. Marxism is now increasingly being accepted as a science which one must take note of, even though it is not acceptable in some quarters. In this situation the dialogue in which we should engage — in the most friendly fashion — is precisely on Marxism and its application to Canadian reality. That interest in Marxism is rising can be seen in the increased sale of Marxist literature particularly in the universities. Unfortunately we are not giving enough attention to how Marxist literature could be brought to those workers who are beginning to turn to the left, those who are not mesmerized by "people's capitalism" or the "affluent society". It is time we corrected this situation, seeing our efforts to do so as part of the stimulation of socialist thinking and action in the broad labor movement.

Next year we shall be marking two significant events — 100 years of Confederation and 50 years of the Great October Socialist Revolution. After a hundred years the Canadian people are still striving to establish their identity and safeguard it from U.S. imperialism. After a hundred years we have still to resolve the crisis of Confederation in the only way it can be resolved — on the basis of a voluntary, equal union of the French- and English-Canadian people and a constitution that embodies it.

In 50 years the Soviet Union, on the basis of working-class power, rose from an economically backward country into one of the mightiest powers in the world, standing as a beacon light to all those who are striving for peace, freedom, independence and socialism. Its existence and the emergence of a world socialist system are helping to transform the world.

We need to do everything we can to make these events into mighty demonstrations of peace and friendship between our two countries and peoples.

In presenting the keynote address, it was not my intention to cover all aspects of the policy statement or other resolutions before you, but rather to highlight some developments that have a bearing on our discussions. The panels and the general discussion should help us hammer out those policies which will advance the cause of peace, independence, democracy and socialism, strengthen our fight for unity and lead to the building of the Party and the press.

I am sure the debate will be sharp and critical, all directed to one crucial point — how to make our Party an effective and vital force in the political life of the country; all of it beamed to strengthening our ties with labor and the youth; all of it leading to strengthening the unity of the working class and democratic forces of our country.

Our Party which has withstood great difficulties over the years is now confronted with new possibilities of advance. How well we take advantage of these possibilities depends on us, on our work, devotion, tenacity, yes, even stubbornness. All of us take pride in our Party and in its great contributions to the working class and democratic forces of our country. This is all the more reason why we express confidence today in the Party's ability to find the road forward that can lead us to the broad highway of advance.

Let us make our Party the party of all those who want to work for a more just, more humane society, a socialist society, the party which step by step and stage by stage indicates to the working class and its allies the way forward to the achievement of this great goal.

CLOSING REMARKS

Comrade Chairman and Comrades:

Now that the Convention is over, how do we estimate its work? What conclusions can we draw from it?

I am sure all of us would agree that it has been a good and hard-working Convention. More than that. It has also been a critical and constructive Convention. It could have been more critical. It could have probed much more into the many complex problems we are called upon to solve. Generally speaking, however, it has been creative in its approach. This positive feature was seen in the fact that, notwithstanding varying points of emphasis which arose in the course of the discussion, at the end there was complete unanimity on the basic policies and line of the Party. The adoption of the policy statement and of other resolutions before the Convention clearly established this fact.

What stood out at this Convention was the spirited and confident note evidenced throughout the discussion. I am sure all the comrades who struck that note did so fully aware that we still have a rough road ahead. What then is the source of this confidence? The first source is the changing and more favorable political climate in Canada, the second is the changing situation in the world, each interacting with and influencing the other. What is characteristic of the present situation is that imperialism, notwithstanding its aggressiveness, has been suffering severe defeats. What is equally characteristic of the present situation is that world socialism, the national liberation movement and the working class in the developed capitalist countries continue to gather strength. On a world scale imperialism is in retreat while the forces of peace, democracy, independence and socialism continue to advance.

It is these objective realities that lead us to conclude that the spirit of confidence expressed in the Convention is not just a wish but based on a changing situation. Our discussion mirrored this change and reflected in its own way the growing struggles of labor and the people, and the impact world events have on them. This we should never lose sight of, despite the difficulties we still have and the problems we need to resolve, bearing in mind that it is these objective realities that are determining the course of world events and of world history.

Because our confidence is not a purely subjective one, we want to make sure it will find its reflection in the way in which the Party is able to advance and bring to labor and the people the policies we have been discussing over the past three and a half days.

There is also another feature of our Convention we need to note — the democratic way in which the Convention handled itself, the participation of almost every member in the discussion, either from the floor or in the panels. Where else in Canada could there be, if one wants to use the term, such a "free-wheeling" discussion, such an exchange of views, tolerance of opinion, at the same time arriving at conclusions that represent majority opinion and become the law for the Party as a whole? This is the way in which we need to work, and learn to work far better than we do. In any case I think we can say with truth and pride that our Party is the most democratic party of any in Canada. Nor is this accidental. It derives from our efforts to find the most peaceful path to the achievement of socialism in Canada, through the extension of democracy all down the line and, to make that possible, to unite behind the working class all the democratic forces of the people.

What has also given this Convention its special stamp is not only the changing realities but also the spirit the younger comrades have brought to it. There is no question about that. The representation here shows that the Party has begun the process of revitalization and renewal, a task we set ourselves at the last Convention. This is a beginning, a good beginning. But I think we must also say that we cannot be satisfied, that we have much further to go. We work not only to become a party of the working class based solidly on the industrial workers of this country; we work not only to become the party of the nation in French and English Canada alike; we also work to become the party of the youth.

In saying this we are required to work in such a way that working youth, student youth, the young generation generally, see in our Party their hopes and aspirations not only for today but for tomorrow. If we emphasize the importance of work among young people it is not because we consider the older generation less important. Our emphasis arises from the fact that the changing population must find its reflection in our Party. The fact is that if the Party is to have a future, part of that future lies in the strength of our Party among young people.

Not least, this Convention showed that our Party with all its difficulties and weaknesses, is not as isolated as we think. The truth of this is to be seen in the fact that the capitalist press, radio and TV, were compelled to note that our Convention took place, were compelled to write and speak about it, were compelled to comment on it. One would think that a "dying party", which is what the press previously called us, could be easily ignored. Apparently the news media were compelled to note that we are very much alive and kicking. This means that socialism, that the Communist Party and its policies, are news today in this country. It also means we need to work to ensure that what we have to say is presented in ways which will impel the capitalist press to note our proposals. The stronger our Party becomes, the wider its base in the labor and democratic movements and among youth, the more likely is this to be the case.

I think we can say then that this Convention laid a good foundation, but only the foundation, for serious advance. Now the real task, the real job begins — what in our judgement are correct policies, good policies, for labor, the youth, for all sections of the working people, must be brought to these sections of the population. This is the challenge before us now.

I want to express again on your behalf warm thanks to Maria Maluende, warm thanks to comrade Claude Lightfoot for their greetings and for the greetings of all fraternal parties. These greetings showed that we are surrounded by many, many friends throughout the world. This is a great source of strength for our Party. For us, solidarity is not just a word. It has a very deep meaning. It has a deep meaning because we must never forget that our cause, the cause of democracy and of the working class is tied up with the struggles of the people throughout the world. Where imperialism loses, progress advances in Canada. Therefore solidarity for us is not a word, solidarity for us is the very heart of our being and our existence.

Here we have special responsibilities to the peoples of Latin America — to do everything we can to assist them in their struggle against U.S. imperialism. Every time a people of Latin America breaks away from imperialism, as heroic Cuba did, it strengthens the fight for independence in Canada and advances the cause of democracy and peace. We therefore cannot be indifferent to the heroic efforts of the peoples of Latin America to achieve their independence and freedom, nor to the acts of provocation by U.S. imperialism against Cuba or other peoples.

We have an obligation to the Communist Party of the United States and to the progressive movement in the United States. In a very real sense the defeat of reaction, the defeat of the "war now" crowd, the defeat of the ultra-right would be, as Claude very aptly and ably indicated to us in his greetings, an enormous source of strength for progress in Canada.

Nor is it only our struggle. What we need to understand and show the Canadian people is that the cause of progress in Latin America, the cause of progress in the United States is tied up with the efforts of the Canadian people to undermine United States domination of our country and to strengthen the forces of national independence and peace on a world scale. So that here again solidarity is not an empty word, solidarity is not the duty of Communists only, solidarity is an obligation for all democratic Canadians.

I am sure this Convention, in the applause it gave to the greetings from fraternal parties, understood this well. Our Party will never fail in its international responsibilities as it will never fail in its struggle to defend the true interests of the Canadian people. We see this as one struggle.

The discussion at this Convention has been very fruitful and helpful to the Party. But I think all of us would agree on the need to dig much more deeply and concretely into Canadian reality and the processes at work today that are stimulating new alignments in Canadian political life.

It is sometimes easier to speak of the new than to see and understand what is new. It is sometimes easier to speak about the old than to say what is old and needs to be thrown away. Not everything that is old is wrong. Not everything that is new is good. Here as in everything else we start from a class viewpoint, the interests of the working class and the cause of socialism. It is from this vantage point that we need to study what is new so as to enable our Party to play an increasingly effective role in the labor and democratic movements.

This has a direct bearing on what we have been discussing at this Convention and what our Party has been discussing over the past number of years — how to help the working class advance the fight for socialism.

What is the path to socialism in our conditions? I am not speaking here of what socialism will be like, but the path to socialism. Wanting socialism is not enough. A Marxist party, a Communist party, if it is to live up to its responsibilities needs to help the working class find that path, help it to unite, ensure that it has allies in that struggle, concentrate its fire on the most reactionary forces that impede its advance, concern itself with all questions no matter how big or small that affect the interests of the working class. Those who advance general propaganda slogans while ignoring the real movements of the people neither move the working people nor help to advance the struggle for socialism.

What is decisive at this time is the need to find the links through which our Party will be able to play an increasingly important role in the labor and democratic movements of our country.

Just look at what is shaping up in our country. We see a whole number of streams developing at the present time. There is the movement for peace. There is the movement in French and English Canada for a new Constitution and for democratic action against foreign control, against United States domination. There is the growing militant strike movement for higher wages and better living standards. There is the upsurge of working-class action against the social and economic effects of automation which lead the workers more and more to press for social change and for a fundamental change in society. There is the developing movement on the part of growing numbers of the Canadian people for the extension of democracy. Each movement stands on its own feet. At the same time they are all united by common bonds — the struggle against foreign and Canadian monopoly. Each unites different sections of society but combined they constitute a growing force which can bring about a sharp change in the relationship of forces in our country. If we do not see these national, democratic and social movements as an integral and inevitable part of the struggle to advance to socialism we will be talking about socialism, comrades, but we won't advance the cause of socialism.

I think we need to see these developments as the decisive movements today. No one can say what may cause sudden sharp changes in the political situation. At one time we thought an economic crisis would be the catalyst of social change. No one can say that we will go through the period of 1929 again, and certainly it would be wrong for us to sit back and wait for such a development. No one can deny that these various streams and movements of the people may make up the ingredients that could become the catalyst of social change in the coming period of time.

Our Party needs to keep its eyes open and play its role on all these fronts as part of these movements, while at the same time strengthening its independent and distinctive role and making its specific contribution to uniting them into a powerful majority that can go to bat and finally curb and destroy monopoly power in this country.

In this sense, we are carrying on a race against time. If we were only to see the leftward trend now developing in Canadian political life and fail to see the right-wing forces trying to check it, while developing their own offensive against this leftward turn, we would be closing our eyes to reality. There is a race on today between the rising progressive movements of the people and the right-wing elements in Canadian political life who are trying and will increasingly try to turn Canada to the right. This is all the more reason why the proposals we have advanced for unity of the democratic forces in Canada are of basic importance. All our work must be directed to enable all the forces of democracy and of the left in this country to find the basis of co-operation and of unity so as to make them the decisive current in Canadian political life.

Here is where the responsibilities of our Party come in. I think the biggest challenge this Convention has put before us is that we have to learn the art of speaking to millions of Canadians, not to a few, not to a hundred, not to a thousand, but to millions of Canadians. But it is not only necessary to learn to speak to those millions. We must learn to work in a way to increasingly earn the right and the privilege to become the voice and conscience of millions of Canadians. We appreciate that this is a process. We cannot give a timetable when this will be realized. But we believe that the policies this Convention has advanced give us the material out of which we can move in that direction. And from this point of view I think we have reason to say we are optimistic about the period ahead, optimistic about the future. In fact we are an optimistic Party. Our optimism is not based on wishful thinking. It is rooted in the reality of our time.

We are not like the pessimist who says "Stop the world, I want to get off". We don't want to stop the world, we want to change it into a better place for mankind. We don't want to get off the world. We want to be active participants in making and shaping history for the good of man. That is our role and that is the aim we set ourselves.

Well, comrades, I want to thank you very deeply for the honor you have bestowed on me in electing me the General Secretary and Leader of the Party. It is a great responsibility. I don't want to promise an easy road. There are no easy roads. If there were such easy roads we would have found them by now. We face a hard, difficult road ahead. All of us are conscious of that. All of us understand it will require the collective efforts, the strength, the wisdom of the whole Party to find, step by step, the ways to build up the strength of the communist movement and the strength of the labor and democratic forces of our country.

All I can say is that I will uphold and defend the policies of the Party and fight for them to the best of my ability. I will fight continually for the unity of our Party which is the source of our strength and the strength of the working class and of democracy. And I am sure that with the co-operation of all members we will be able to apply our generally good policies in ways that can bring results to our Party and democracy in Canada. The real test for us now that our Convention is over is to see to it that these policies become a subject for discussion in our Party, a subject for discussion in the labor and democratic movement, directed toward building our Party and our press and directed toward advancing the cause of peace, democracy and socialism.

Chatting early this evening with one of the delegates, he made a point which I thought was well put. He said, "You know this Convention has unleashed a lot of energy." I think he is right. This Convention has unleashed a lot of energy. Now our task is to use that energy, to apply it in such a way that we can begin to move little mountains and eventually be able to move the big mountain in this country.

Keynote address and closing remarks,
19th Convention, Communist Party of Canada,
May 21-24, 1966.

II

Unity of the left to defeat
U.S. aims and monopoly

This has been a hot summer characterized by Israeli aggression in collusion with U.S. imperialism against Arab states, by further U.S. escalation in Vietnam and by the "rebellion of the poor" in the slums and ghettos of the USA.

It adds up to the fact that we have entered a more dangerous phase in international relations. There is a direct connection between U.S. imperialist aggression in Vietnam and Israeli aggression against Arab states, as there is a connection between the Israeli aggression and the military fascist putsch in Greece, threats to the independence of Cyprus, the mercenary war in the Congo and the conflict in Nigeria.

These are all links in one chain, part of the global strategy of U.S. imperialism. This strategy is directed to crushing the national-liberation movements, interfering in the internal affairs of other countries, regaining lost positions and changing the balance of power on a world scale in favor of imperialism.

However, U.S. imperialism's counter-offensive is everywhere meeting with increasing resistance. More and more people can now see the sharp division between those who are for peace and a peaceful solution of outstanding questions and those who are striving to change international relationships by war and threats of war. With every passing day the truth is being driven home that imperialism by its very nature is a direct menace to the peace of the world, a source of war, exploitation and oppression of other peoples. Despite the U.S. government's efforts, together with the West

German militarists, to keep NATO together it is showing signs of increasing disarray. The more U.S. imperialism tries to drag its allies into active support of its aggression in Vietnam, the deeper grows the crisis in the NATO camp.

Despite its continuing escalation of the war, U.S. policy in Vietnam has reached an impasse. But, instead of ending its bombings, it is accelerating them. Instead of withdrawing its troops, it is increasing their numbers. Voices are now being raised in the U.S. Senate preparedness sub-committee demanding a widening of the air war that would include "closing the port of Haiphong, isolating it from the rest of the country, striking all meaningful targets with military significance and increasing the interdiction of the links of communication from Red China." These proposed acts of U.S. brinkmanship may also include an invasion of the Democratic Republic of Vietnam and the extension of the war in Southeast Asia.

Despite the Israeli military victory in the Middle East, it did not accomplish its main purpose — to overthrow the progressive Arab governments. Nor did it undermine Arab unity or break growing co-operation between the socialist countries and the progressive Arab states. Indeed, this act of aggression in collusion with imperialism has weakened U.S., British and West German imperialist influence in the Middle East and accelerated the processes which will lead to the Arab peoples becoming masters of their own economies and internal social development.

Second thoughts are now developing among those who were temporarily taken in by the false claim that Israel was in danger of being destroyed, claims which were unfortunately given credence by the harmful and dangerous statements of some extreme nationalist spokesmen in the Arab world. Such second thoughts must necessarily include agreement that the government of Israel withdraw its troops to the June 5th line, and that the Arab countries withdraw their state of war declaration as a basis for achieving a political settlement of all outstanding questions, thereby laying the groundwork for peace and security in the Middle East.

One cannot however close one's eyes to the counter-offensive of U.S. imperialism and of the colonialists, and the strategy of the USA in promoting local wars while using the peoples' sentiments for peace and the desire and efforts of the socialist countries to prevent war as a form of blackmail, a means through which to change the balance of forces on a world scale.

This strategy can be defeated provided there is unity and co-ordination of effort by all anti-imperialist and socialist forces in the world. The necessity for this was never more obvious than it is today, and its absence is used by U.S. imperialism to continue its counter-offensive. An anti-imperialist united front based on the cohesion of the socialist states and Communist and Workers' Parties could deter imperialist aggressive aims, could make more effective the aid given Vietnam by the socialist countries and all progressive forces throughout the world, and could compel the Israeli government to withdraw its troops to the June 5th line.

Unfortunately such unity is being hindered by the splitting and provocative actions of Mao Tse-tung and his group in China, actions which objectively play into the hands of U.S. imperialism and encourage it to continue its reckless course of escalation and brinkmanship. This cannot but be condemned as a disservice to the cause of peace, national liberation and socialism.

The varied actions of the peace movements, the NDP, the youth movement and sections of the trade union movement all reflect the rising tide of opposition to U.S. aggression and to the craven subservience and complicity of the Pearson government with U.S. criminal action. Instead of the government using the growing isolation of the USA arising from its aggression to strengthen the independent voice of Canada in world affairs, and particularly with regard to Vietnam, it appears to be acquiescing in that policy more than ever, hoping thereby to get additional war orders for U.S.-owned aircraft and other industries in Canada, extend integration in other industries following upon the auto pact and ease Canada's international balance of payments.

That this is the reason for the government's "quiet" diplomacy is seen in the interview with Prime Minister Pearson in the July issue of *Maclean's* magazine. Said Mr. Pearson: "If I thought a public statement or a public posture by me or Mr. Martin would help to bring about an end to the fighting, I wouldn't hesitate to make it." But — "We can't ignore the fact that a first result of any open breach with the U.S. over Vietnam would be a more critical examination in Washington of certain aspects of our relationships from which we get great benefit. It's not a very comforting thought, but when you have 60 per cent or so of your trade with one country you are in a position of considerable economic dependence."

This statement of Prime Minister Pearson has again revealed that peace and genuine independence for Canada are inseparable, that if Canada is to pursue an independent foreign policy it must achieve democratic control over the economy through nationalization; and that the achievement of this objective requires an independent foreign policy, including withdrawal of Canada from NATO and NORAD and the adoption of a position of neutrality. In saying this we must reiterate what was emphasized at our last Central Committee meeting: the fight for peace and dissociation of Canada from U.S. aggression against the Vietnamese people would today be the most effective way of strengthening Canadian independence.

Prime Minister Pearson, however, presents only half a truth when he infers that Canada allegedly benefits from the U.S. war in Vietnam. The fact is that while that war may benefit some U.S.-owned corporations in Canada it is having a serious effect on the Canadian economy and on the Canadian people. It is the prime cause of inflation, of rising prices and taxes and of eroding purchasing power for the Canadian people. Contrary to what Prime Minister Pearson says the Canadian people are paying for the U.S. war at the expense of their living standards. At the same time this war is responsible in large measure for the government's current economic drive and the efforts afoot to scuttle social welfare measures.

Medicare which was to have been implemented in 1968 is presently under attack. While Conservative and Social Credit spokesmen lead the attack, the insurance companies are not far behind. On the one hand they argue that Canada needs to decide on priorities and that education comes first, ahead of medicare in terms of priorities. On the other hand they argue that if medicare is to be enacted it should be emasculated of its content and be carried out on the basis of need. In practice this means applying a means test and eliminating the universal character of this long overdue measure.

Decent housing for Canadians has become one of the first victims of the "economy" drive despite the persistent and acute housing shortage in the growing urban centers of the country. It is a commentary on government and monopoly policy that while Canada has one of the highest living standards of the world, it is twelfth in ratio of housing completions among the highly-developed capitalist countries.

Proposed improvements in unemployment insurance rates which were to have been implemented in this session of Parliament have become another victim of the economy drive and shelved to next year.

At the same time the Freedman Commission recommendations on technological change appear to have been permanently discarded, while the Labor Standards Act which was to have made the 40-hour work week applicable in industry under federal jurisdiction is not being enforced by the government, thus compelling seamen to strike to assure its implementation in the shipping industry.

While cutting down on the vital needs of the Canadian people and compelling them to pay the cost of the Vietnam war and the economic slowdown, the government twiddles its thumbs when it comes to curbing price rises. Prices continue to go up on food, clothing and rents while taxes continue to rise, thus eroding purchasing power and the real living standards of the people. The government is equally slow when it comes to implementing the Carter Commission proposals, with increasing indications they too will be shelved as a result of monopoly pressures.

At the same time there is a growing concentration of monopoly in all aspects of the economy. The *Financial Post* drew attention to this recently pointing out that 100 companies, most of them foreign-owned and controlled, dominate the economy. As it said, "No matter which yardstick is used, there is no denying the domination this relatively small number of large corporations exercises over the Canadian economy. They account for 42 per cent of sales of all Canadian companies, excluding merchandising and financial institutions, and account for 65 per cent of earnings of all Canadian industrial, utility and resources companies."

This concentration of power and of production, which in turn influences prices, is left untouched by the government. Indeed, government policy is directed to facilitating the process of concentration, as the Kennedy Round proposals indicate, even though it will adversely affect employment for numbers of workers and further tie Canada to the U.S. economy.

At home the crisis of Confederation has reached a new stage in its development. For a time it appeared as if the establishment was successful in pushing this question into the background, using Expo as a means of so doing. The de Gaulle visit and his intervention, as well as the different reactions to his remarks in French and English Canada, revealed the depth of this crisis. In fact the upsurge of opinion in French Canada on this question has demonstrated unequivocally that it cannot be kept under the rug any longer.

It is this which is compelling the old-line parties to manoeuvre if they are to maintain or gain a firm foothold in Quebec and advance their political fortunes.

The struggle for national self-determination is likely to grow in intensity in French Canada and lead to an upsurge of mass action in the coming period. What it indicates is that the "quiet revolution" is increasingly taking on the character of a democratic revolution.

It is on this basis that a voluntary equal partnership between the English- and French-Canadian people can find expression in a new Constitution.

It should be obvious that this new stage of the struggle requires a shift in emphasis by the Party, particularly in

English Canada. Hitherto we have been stressing the need for a new Constitution. What we need to place in the fore-front at this time is the core of the problem — that of the right to national self-determination, including the right to secede. We are aware of the fact that this is not understood and will require thorough-going explanation, but it is a responsibility the Party must undertake. In French Canada the Communist Party of Quebec is called upon to enter into vigorous debate with others, including the separatists, on this issue to help strengthen in every way the conscious role of the working class in the struggle to achieve national self-determination. It is by relating the national and democratic issues to the basic social and economic issues confronting the working class that the Party can begin to play an ever-growing role in the political arena.

The demand for national self-determination in French Canada finds its counterpart on an all-Canadian scale in widening opposition to monopoly and its policies. Workers are rejecting out of hand proposals for labor-management co-operation. The strike movement is continuing unabated as workers strive to win a larger portion of the wealth they produce and to overcome wage differentials between U.S. and Canadian workers, as the auto workers aim to do. At the same time a stronger trend toward unity is making itself evident in the trade union movement, exemplified in the merger between the Mine Mill and Steel Unions and in new approaches being developed between the CNTU and the Quebec Federation of Labor. Increasingly the trade union movement is concentrating attention on the organization of the unorganized, particularly in the professional and white-collar fields, alongside efforts at achieving mergers of unions to meet the challenge of monopoly control and technological and structural changes in the economy. New sections of working people are being organized, adding to the economic and political strength of labor and the democratic movement.

University students have advanced the slogan of "student power" through which to democratize university life and give them a say, a demand which is also being taken up by high school students. At the same time a growing trend leftward is discernible among sections of students.

Farmers who for some time seemed to be outside the growing democratic movements of the people are beginning to move in defence of their interests, advancing varied and militant forms of struggle — from marches, to boycott, to strike — in order to improve their conditions of life.

Workers, farmers, students, housewives, professional and other groups, all these are in action against monopoly and its policies. The ingredients of an anti-monopoly coalition are in the making and being added to by the national and democratic movement in French Canada for national self-determination and equality and by the growing trend toward independent labor political action among Quebec workers. The groundwork is thus being extended for ever-widening independent political action in English and French Canada.

None of the basic economic and social problems confronting the country and the Canadian people can or will be solved by state-monopoly capital. As the evidence shows state-monopoly policy is directed to strengthening monopoly capital at the expense of the people.

To prevent a shift to the right and begin to tackle the fundamental problems before the country in a radically new way obviously requires a shift in the balance of political and social forces in the country in favor of working-class and democratic forces. This is a process which will take a longer or shorter period of time depending on a number of circumstances, not least on the extent to which unity and co-operation of the left is achieved.

This is why we place the struggle for unity of the left to the fore at this stage. However, it is not enough to want unity. What we need is a concrete examination of the scope of the problem, our experiences in the struggle for unity and what we should focus on at this stage to advance the struggle.

The NDP has so far rejected the idea of co-operation of the left, including our Party, and taken the position that unity can be found within the NDP.

This line of argument, pushed by the right wing, attempts to slur over the essential content of our struggle for unity which is directed to help the labor movement assert its class independence and begin a systematic struggle against the capitalist system. The unity the right wing speaks of, which at the moment typifies the reformist thesis, does not include this political conception even though the unity they have in mind serves to safeguard some of the economic, social and political rights of the workers.

On these questions there is a fruitful basis for co-operation. The experience of the past period has shown that it is possible to achieve co-operation with NDPers and others on a wide range of questions — be it in the fight for peace, foreign policy, on economic issues, work in trade unions, municipal, provincial and federal elections, during strikes, in the struggle for democracy, or in the various organizations of the people. However, this co-operation is still limited to individuals and has not yet developed between parties.

This socialist left will be stimulated, as will co-operation between our Party and others, only as a result of sharp struggle against right-wing policy and activity. In fact it is such an ideological struggle, against right-wing views, that will strengthen socialist convictions and the socialist perspective and begin to change the relationship of forces within the labor movement.

Such criticism is all the more necessary in light of the position of the NDP on some key questions, particularly evident at the recent NDP convention. That convention, arising from the efforts of the right wing to appear respectable, evaded coming to grips in any full way with the issues of Canadian independence, economic domination, foreign policy and the constitutional crisis.

It side-stepped nationalization, reiterated its position of co-operative federalism and special status as a substitute for national self-determination, avoided coming to grips with U.S. imperialism and its drive to world domination. Essentially, the right wing's program seems directed to proving it can manage capitalism better than the old-line parties can.

It seems to us that what we should now focus on is the working out of demands that reflect the real needs and possibilities of the labor movement and will facilitate its advance. What we have in mind is the elaboration of a common program for which our Party should campaign and which in turn could stimulate the trend toward unity and co-operation of all the forces of the left.

What should such a common and minimum program consist of? Should it be a program of socialism or a more immediate program of action? Our view is that it should be a basis for united action, a stimulation of mass movements and united action, a means through which to build unity and co-operation of the left. We believe such a program should include the following main themes: peace and neutrality, independence and nationalization, the right to national self-determination, the technological revolution and social progress, the extension of democracy and trade-union rights. It should include proposals for a new deal for the farmers and for the youth, and proposals to overcome the problems of housing, taxes and prices.

We should also see this campaign as part of our preparations for a federal election, which rumor has it will take place next year and for which all political parties are now preparing. The elections in Ontario, Saskatchewan and New Brunswick will in a sense be the curtain raisers for it. Our Party, particularly in Ontario and Saskatchewan, will on the basis of our electoral policy work for the strengthening of the progressive forces in the legislatures, while advancing their own program and candidates where possible.

To focus on the central questions and at the same time pose the necessity for a truly democratic alternative requires that the Party run candidates in a selected number of constituencies in the country.

There is also another aspect, related to the question of what ideological roadblocks stand in the way. We do not make ideological unity a basis for co-operation, but at the same time we know that ideological questions if not cleared up hinder the development of unity and co-operation.

Over the past number of years our Party has elaborated its position with respect to the possibility of a peaceful advance to socialism in our conditions, as we have rounded out our position on the non-inevitability of world war. We have done a considerable amount of work in overcoming sectarian attitudes toward social democracy on the question of multi-party government in the period of socialist construction.

These efforts, and the consistent struggle of the Soviet Union for peace and peaceful co-existence, have done much to break down prejudices and helped create a better atmosphere within which to work.

However, the divisions in the world communist movement have raised anew a host of questions which need to be battled out among the "old" left and the "new" left. These include questions such as that of the relationship of the struggle for peace and national liberation, freedom and democracy, of the paths of transition to socialism, the peaceful and non-peaceful paths to socialism, of the multi-party system and the political rule of the working class, of proletarian internationalism. Where the divisions tend to focus most is on the rights of the individual and democracy under socialism.

Looked at from one side, these questions could be considered part of the public discussion on the path to socialism in Canada that we must join in. At the same time they emphasize the need to strengthen work in the ideological and educational field and in the battle of ideas, seeing in this an important part of the struggle for unity.

If we see this as an integral part of the work on the Party program we should agree that more time will be required to complete the draft of such a program and that much more needs to be done to involve the entire Party in discussions around it.

Extracts from report to meeting,
Central Committee, Communist Party of Canada,
September 16-18, 1967.

(Canadian Tribune, September 25, 1967)

III

Strengthen the struggle
for working-class rights,
for peace and democracy

Comrade chairman, fraternal delegates, delegates to the 20th Convention:

I think it can be said that our Party has been involved in a frank, open and critical discussion these past few months, perhaps one of the best and richest discussions we have ever held. This wide-ranging discussion covered many facets of Party activity, as it was bound to. All or most of it centered around the crucial question — how to revitalize the Party and make it a more effective instrument of the working class in its struggle for economic well-being, democracy, peace and socialism. This is really the heart of the question before this Convention.

The pre-Convention discussion also showed an increasing awareness in the Party, and not in the Party alone, that we are entering a new phase of struggle, a phase which will test the vanguard role of the Party, its ability not only to relate to but give ever-increasing leadership to the growing struggles of the working class, students, and farmers.

Above all it showed the determination of the Party to strengthen its unity, not in a formal sense, but on the basis of the principles of scientific socialism, on the basis of a firm and clear line.

This Convention is, in a sense, both a continuation and the conclusion of the pre-Convention discussion. The delegates have the responsibility of deciding whether the draft resolution meets the needs of the situation and the tasks of the Party. While this is the main political document before the Convention, a number of policy statements will be introduced in the course of the discussion on important and topical issues.

At this time I would also like to add my voice to that of the chairman in welcoming the fraternal delegates to our Convention. It is no fault of ours that not all the fraternal delegates invited were able to come here. This fault lies with the government which has refused to give these fraternal delegates visas. This Convention should register its strong condemnation of the government's action. It is an interesting commentary on the state of affairs of our country that while fascists and criminals have no difficulty gaining entrance into Canada, advocates of peace and friendship with our country and people do.

To those fraternal delebates who are present, we extend our hospitality and a fraternal handshake. Their presence here is a source of inspiration for us, a vivid and living expression of that internationalism which binds us all in the common struggle against imperialism and for peace and socialism. We look forward with great interest to their fraternal greetings.

Now if I may, I would like to deal with some aspects of questions related to the draft resolution.

THE WORLD WE LIVE IN

We live in a world of sharp contrasts and contradictions. Science and technology have made a fantastic leap forward. Space is being conquered and man has begun to reach for the stars. And yet at the same time two-thirds of humanity live in extreme poverty and want, while vast resources which could be used to overcome this situation are squandered in an uncontrolled arms race. Meanwhile, peace which is the hope of mankind is in a precarious state with the threat of a nuclear holocaust ever present.

Canada is also full of these sharp contrasts and contradictions. The concentration of wealth and power in fewer and fewer hands continues. Multi-national corporations, in the main U.S.-owned, increasingly dominate the economic and political life of the country. Science and technology, which could bring abundance and ease man's labor, are instead subordinated to the interests of profit and create insecurity and unemployment. Underneath the so-called affluent society mass poverty exists while exploitation of the working people increases in intensity.

State-monopoly capitalism which claimed to have found the secret of eternal youth is showing increasing signs of instability. The currency crisis internationally, the breakdown of the International Grains Agreement, and chronic inflation internally, indicate the growing sickness of a system of exploitation which is more and more unable to fully satisfy all the needs of the people.

People now sense there is no need for such a state of affairs. More and more of them see the difference between what is and what could be. That is why they do not take kindly to those who tell them to wait for tomorrow, the next day or next year. They want their high hopes and expectations realized today. It is this which is at the heart of the democratic upsurge in our country today. It is this which explains the restlessness in the working class, the rebellion among students, the insistence of farmers on a better deal.

This upsurge is in reality part of a movement embracing many continents and peoples. It is a reflection of the deepening crisis of imperialism in the same way that it mirrors the growing power of the socialist world. Try as it might, imperialism has been unable to check the irresistible movements of the people striving for freedom and independence. It has been unable to do so because of the new balance of power in the world arising from the emergence of the socialist system of states. It is this which gives confidence and strength to the democratic upsurge of peoples everywhere. Canada is not excluded from this process.

This growing demand for meaningful change coincides with a growing disillusionment with the Trudeau government.

Looking back it is now clear, as the Communist Party warned, that monopoly chose Mr. Trudeau, or took a chance with him, to deflect the desire for change into harmless channels. Monopoly was well aware of this upsurge of sentiment and with the able assistance of the mass media built up the so-called mystique of Trudeaumania.

Whether Mr. Trudeau was a willing partner of monopoly in this game, or thought he could decide policy independently of and contrary to the basic interests of monopoly, is beside the point. What is to the point is that since the election none of the high hopes and expectations of many of those voting for him has materialized. They have not materialized because it is impossible for Prime Minister Trudeau to pretend to be for meaningful change while supporting monopoly policies. The Trudeau government is the instrument of monopoly, not the people. No one should have illusions on that score.

This is why the war on poverty and for a Just Society has not got off the ground, why the housing crisis remains as acute as ever, why the crisis in the countryside mounts; why the Carter Report on Taxation, the Watkins Report on Foreign Ownership, the Freedman Report on Technological Change, all gather dust; why prices, taxes and rents continue to climb, and the roots of the rebellion in the universities are ignored.

Nor has the review of foreign and defence policy fared any better. The general expectation of a change in policy has not been fulfilled. After nine months review one could expect a robust child to be born. Instead we have what appears to be a miscarriage with a few trimmings thrown in as a gesture to public opinion. Trudeau seems to have taken over the mantle of Mackenzie King — NATO if necessary but not necessarily NATO — but in the end there is no basic change in policy.

The fact is that the government never intended to change its policy toward NATO. All the motions it went through were part of a calculated game of horse-trading with the Nixon government based on the idea that if a deal could be worked out on oil and wheat, the Canadian government would remain in the NATO alliance. Whether this includes acquiescence with the ABM system, including a possible agreement to allow them to be placed on Canadian territory, remains to be seen. In any case, the statement of Prime Minister Trudeau that he still has to make up his mind whether the ABM system is good or bad, politically and morally, is not a good omen, particularly in light of the fact that missile research for the U.S. government has been going on for some years in Canada. On both counts it is a new type of barter deal, with world peace and the Canadian people the victims. Whether it will come off remains to be seen. In the meantime the Canadian people will continue to be saddled with the NATO military alliance which subordinates Canada to the imperialist aims and adventures of the Washington-Bonn axis, and to continental defence which is another name for further subordinating Canada to U.S. imperialist interests.

What then remains of Canada's independent posture in foreign affairs promised by Prime Minister Trudeau? To paraphrase him, the elephant grunted and produced a noose for the Canadian people.

Neither has Prime Minister Trudeau fared any better on the question of English-French relations, one of the main reasons he was pushed forward as prime minister by the establishment and monopoly interests. The policy of "One Canada, One Nation" which was the centerpiece of his election campaign satisfied the establishment but it could not resolve the crisis of relationships which have their source in national oppression and economic inequality of the French-Canadian people. Bilingualism and biculturalism cannot wipe this out. Neither can the substitution of civil rights for individuals replace the collective rights of the French-Canadian nation. The crisis will therefore continue to deepen as long as the reality of the two nations and its consequences are ignored and not embodied in a new relationship of equals in a voluntary partnership based on a new Canadian Constitution.

Such a Constitution must be based squarely on recognition of the right of the French-Canadian nation to self-determination, the recognition of its right to a national state.

The Communist Party stands opposed to the fragmentation of Canada, a process that would weaken the political unity of the working people of both nations against their common enemies — monopoly capitalism, Canadian and American imperialism.

The position of the Trudeau government opens the door to such fragmentation in English Canada also, stimulated further by a policy of continentalism and subordination to U.S. imperialist aims.

The failure of the Trudeau government to come to grips with these basic questions in any fundamental way is leading to growing disillusionment, particularly among those young people who thought Prime Minister Trudeau was really out to change the situation in a radically new way. The mystique of Trudeaumania has not faded but it is fading. What is evident is that monopoly's effort at diverting the widespread desire for change is not succeeding, nor has it been able to check the growing process of radicalization shaping up in the country. It cannot do so because the root of that radicalization is the growing crisis in Canadian society, a crisis reaching into the economy, the state structure, the tax system, the educational system, a crisis which cannot be dealt with by superficial, partial or limited measures but requires fundamental changes in society itself.

THE WORKING CLASS — THE HEART OF A NEW POLITICAL ALLIANCE

Only a powerful democratic movement united in its aims can bring such changes about. The components of such a democratic alliance are beginning to take form in the growing national, democratic, anti-monopoly and anti-imperialist actions in English and French Canada alike. However, we are only at the beginning of what the draft resolution calls for, the forging of "a new alliance, a national, democratic, anti-monopoly and anti-imperialist coalition, led by the working class", and it may be necessary to pass through various stages before reaching that objective. In any case, it is to the working class we must turn because it is the principal driving and mobilizing force in bringing about this democratic alliance. Without it or against it there will be no democratic alliance and no effective or conclusive struggle for fundamental change.

Those who consider the working class a conservative and declining force are selling the working class short. Everything shaping up in the working class disproves the false argument that the working class has become satisfied with its way of life in today's society, that it has become bourgeoisified and middle class in its outlook, or that technology, according to Mr. McLuhan, has replaced the doctrine of the class struggle. The contrary is, in fact, the case. Technological change has, alongside exploitation and dissatisfaction of working people with their way of life, sharpened the class struggle, not toned it down. It is stimulating class consciousness, not eliminating it. It is compelling workers to move toward independent labor political action, not away from it. This process will grow. The laws of capitalism will see to that. The fact of the matter is that state-monopoly capitalism is faced with growing difficulties. True enough, under capitalism great wealth has been created. But capitalism has created poverty also. Social inequality grows. The polarization of class forces continues, seen on one hand in the growing concentration of power in the hands of monopoly, and on the other in the growth of the working class and its organizations.

We are aware of the fact that capitalism strives to corrupt sections of the working class, stimulates opportunism and reformism in its ranks in order to divide and deflect it from the path of revolutionary consciousness. Slowly but surely there is growing up in the working class an understanding of the necessity for radical changes in an economic and social system based on exploitation.

It is not only the apologists of capitalism who try to convince themselves and the working class that it has become a self-satisfied and conservative force in society. This same line is peddled in the trade-union movement by the right wing as a pretext for dampening down the rising militancy in the organized labor movement and holding the working class within the confines of the capitalist structure. However, it is not the working class that is conservative but some of its leaders who are out of touch with the new needs and the new moods of working men and women, young and old.

The fact that the working class is not yet seized with the need to bring about a revolutionary change of society is not to deny its revolutionary potential as the historical grave-digger of capitalism. Students may appear to be more militant in striving for change. But wanting change is not sufficient. What class does one rely on to bring it about? The middle class, the farmers or the students and intellectuals? This is not to deny that important sections of them can and will become allies of the working class in the struggle for revolutionary change. But by themselves they can do nothing to achieve it. If we focus on the working class, a growing class and not a declining one, it is not because we idealize it or have become mesmerized by it but rather to point out that by its strategic place in production the working class is impelled to fight exploitation and eventually change the system which exploits it.

It is argued in some quarters that the working class is too uneducated and backward to build a new society. The fact is however that the technological revolution is creating a more educated, more highly skilled and intellectually more mature working class capable of being the motive force of social progress, and equally able to take the management of production into its own hands.

Any tendency to downgrade the historic role of the working class and its revolutionary potential, to by-pass it and seek some other force, some "easier and faster road", is doomed to failure. There is no other force and there is no other road in conditions of an advanced capitalist country. The answer to those who want social change and seek to bring it about is to ally themselves with the working class and above all with the revolutionary party of the working class, the Communist Party.

The crux of the matter is that the working class alone is the force on which all progressive forces of society can rely, that the working class alone is the mainstay, the chief organizing and creative force in the construction of a new society. This means that those who are looking to the future and working for it must look to the working class, base themselves on the working class, start from the working class in developing effective policies of radical change.

The working class which has shown its capacity to build the trade union movement of today, to begin the process of independent labor political action, to conduct a ceaseless struggle for social progress and democratic advance, will also find within itself the revolutionary potential to bring about a basic change in society. We are all aware that a great effort, time and experience will be required to reach that objective. One thing is clear. Reformism will not take the working class there. Only a revolutionary party ceaselessly fighting side by side with the workers on all questions, no matter how big or small, a party that always holds forth the socialist perspective while fighting on every question of concern to the working class and democracy, will help to imbue the working class with that understanding and consciousness of its historic role in transforming society. We are such a party. It is to the working class that we turn in building the democratic alliance, for it is the working class and the class struggle which is the axis around which all forces of social progress revolve and will eventually unite.

The most important task of the Party therefore is to strengthen its links with the working class — the organized working class in the first place. Without this, the Party will be suspended in mid-air, unable to change the situation. The daily struggles of the workers against capital, of the people against monopoly, must be the basis of the work of the Party from first to last, the focal point of the work of the entire Party and all its members.

All the signs point to a sharpening of the class struggle as the working class is impelled to fight back against monopoly's offensive. Restlessness in the working class is rising as it sees its standards constantly eroded by rising prices, taxes, rents and interest rates. This indirect form of wage-cutting coupled with the facts that wage increases won through struggle lag behind increased labor productivity, of speed-up and a rise in monopoly profits are compelling workers to engage in sharp struggle with employers for a larger share of the wealth they produce. This will particularly be the case this year with half a million workers in negotiations.

It is with an eye to this situation that the government is permitting unemployment to rise to five per cent and over, at the same time trotting out the bugaboo of inflation to press workers into accepting cheap settlements. However, while monopoly makes a big to-do about inflation, it is not too concerned with it because this gives it the opportunity to jack up prices and amass additional profits. It is not inflation they are concerned with so much as the growing strength of the working class.

It is this they are trying to change through more direct state interference in the trade union movement, in the collective bargaining process and by efforts at regulating wages. Through such measures, state-monopoly capitalism is striving to integrate the working class into the capitalist system and weaken its ability to struggle against monopoly and its policies. The Woods Task Force proposals are of that character, covered up with a little bit of jam to hide the poison. Unfortunately, some union leaders seem prepared to buy them instead of fighting for a Labor Bill of Rights with enlargement of the scope of collective bargaining, which the technological and scientific revolution makes imperative. Workers don't want to be mere cogs in a wheel. They want the power to decide, to have a say over technological change.

Despite these and other roadblocks put in its way by monopoly and governments, the trade union movement continues to grow. It has begun to reach out into new sections of the working class, including the white-collar and professional workers. The militant struggles of many of these workers disprove the argument advanced by some right-wing trade union officials that trade union principles would have to be watered down in order to organize them. Indeed, in the recent period these workers have shown a marked ability of developing varied types of strike action which could prove useful to other sections of organized labor.

The very growth of the working class and of the trade union movement creates its own problems. The influx of young people into industry has added a new quality and militancy to the trade union movement, but it has also led to stresses and strains because of the seeming conflict of interests between the young and older workers. This seeming contradiction must be overcome in the interests of strengthening the unity of the working class and trade union movement. Our Party must give increasing attention to this question, at the same time working to extend its influence and organized strength among these young militant workers.

The same thing applies with equal force to the growing body of working women who constitute an increasingly important part of the working class and are a vital factor in the struggle for peace. Their specific needs, including the battles for equal pay for equal work, the upgrading of skills, maternity benefits and crèches for the children of working mothers require more aggressive attention by the trade union movement and by our Party.

Not least, the growing number of union mergers characteristic of the recent period has opened the window for fresh progressive breezes to enter the trade union movement. An important by-product of this has been the elimination of anti-communist clauses in the CLC and in some labor councils. This cannot but help strengthen the trend toward trade union unity around left policies.

The Communist Party supports the efforts of workers to achieve substantial wage increases. No guidelines set by governments on behalf of employers should be allowed to stand in the way of their achieving what their united strength makes possible. Our Party likewise supports the efforts undertaken by the trade union movement to organize the unorganized, seeing in this a decisive element in changing the balance of power in favor of the working class.

One of the questions to which our Party should give particular attention is that of the guaranteed annual income. There has been much talk of a war against poverty. That problem could be got at by a guaranteed annual income. Our Party fought for "work or wages" in the 30's and this became a rallying point for the unemployed. There is no reason why our Party should not now advance the demand for "work or an income" around which to mount an effective struggle against poverty. In advancing this demand, however, we stand opposed to those sections of monopoly and their governments who are beginning to play with this idea as an answer to the displacement of workers by the technological revolution, seeing the guaranteed annual income as a form of glorified dole. We are equally opposed to those monopoly interests and their governments who see in this a way of getting rid of those measures of social security the working class won through hard and bitter struggle.

Our Party opposes any trade-off of this kind. The organized working class is fighting for a guaranteed annual wage and for guaranteed weekly wages. It has fought and will continue to fight to extend social security measures, particularly maternity and sickness pay benefits, as it will continue to press for increases in family allowances, unemployment insurance and pensions. At the same time it is in its interests to press for a guaranteed annual income for all Canadians as a right. As this is won it could replace welfare payments. Such a guaranteed annual income could be enacted either by a negative income tax or in other ways to provide an adequate standard of living.

To the argument of where the money is to come from to cover the costs of such programs, we would reply: take it out of the defence budgets and by democratic reform of taxation including a capital gains tax.

Our Party should be a foremost champion of such a measure and press for its adoption by the federal government.

THE YOUNG GENERATION AND STUDENTS —
IN UNITY WITH WORKERS

The growing demand for change finds particular reflection among young people. One of the most significant developments of the recent period has been the radical upsurge among young people. Among working-class youth this finds its reflection by their entry into the trade unions and in active participation in the class struggle. Among students it finds its reflection in a growing demand, backed by various forms of action, for democratic reform of education and for a voice in the administration of university life. A growing body of students link the struggles for a democratic restructuring of society and for an end to monopoly control. This development is of considerable significance, adding an additional force to the growing movement for far-reaching change in our country.

Our Party has been slow in understanding the underlying factors that give force to the growing rebellion among students. A tendency exists to look at the social composition of the students, which in fact is changing as a result of the technological and scientific revolution, and not at what is primary — the criticism of a system which breeds wars, racism and oppression and cannot satisfy all the needs of the students or give them a meaningful future. The rebellion among students is thus an additional proof of the deep-going crisis of the capitalist system.

Communists do not stand aside from this movement among students. They actively participate in it. Their task is to bring Marxism, the science of scientific socialism to students, at the same time explaining and exposing the dangers inherent in anarchist and pseudo-revolutionary theories spread among them — theories and practices which are harmful and self-defeating. Communists work to strengthen students' understanding of the leading role of the working class in the struggle for a radical change of society. They are foremost champions of the demand for democratic reform and modernization of education, a modernization which should ensure its Canadian content. Communists must systematically combat all theories which separate the students from the working class.

One theory holds that only the students are capable of moral revolt, that the working class is incapable of it because it is satisfied with its material conditions of life. Another theory holds that the students are a new basic class in society, replacing the working class in the system of capitalist relations of production.

Both theories draw the same conclusion — that the student youth are the main or sole revolutionary force in society today. On the surface this seems so if one looks at the more radical slogans and sharper forms of struggle of students, a situation explained by the fact that reformism and a trade union outlook are still dominant in the working class, fed and stimulated by monopoly's ability to make concessions and by right-wing control of these working-class trade union organizations.

Lenin in *"Left-Wing" Communism* correctly stated that "anarchism is not infrequently a kind of penalty for the opportunist sins of the working-class movement."

But this temporary situation cannot negate the fact that no basic change can be effected in present-day society without or against the working class and its revolutionary party, the Communist Party.

The various tendencies finding expression among students won't be overcome on their own. They will be overcome in alliance with the working class. The basis of such an alliance exists in the fact that the working class is as concerned as the students with the need to win peace and the democratic restructuring of society, including democratic reform of education.

The task of forming such an alliance is inseparable from strengthening Marxism and building the Communist Party among students and intellectuals. The fact is that the student rebellion in its own way reflects the new role intellectuals are beginning to play in the life of capitalist society. Thus when we speak of an alliance of students and the working class we do so in the context of the widening of the national democratic, anti-monopoly and anti-imperialist movements into a majority movement of the Canadian people, led by the working class.

Our Party must work to help bring such an alliance about.

In examining these developments in the young generation we cannot but conclude that we need to work for the establishment of a Communist youth organization, an organization based on the class struggle and on socialism expressed through the political power of the working class and its allies. We are mindful that the task of building such an organization will not be easy. On the other hand the growing interest in Marxism and socialism, the ferment taking shape among young people, indicate that an objective base exists for such an organization fraternally related to the Communist Party.

Once this Convention determines the orientation the Party will take with respect to such an organization, the leading bodies of the Party will have the responsibility of elaborating program, structure, organizational forms and leadership to implement that orientation.

Side by side with building such a youth organization, our Party should redouble its efforts to attract revolutionary-minded young workers and university students into its ranks. We see no contradiction in building a Communist youth organization that can attract working youth, teenagers and young people generally to the banner of Marxism-Leninism, and the strengthening of the Party's influence among the young generation.

UNITY OF THE DEMOCRATIC LEFT

As we can see it, the forces opposed to monopoly, and these include the farmers, are growing and will continue to grow. What is decisive now is the strengthening of unity of action particularly of the democratic left and the genuine socialist currents emerging in English and French Canada. Unity of action of those forces will create more favorable conditions for forging a new political alliance, a democratic alliance capable of drastically curbing the power of monopoly and opening the door to socialist advance. The key here is co-operation between the NDP and Communist Party.

Within the NDP a differentiation is underway between those who would tie the NDP to capitalist policies and to the position of "loyal opposition", and those who see the future of the NDP as part of a democratic and socialist alignment. We welcome this development. Indeed the firm and patient struggle of our Party for unity of action, against reformist ideology and for the socialist perspective will facilitate this differentiation in a positive way.

While we seek all forms of co-operation with the NDP on questions which advance the interests of the working people and democracy, we at the same time compete with them in the working-class and democratic movements.

The struggle for unity of action and the strengthening of the independent role and work of the Party are therefore not contradictory aims. They facilitate and complement each other. But it should be clear: the stronger the Party the more likely will unity of action be achieved. The more it makes its presence felt the sooner will unity of action come about. To build the Party is to build the motive force of united action.

Similarly, the struggle to bring about a new political alliance and a new majority in Parliament is not in contradiction to the strengthening of the mass movements of the working class, students, farmers and other sections of the people. If we emphasize mass actions and movements of the most varied kinds, led by the working class, it is because they are together the decisive factor in the struggle for democracy, peace, the well-being of the people, and the struggle for socialism itself, as they are the decisive element in forging a new political alliance. In short, mass actions at every level will complement and reinforce parliamentary activity.

THE INTERNATIONAL SITUATION

We cannot separate domestic from international developments. The Canadian people are affected daily by these events which could determine their future, indeed their very lives.

A fierce struggle is going on between imperialism and socialism on all fronts. Imperialism is striving might and main to reverse the course of history, weaken and undermine the positions won by the working class and national-liberation movement throughout the world. It uses various forms of struggle, be it ideological subversion or military measures, to accomplish its aims. It is much easier to see its hand when it takes military action as in Vietnam or elsewhere. It's not so easy to see its hand when it undertakes ideological subversion. We, like many other parties, have been slow in seeing this side of imperialist strategy and have tended to underestimate this more cunning and subtle line which is directed to establishing Trojan horses within the socialist camp, within the national-liberation movement, within Communist and Workers' Parties. In reality of course ideological subversion and military action are part of one package, to change the course of world history and alter the balance of world power in favor of imperialism.

This is the essence of the struggle on a wide number of fronts in the world today — in Vietnam, in Europe, in the Middle East, in Africa and in Latin America.

Worldwide pressure finally compelled the U.S. government to agree to negotiate in Vietnam. The world hoped this would lead to an end to U.S. aggression. It is apparent, however, that the decision to negotiate which was forced on it by the heroic resistance of the Vietnamese people themselves, the pressures of American public opinion and the increasing support given the heroic people of Vietnam by the socialist countries, have not yet led U.S. imperialism to conclude that it should withdraw its troops and bases from that country. President Nixon's warning about stepping up escalation again, an escalation that has already begun, coupled with Mr. Laird's statement that U.S. troops will stay for an indeterminate time in South Vietnam, is a clear warning to the world that a period of sharp and dangerous struggle still lies ahead, and that efforts need to be redoubled to compel the complete and unconditional withdrawal of U.S. troops from Vietnam. This is a most important task today.

The situation is further aggravated by the ceaseless efforts of West German imperialism to rearm with the connivance of NATO and try to get its finger on the nuclear trigger, with the aim of recarving the map of Europe. West German imperialism is today the chief obstacle to a detente, to peace and international security.

The situation is further sharpened by the refusal of the Israeli government to arrive at a political settlement in the Middle East, based on the UN Security Council resolution which provides the basis of a just settlement.

Not least, the international situation is aggravated by the decision of the Nixon government to go ahead with the construction of an ABM system that could likely trigger a nuclear arms race, hinder negotiations for nuclear disarmament and threaten the security, indeed, the very survival of Canada. As the Communist Party stated in March ". . . the Pentagon is prepared to defend the USA to the last Canadian."

These developments taken together show that imperialism is intent on sharpening international tensions and on preventing an international detente. Mr. Laird's statement that the ABM system is a "building block to peace" merely updates John Foster Dulles' discredited and bankrupt policy of "peace through strength" and "negotiations through strength". Implicit in that theory is the aim of imposing an imperialist peace on the world with the use of an overwhelming superiority of nuclear weapons. John Foster Dulles' policy could not succeed and neither will President Nixon's and Mr. Laird's. They arise from a mistaken conception of world reality, an overestimation of the strength of U.S. imperialism and an underestimation of the strength of the socialist world and of the forces of peace on a world scale.

This is not to suggest that no real dangers for world peace exist. They do. Imperialism, while weakened, is not a paper tiger. It still has powerful claws and the more defeats it suffers the more desperate and dangerous it becomes. Imperialism continues to seek out soft spots to instigate local wars as in Vietnam and in the Middle East. Nor can one close one's eyes to the danger of a third world war that by the nature of things would be a nuclear war. This is why the greatest of vigilance is demanded on the part of all those concerned with the maintenance of world peace. But more than vigilance is demanded to prevent a third world war, safeguard peace and free the peoples oppressed by imperialism. To achieve success in such a struggle requires unity of all peace-loving and democratic forces and above all, unity of the socialist camp, of Communist and Workers' Parties throughout the world.

The struggle for peaceful co-existence is an integral part of the fight for world peace. However, as we have had occasion to say more than once, peaceful co-existence does not mean maintaining the status quo between capitalism and socialism, between the national-liberation movement and imperialist oppression or between capital and labor, the people and monopoly. The worldwide struggle between capitalism and socialism also goes on in our own country, represented in the struggle between democratic and socialist advance and monopoly rule. The struggle against monopoly and imperialism and their defeat will in the final analysis rid the world of oppression and of war.

In the increasingly complex conditions of the struggle for world peace our Party must sharply attack all views which base themselves on the inevitability of world war and therefore oppose the policy of peaceful co-existence and of international detente. By the same token the Party must equally combat views tending to underestimate or ignore imperialism's offensive and reactionary drive, its continued resistance and opposition to international detente. To close our eyes to both views could lead to passivity when what is required is ever-increasing and wider public action to check and reverse the course of imperialist strategy.

The defeat of U.S. imperialism's global strategy is of direct concern to the Canadian people. Such a defeat would weaken U.S. imperialism and thus make easier the struggle for Canadian independence. Canada's independence is undermined by continued membership in NATO and NORAD. Canada's independence, indeed its very survival, is threatened by the ABM system which can trigger a nuclear arms race and even, as Prime Minister Trudeau admitted, "engulf the world in a nuclear holocaust."

The cause of peace, of Canada's sovereignty and independence, is thus joined.

This is why the Canadian people should demand of the U.S. government: bring all the U.S. troops back home from Vietnam. Let the Vietnamese people decide their own destiny without outside interference.

This is why the Canadian people should insist that a political settlement be arrived at in the Middle East on the basis of the UN Security Council resolution.

This is why the Canadian people should solemnly declare: we will not take up arms in support of West German revanchist aims and of the neo-nazis. Moreover they should underwrite this pledge by demanding a European security pact, recognition of the Oder-Neisse line, the German Democratic Republic, special status for West Berlin, no nuclear arms for West Germany and the annulment of the Munich Pact.

This is why the Canadian people should insist that the ABM system be scrapped and that meaningful negotiations be started with the Soviet Union directed to reverse the sterile, wasteful and dangerous competition in armaments. This is why the Canadian government should recognize one China, which includes Taiwan, and work for China's entry into the UN.

No least, this is why the Canadian people should continue to press for Canada's withdrawal from NATO and NORAD and for a drastic reduction in the defence budget. Canada must get out of NORAD and NATO and the Canadian troops in Western Germany brought home. Canada's best interests lie in pursuing a policy of military non-alignment and working for the dissolution of all military blocs. As a nuclear-free zone, Canada could call for the USA and USSR to respect her position. It is along these lines that Canada could become an effective peacemaker in the world, and strengthen her independence.

In fighting for this program of peace our Party will at the same time strengthen solidarity action with the Communists and democrats of Greece, Portugal, Spain, Indonesia and everywhere else that such solidarity is needed to help defeat fascist, dictatorial and reactionary regimes. The fight to defeat reaction is an integral part of the fight for peace.

The fight to head off the danger of world nuclear war and for peace remains a central part of the work of the Party.

CONSOLIDATE THE UNITY OF THE WORLD COMMUNIST MOVEMENT

I have referred previously to the new offensive strategy of imperialism that includes as one of its aims the fostering of divisions and splits in the world communist movement, the working class and revolutionary forces throughout the world. We cannot but take account of this global strategy to which our Party must reply by working to strengthen international solidarity in every way possible.

The International Conference of Communist and Workers' Parties to be held in Moscow on June 5 can be an important step in this direction. We see this Conference as of decisive importance, opening the door to the consolidation of the unity of the world movement on the basis of Marxism-Leninism and proletarian internationalism. This is why our Party has worked and will continue to work for its successful outcome.

The trend to consolidating the unity of the communist movement, despite many continuing difficulties, stands in sharp contrast to the recent provocative actions of the Maoists on the Soviet-Chinese border. Why were they undertaken? Whose interests do they serve?

One cannot separate these provocative and adventurist actions from the fact that a Party Congress is taking place in China and that the Maoists, faced with internal difficulties and internal opposition, are whipping up anti-Sovietism to drown opposition to their policies.

Neither can one separate the coincidence of these provocative actions from the election provocation engineered in West Berlin by the West German government nor from the U.S. escalation in Vietnam.

Is it not rather strange, to put it mildly, that the Maoists raise territorial claims against the Soviet Union on matters that have been historically resolved while ignoring such questions as Taiwan, Hong Kong and other Chinese territory presently under colonial rule? Is it not rather strange that they raise territorial questions by armed actions and not by negotiations?

Is it not rather strange that precisely when U.S. imperialism is stepping up its escalation against the Vietnamese people, the Maoists stop the transhipment of war materiel from the Soviet Union to the Vietnamese people?

Does it not suggest that Maoism has undertaken a basic shift in policy, one geared to virulent anti-Sovietism, the splitting of the world communist movement and rapprochement with the very imperialists whom they pretend to fight?

It is no accident that reactionary forces in the U.S., West Germany, Japan and elsewhere have suddenly become "friends" of China and try to get close to Mao in whom they see a potential ally in the struggle against socialism.

What is clear is that the strategists of imperialism hope to take advantage of the present situation to bring about a change in the balance of power in their favor. What is equally clear is that Maoism is objectively playing the game of the imperialists — the undertaking of a two-front drive on socialism. Thus do the right and "left" meet.

Our Party condemns these provocative actions undertaken by the Maoists that are nothing less than a betrayal of socialism and of internationalism. These events bring home the fact that what has emerged in China in the course of the so-called cultural revolution is a military-bureaucratic dictatorship, with the Communist Party, the Young Communist League, the trade union movement and the public institutions destroyed and replaced by "revolutionary committees" under the control and direction of the military forces.

They no less bring home the fact that Maoism has moved over from ideological struggle to provocative and adventurist actions against the Soviet Union and socialism, of which the border incident is but a prelude. We would be remiss in our duty if we failed to see that the struggle against Maoism has gone beyond ideological questions and reached a new and dangerous stage. In saying this we also wish to say we are confident that the Chinese Communists who adhere to Marxism-Leninism, and the Chinese people, will eventually assert themselves. Marxism-Leninism will sooner or later win out in its contest with Mao's petty-bourgeois nationalism. The place of China is with the socialist camp, with the world communist movement, with all anti-imperialist forces in the struggle for peace, independence and socialism.

In drawing attention to these more recent events we do not close our eyes to what transpired in Czechoslovakia where an effort was mounted by imperialists and by the rightists and counter-revolutionaries to take that country out of the socialist community. The decisive action of five Warsaw Treaty states prevented this. History will surely record the fact that the imperialist counter-offensive against the forces of socialism and progress, prepared over a long time, suffered a severe defeat as a consequence of this action.

Our October Central Committee meeting supported this action and the steps taken by the Communist Party of Czechoslovakia to normalize the situation. We are confident this Convention will uphold that position.

Developments since show that imperialism has not given up its efforts at preventing normalization, nor have the rightists in Czechoslovakia. The real friends and defenders of socialism in Czechoslovakia are not those who stand in the way of normalization and attack it from the right or from the "left"; its real friends and defenders are those who give every support to the CP of Czechoslovakia in implementing these measures.

If the recent events in China have their "logic" in the left opportunism of Maoism, the events of Czechoslovakia have their "logic" in right opportunism and revisionism. Both left and right opportunism have their roots in nationalism, in a negation of proletarian internationalism, in anti-Sovietism. Both roads finally lead to a weakening of the leading role of the working class and of the Communist Party, and strike at the very foundation of socialism.

History abounds with facts showing that anti-Sovietism

has always been the common factor drawing together all enemies of peace and socialism. This is why those who are concerned with the struggle for peace and for socialism must never forget that the Soviet Union is the decisive factor in the world struggle against imperialism, for peace and socialism.

Saying this is not to deny the independence and sovereignty of each Communist Party. But the assertion of that independence and sovereignty does not and cannot lie through the road of anti-Sovietism. It lies in asserting the independence and sovereignty of Communist and Workers' Parties from the capitalist class and their policies, by standing firm on the platform of Marxism-Leninism and proletarian internationalism. One can't be for socialism and against the Soviet Union. This is why our Party will never take the road of anti-Sovietism, no matter how disguised.

The Communist Party of Canada sees no contradiction between patriotism and internationalism. Our patriotism lies in defence of the true interests of our people. Our internationalism lies in the fight against imperialism, oppression and war and solidarity with the socialist states. This too is in the interests of the working people of our country. True patriotism has nothing to do with nationalism, chauvinism or national exclusiveness.

We stand on the firm ground of proletarian internationalism. It is with this in mind that our Party needs to undertake a consistent struggle against nationalism, chauvinism and separatism. Imperialist strategy focusses on stimulating nationalism to undermine international solidarity. We focus on international solidarity as a decisive component of the strategy of advance in the struggle against the enemy of mankind — imperialism.

THE PARTY

Now to some questions related to the role and work of the Party.

The argument is advanced in some circles that our Party is too conservative and in -fact has ceased to be a revolutionary party. Those who say this tend to mix up pseudo-revolutionary phrase-mongering with serious activity directed to help the working class and its allies find and take the path of revolutionary change of society.

What does it mean to be a revolutionary today?

To be a revolutionary is to relate the Party to the contemporary situation and the tasks which flow from it, and work to win support for the policies of the Party among the people. To be a revolutionary today is to stand with the working class as the main force for social change, with the working people in the struggle to defend their interests. To be a revolutionary today is to work to curb the power of monopoly, for unity of action of the democratic left and for a trade union movement united around militant policies. To be a revolutionary today is to fight to defend and extend democracy in the economic, educational and political arenas. To be a revolutionary today is to be in the front ranks of the fight for peace and against imperialism. To be a revolutionary today is to build the party of socialism, the Communist Party.

Yes, we are a revolutionary party because our aim is socialism based on the political power of the working class and its allies, a Party that properly relates every form of struggle directed to achieve socialism. However, wanting socialism and achieving it are two different things. Impatience is no substitute for hard work, for advancing the strategy and tactics necessary in building alliances, for winning reforms, strengthening the political independence of the working class movement — all essential ingredients in paving the way for socialism.

Our Party is also attacked from a different angle — that we are not relevant in contemporary society because we are a revolutionary party. Those who argue this way suggest that state-monopoly capitalism has found the secret of eternal youth, that all its inner contradictions have been resolved and that socialism will never be on the Canadian agenda. These short-sighted people assume too readily that capitalism on an international and on a national scale has stabilized itself and is now proof against revolutionary change. Everything that is happening disproves this. The fact is that we are now entering a period of growing instability of the capitalist system, a growing and deepening crisis of imperialism, and with it the emergence of growing movements for change. A process of radicalization is underway and, while it is not yet revolutionary in character, there is no arbitrary wall between radicalization and revolutionary change. Indeed radicalization is a prelude to revolutionary change. But this will not come by itself. The challenge for our Party is to imbue this radicalization with revolutionary, socialist consciousness and action, and to advance the issues and slogans that will facilitate this process.

Our Party will not be sidetracked from its responsibilities to its class and the nation, either by pseudo-revolutionary phrasemongering or by the admirers and apologists of state-monopoly capitalism who strive to integrate the working class into the capitalist system and the status quo.

Of course the proof of the pudding is in the eating. It is not enough to say we are relevant, that we are the vanguard. We must earn this every day by our work among the working people, the students, women, farmers and intellectuals. The most important thing we must do in this connection is establish our presence and be part of the growing movements all around us. But in the first place what we must do is strengthen the Party and build it and the press among the industrial workers, the most advanced section of the working class.

This will establish our relevance and vanguard role in a real way. Our work in this connection, and good work has been done by our Party in many fields and on various fronts, needs critical examination at this Convention.

Comrades: This is one of the most important Conventions in our history. Its task is to unite the Party around the political line agreed to here and that is indicated in the draft resolution before you, a resolution unanimously adopted by the Central Committee at its last meeting. The draft resolution establishes an orientation, a direction, a perspective for the period ahead. It also establishes the kind of Party we need to meet the challenge of the 70's. This draft should be the subject of sharp and critical examination by the Convention so that the end result will lead to further strengthening the resolution and making it an effective guide for the whole Party. It goes without saying that once adopted it must be unswervingly applied without reservations and be binding on the Central Committee, the whole Party and all its members. It is necessary to say this because some members of the Central Committee who voted for the draft resolution apparently felt it quite in order, in the course of the pre-Convention discussion, to argue against what they voted for. It is equally necessary to say this because there can be only one line — that adopted by the Convention. There is no other way a Party such as ours can work, unless we wish to transform the Party into a debating society and virtually paralyze it.

Some comrades argue that the Party can and should be united in action and that differences, insofar as they exist on some questions, be allowed to continue. However, we are not only a party of action but also a party of unity of will, that is, a party with a common ideological standpoint, one political and tactical line. To lose sight of this fact would undermine the unity of the Party. To have comrades go their own way, except on those questions of action they may agree with, is to undermine the revolutionary character of our Party.

Some comrades say the differences, insofar as they exist, have to do only with an estimation of the events in Czechoslovakia. Certainly the events there have many lessons for Communist and Workers' parties, many of which are beginning to draw appropriate conclusions from them. However, the pre-Convention discussion showed that differences with the draft resolution exist on a wide number of questions other than the events in Czechoslovakia. They include such questions as the united front and electoral policy, the national question, the task of building a young communist organization, nationalism and internationalism, the struggle on two fronts.

Some comrades say the main danger we are faced with is that of dogmatism and sectarianism, not left and right opportunism and revisionism.

But who can deny that bourgeois ideology has penetrated

the thinking and work of the Party and led to an erosion of Marxism-Leninism? Who can deny tendencies that have arisen to elevate national peculiarities to one of principle and downgrade what is a matter of principle — the universal character of Marxism-Leninism? Who can deny that the capitalist environment and the role of state-monopoly capitalism in making some concessions to the working class have not corrupted some sections of the working class and stimulated opportunism and reformism in their ranks? Who can deny that tendencies have arisen to water down class principles so as to present a more acceptable image of our Party? Who can deny in these circumstances that left and right opportunist tendencies have not affected the work of the Party?

Saying this is not to suggest that a consistent struggle should not be waged against dogmatic and sectarian tendencies. Such a struggle must be waged, and it has particular meaning in light of the dangerous positions being taken by Maoism in China. But it would be foolhardy indeed for the Party to close its eyes to opportunist tendencies which have their social roots in the soil of capitalism and its pressures, a soil in which our Party has to work and which requires steadfastness and firmness on all matters of principle while exercising the utmost flexibility on questions of tactics.

When the Party does not effectively counter bourgeois ideology with socialist ideology, bourgeois ideology moves in. When the Party does not fight opportunism, opportunism takes over. This is why the struggle against left and right opportunism is a long-term struggle.

There can be no question therefore about the need to fight on two fronts, against left and right opportunism and revisionism, and against dogmatism and sectarianism — while focussing our attention at this time on the struggle against opportunism and revisionism as the main danger.

In saying this we are not labelling anyone, but rather establishing what it is we have to fight against. What is basically involved is the ideology of the Party, its place and role in the struggle for socialism.

If these questions are brought forward it is not to aggravate the situation, but rather to call upon the Convention to ensure that out of frank and open debate the Party's unity will be strengthened on the basis of its principles and policies.

The Party cannot have two lines of policy. The Convention must resolve this question and elect a leadership that will apply itself to the line and policies adopted, and work to build a strong, united Party.

Unity around a firm, clear line does not mean that discussion should or will end in the Party. There are a number of programmatic questions our Party needs to go into in a thorough-going fashion so that by our next Convention we can update our program in conformity with changes taking place since it was adopted. These include questions of the peaceful, parliamentary road to socialism, and multi-party government. The discussion on these questions should help to strengthen the Party ideologically at the same time as it should assist in outlining the path to socialism and the building of a socialist society in Canada.

Our discussions will be helped by virtue of the fact that next year we shall be commemorating the life of that man of genius — Vladimir Lenin — and above all his theoretical and practical work which led to the success of the Great October Revolution and with it the beginning of the process of changing the world. Only Marxism-Leninism provides real answers to the questions confronting mankind and only socialism opens up prospects for solving the problems of the present-day world. Lenin fought consistently against opportunism and sectarianism and for the creative development of Marxism. This we must always remember.

It is with this in mind we should likewise prepare for the 50th Anniversary of our Party in 1971. Our Party not only has a rich past full of contributions to labor and democracy. It has an even richer future. This Convention has the task of laying the groundwork today for that future. Above all it needs to give meaning and substance to the widespread desire for change permeating ever-growing sections of the Canadian people. The best way to do that is to build the

Party of socialism. This is the most important task of this Convention. This is the real challenge of the 70's.

Keynote address, 20th Convention,
Communist Party of Canada,
April 4-6, 1969.

IV

Speech at the International Meeting of Communist and Workers' Parties

Our Party and many progressive people in Canada welcome the fact that this conference is taking place. The Communist Party of Canada has long pressed for such a world gathering as an urgent necessity, both to assess the march of events since 1960 and the new problems that have been posed by history, and to consolidate the unity of the international communist movement.

The fact that it is being held is of great historical moment. The enemies of peace and socialism hoped it would not take place. Their hopes have not been realized. Now that it is on, they hope nothing will come out of it, that unity will not be achieved. We are confident, however, that their hopes will be dashed again, and that all of us, conscious of the great responsibility we bear before the peoples of our countries and the working class of the world, will work to assure the success of this conference and not allow temporary differences to stand in the way.

Our Party is in full agreement with the main document before us. It was unanimously endorsed by our Central Committee following our 20th National Convention in April, which by resolution instructed the Central Committee "to work for the success of the international conference". We believe the main document correctly assesses present-day phenomena in their complexity and contradictions, the strategy of imperialism, and the tasks and responsibilities confronting us at this stage. We believe it will help to overcome tendencies which have arisen to one-sided interpretation of some questions related to the struggle for peace, democracy and socialism, and will thereby make the work of the Communist and Workers' Parties in the coming period more effective.

We cannot agree with the viewpoint that only one part of the document should be adopted. We believe a correct rounded-out analysis of imperialism and its strategy at this stage is fundamental to reaching appropriate conclusions with respect to the tasks we must undertake. Nor can we agree with the viewpoint which fails to take into account and draw all the necessary conclusions from the global strategy of U.S. imperialism and its allies, their efforts to undermine the unity of the socialist countries and the Communist parties to separate them, weaken them from within and lay the groundwork for the restoration of capitalism in one country after another, and the threat this poses to world peace. Any complacency in this regard would seriously weaken the forces capable of resisting and checking imperialist aggression.

Differences in estimating the aims of imperialism and the relationship of forces on a world scale lead to different conclusions for action and undermine the cohesivenss of the world Communist movement. Our Party agrees with the analysis on this question in the main document. This is the basis for our support of the conclusions arrived at, as it is the basis for our well-known position with respect to the events in Czechoslovakia. Our Party Congress expressed full support and solidarity with the present leadership of the Communist Party of Czechoslovakia in the steps it is taking to normalize the situation and strengthen socialism.

In the fact of U.S. global strategy, we see the maximum co-ordination of action by all Communist and Workers' Parties as a prime necessity. Any other position would be narrow-minded in the extreme. Any thought of "going it alone" in face of imperialism's "bridge building" and subversion, on the assumption that it would bring some immediate gains to this or that Party, is indeed a short-sighted policy which will help neither the Party concerned in the long run, nor the anti-imperialist struggle.

One should have no illusions about the peaceableness of imperialism. Imperialism will only negotiate seriously based on the unity and cohesion of the socialist states and all anti-imperialist forces.

II

The international tasks projected in the main document fully correspond to the national tasks of our Party. Indeed, most of the points in it are also embodied in the main resolution of our 20th convention. That is only natural, for how can there be a conflict of interest between national and international tasks in the face of the global strategy of imperialism?

The defeat of this strategy is an essential prerequisite for assuring the peace, independence and sovereignty of Canada, as it is for other nations. Every setback for U.S. imperialism strengthens the patriotic and peace forces in our country. The growing pressure of Canadian public opinion to extricate Canada from the suffocating embrace of American imperialism has compelled our government to begin a review of its foreign policy with respect to Latin America, China, Africa and its commitments to NATO. Of course this also partially reflects the efforts of sections of Canadian monopoly to exploit contradictions between imperialist states to their own advantage.

As is already known the Canadian government announced that it has decided to carry out a phased and controlled withdrawal of a part of its armed forces from the NATO alliance in Western Germany. However, it was quick to add that the number of troops to be withdrawn and the timing of the withdrawal were subject to consultation with its allies. Even this timid step was sharply attacked by the American, British and West German governments, which are fearful that this example might be followed by other NATO countries. They are striving to compel the Canadian government to retreat from its stated position. This is flagrant interference in Canadian affairs, an attempt to deny the Canadian people their sovereign right to determine the foreign policy of their country. This pressure from foreign states coincides with the efforts of the industrial-military complex in Canada which is closely related to the U.S. military-industrial complex, to tie the country permanently to NATO and the NORAD military alliance, to the Washington-Bonn war axis as a means of securing war orders from the United States and Bonn at the price of the sovereignty and independence of our country. This same industrial-military complex is pressing the government to acquiesce in President Nixon's Anti-Ballistic Missile (ABM Safeguard) system, which opens the door to a nuclear arms race and directly threatens Canada with destruction in the event of war.

The review announced by the Canadian government does not add up to the adoption of an independent foreign policy in the interests of Canada. This has yet to be won. The government seems to veer in favor of "continental defence" as a substitute for an independent foreign policy. The Communist Party of Canada calls for a truly independent foreign policy along the following lines: withdrawal from NATO and NORAD and adoption of a policy of military non-alignment; a declaration that Canada is a non-nuclear zone; support for a European security pact and recognition of the German Democratic Republic and the postwar borders in Europe; the recognition of one China; support to the 10-point program of the National Liberation Front as the basis for a just settlement of the war in Vietnam; a political solution of the Near East crisis based on the UN Security Council resolution of November 1967; support to the colonial peoples fighting for their liberation; extension of trade with the socialist and developing countries on a mutually advantageous basis; disarmament.

This program meets the interests of the Canadian people, strengthens Canada's independence and security and, we believe, is a solid contribution to the worldwide struggle against imperialism.

There is a direct relationship between the struggle against imperialism and the struggle for peaceful co-existence. Some see the struggle for peaceful co-existence as a rejection of the struggle against imperialism; others see the struggle against imperialism as a rejection of the struggle for peaceful co-existence. In reality, there can be no such contradiction. To achieve peaceful co-existence and international detente imperialist aggression must be defeated. The struggle against imperialism and for peaceful co-existence opens up opportunities for the broadest unity to achieve social advance on all fronts. This is the basis for the unity of all the Communist and Workers' Parties and all forces for peace, democracy, national independence and social progress in the world. The strategy of unity advanced by the main document will make the forces of progressive humanity invincible.

III

Our Party sees the working class as the decisive leading force of the struggle against imperialism. Indeed, without the leadership of the working class no effective struggle can be waged against imperialism, against monopoly. In Canada the struggle against monopoly is mounting, the class struggle is growing sharper. Every effort of the monopolists and their stooges to build up the concept of "class harmony" and "class partnership", directed to preserve the privileged position of corporate wealth, is collapsing in face of the growing confrontation between labor and capital.

In the recent period, in an effort to disorientate the working class, the apologists of capitalism have tried to convince the workers that the scientific and technological revolution "has made the doctrine of class struggle obsolete". The workers are repudiating this classless position by their actions. The class struggle of the workers is mounting. Chronic inflation, sharp rises in taxation, a four per cent annual increase in prices, high rents and interest rates, increased exploitation, job insecurity and growing unemployment — arising from the scientific and technological revolution — all these have led to growing strike action. There is a new spirit of militancy and consciousness in the working class, in which the young workers are playing an important part. The aims set by the workers are higher. While largely concentrated around wage demands, they are also increasingly taking up the fight for job security. These actions and others that will follow, are a fitting reply to those who consider the working class a spent, bourgeoisified force, unable to fulfil its historic role.

Monopoly is striving to change this situation by anti-labor legislation which would seriously curtail the rights of the workers to defend their vital interests through strike action. This is being pressed for with the specious argument that the working class is too strong and needs to be curbed so as to restore "the balance of power". In this way capitalist propaganda tries to obscure the fact that it is monopoly capital that is *in* power. The working class is answering that propaganda by the demand for a say in regard to technological changes and all other questions affecting its vital interests. The growing monopoly offensive is being met by the growing unity of the workers, expressed among other things in such actions as the removal of the anti-communist clauses from the by-laws of the trade union centre and labor councils, and the growing trend of merger of unions in a number of industries in the face of monopoly concentration and the emergence of conglomerates.

The growing strength of the organized industrial working class and its consistent struggle against monopoly have been an important factor in stimulating organization among professional and white-collar workers, as it has indirectly influenced the movement among the youth, particularly student youth, among whom anti-imperialist sentiment is rising. At the same time the inexperience of youth attracted by pseudo-revolutionary phrases has tended to separate them from the working class and Communist Party. Our Party's efforts are directed to unite this movement with the working class, to create among its participants an understanding of the leading role of the working class in the revolutionary process, to bring scientific socialism, the teachings of Marxism-Leninism into the youth and student movement.

The increasing stranglehold of monopoly capital in agriculture, the technical revolution in farming and the chronic agrarian crisis, including the problem of markets, are calling forth a new wave of struggle and unity among masses of farmers. The process of differentiation is growing in the countryside, with the wealthy farmers aligned with monopoly and the masses of working farmers beginning to turn to labor-farmer unity for effective struggle against the monopolies. A new significant development is the movement to establish an all-Canadian farmers' union through which the working farmers could defend their interests.

These movements and struggles against monopoly capital and its policies are augmented by widespread sentiments and actions for peace and around democratic issues, for civil and labor rights and particularly the demand of the French-Canadian nation for the right to national self-determination. The demand of French-Canadians for control of their national state in Quebec, within a reconstructed federal Canadian state, is laying the basis for uniting the national-democratic forces of French-Canada with the working people of English Canada in the common struggle against U.S. and Canadian monopoly. The opposition to the American domination of the Canadian economy and foreign policy has become a major factor of Canadian politics.

It is around the issue of Vietnam that opposition to the U.S. dirty war has been most strongly expressed. Both moral and economic factors are involved here. The Canadian people have felt the economic effects of that war in inflation and rising prices, in a distortion of the international balance of payments, and a currency crisis which could lead to devaluation of the Canadian dollar. At the same time moral revulsion against U.S. aggression has brought new sections of people, young and old, into opposition to U.S. policies and strengthened the demand that the government publicly repudiate these policies, that Canada adopt a truly independent foreign policy. It is this sentiment which has prevented the U.S. government and its supporters in Canada from stopping the entry of draft resisters and deserters from the U.S. armed forces into Canada. It is not accidental that it was in Canada that the Hemispheric Conference against the War in Vietnam took place. Nor is it accidental that considerable material and medical aid has come from the Canadian people to assist the National Liberation Front in its just struggle. Not always clearly, those Canadians see in the Vietnam struggle an assist to their own struggle against U.S. imperialism. For the Canadian people the struggles for peace and independence are in reality one struggle.

All these movements reflecting the desire for deep-going change create the basis for an anti-monopoly, anti-imperialist coalition, led by the working class. This is what our Party is striving to achieve in its work to bring about fundamental social change in Canada. We recognize that this is an intricate and complex process and that a major responsibility falls upon the shoulders of our Party — to help unite these various currents, strengthen its own influence and organized strength, and imbue the working class with consciousness of the role it must play. Here, neither impatience and adventurism, nor adaptation to capitalist pressures will serve the interests of the working class. It requires firmness in principled questions and the utmost flexibility in tactics to accomplish these aims.

Lenin, many years ago, emphasized that the most important task before Communist Parties in the capitalist countries is to search out the forms of transition or the approach to the proletarian revolution. We are guided by this in our work to bring about a democratic alliance which could take Canada on the high road to socialism. Therefore we see no contradiction between these national tasks and our international responsibilities as outlined in the main document before us.

IV

The divisions in the international communist movement have created many problems for our Party and the international movement. This has benefitted only imperialism, which plays upon and inflames nationalism as a means of undermining the unity of action of Communist and Workers' Parties and of the anti-imperialist forces throughout the world.

Our Party is deeply concerned about the actions taken by the Maoist group to split the international communist movement. The Maoists speak about fighting imperialism but in their daily practice and in their basic policies split the forces which can effectively oppose imperialism.

We are equally concerned about their territorial ambitions. Our 20th National Convention sharply condemned the provocation perpetrated by the Maoists on the Soviet-Chinese border as contrary to all ordinary relations between states, let alone to socialist internationalism. This going over from polemics to military provocation, from ideological struggle to state actions, shows how far the Maoists have departed from their commitments and responsibilities to the socialist community and the cause of peace and socialism throughout the world. Their adventurist positions on the main questions of war, peace and revolution, further underwritten in their 9th Congress, are anti-Leninist. Maoism is an anti-Leninist disorder, an expression of petty-bourgeois nationalism. It is a departure from Marxism-Leninism which they have replaced by Maoism. This opportunism masked with left phrases is a negation of proletarian internationalism, a form of virulent anti-Sovietism, and in the final analysis strikes at the very foundation of socialism.

We are confident that the Chinese Communists who adhere to Marxism-Leninism, and the Chinese people, will eventually assert themselves. Marxism-Leninism will sooner or later win out in its contest with Mao's petty-bourgeois nationalism. The place of China is with the socialist camp, with the world communist movement, with all the anti-imperialist forces in the struggle for peace, independence and socialism. The defeat of Maoism ideologically, on an international scale, the strengthening of our unity on the basis of Marxism-Leninism, are a significant contribution in this direction.

We see the Lenin centenary as an important part of the ideological struggle of Leninism against petty-bourgeois nationalism, against opportunism and revisionism and in the building of a working-class party independent from the bourgeoisie, firmly based on the principles of Marxism-Leninism.

It's become fashionable in some quarters to criticize the

91

Soviet Union in the illusory hope that it will make our Party "respectable", forgetting that history abounds with facts showing that anti-Sovietism has always been the common factor drawing together all enemies of peace and socialism. All of us who are concerned with the struggle for peace and socialism must never forget that the Soviet Union is the decisive factor in the world struggle against imperialism, for peace and socialism. This does not mean that any one party is in a privileged position in regard to the others in the world communist movement, but facts are facts, and it is the Soviet Union and the CPSU that carry the main burden and responsibility in the worldwide struggle. Anti-Sovietism, no matter how refined, as any weakening of the socialist countries, plays into the hands of the enemies of the workers of the world.

Each Communist Party is independent and sovereign, responsible to the working class of its country, but it is also responsible to the international working class. Some say that international connections and conferences hurt the Party's influence within our own country. This is sheer nonsense. The present international conference will unquestionably strengthen the unity, influence and prestige of Communist and Workers' Parties in all countries and our Party will enjoy the benefit of all this. For a party to see only one side of its responsibility will cause it to fall prey either to nationalism or national nihilism. In our view the independence and sovereignty of Communist and Workers' Parties find expression in independence *from* the capitalist class and its policies and by standing firm on the principles of Marxism-Leninism and proletarian internationalism.

From our own experience our Party has recognized the need for a systematic ideological struggle against revisionism, opportunism and nationalism, all of which express the pressures of the capitalist environment and could lead to the transformation of the Party into a social-democratic type of party. Recognizing this danger our recent convention, expressing the conviction of the overwhelming majority of the members of our Party, called for a resolute struggle against right and "left" revisionism and opportunism which in our view are the main danger at this stage, and also to continue combatting dogmatic, sectarian tendencies.

From our Party's experience we can fully endorse the statement of comrade Brezhnev about the benefits derived from the various forms of discussion of mutual problems and co-operation between the parties of different countries. Such discussion and co-operation, we believe, help to establish ideological unity — unity based on principle because no other unity can be lasting or durable — in the international communist movement.

The highest expression of that international communist discussion is this historic world conference which we are attending. The workers of all countries are looking to us to emerge from our discussions with the maximum of ideological unity as the greatest asset in bolstering and extending our unity of action. We must not disappoint them. We must find the strength and will to overcome whatever differences there may be among us and emerge with a unanimous agreement, for which we believe the main document before us offers us the basis. We are sure that this can and will be achieved.

As far as our Party and delegation are concerned, we are prepared to sign this document as it presently stands.

Moscow,
June 5-17, 1969.

V

International Meeting — an historic event

Sometimes one has to look back at an event to see it in proper perspective. From this vantage point it can be truly said that the International Meeting of Communist and Workers' Parties was a major success, indeed a turning point for the international communist movement, for the working class and the liberation movement.

One has only to consider the reaction of the mass media to see how true this is. From the period of its preparation right up to its opening session, the capitalist mass media took the position that the International Meeting would never be held, that differences among some parties were so acute as to make such a Meeting impossible. As is known they were proven wrong. Seventy-five Communist and Workers' Parties came to the meeting, two of them, the parties from Cuba and Sweden, in the capacity of observers. In face of this reality the mass media shifted gears and solemnly declared nothing much would come out of the Meeting, hoping that the splitting policies of the leaders of the Communist Party of China on one hand, and the events in Czechoslovakia on the other, would paralyze its work. They backed their hopes by picking out bits and pieces from the contributions of some delegations to create the impression that the Meeting would be rent asunder. What they did not take into account was the high sense of responsibility of the delegations both to their working class and people and to the international working-class movement, their determination to overcome temporary disagreements or subordinate them to the over-riding need of strengthening the unity of action of the international communist movement against imperialism.

This found its expression in the adoption by the Meeting of the main document before it, "Tasks at the Present Stage of the Struggle Against Imperialism and United Action of Communist and Workers' Parties and All Anti-Imperialist Forces"; a statement on "Independence, Freedom and Peace for Vietnam"; an Appeal in Defence of Peace; an Address on the Lenin Centenary; a statement in support of the just struggle of the Arab peoples against Israeli aggression; a statement of solidarity with Communists and Democrats of Greece and of Haiti; an address to Indonesian Communists. In addition it was agreed to work for the convening of a world congress of all anti-imperialist forces, and a world conference against racism.

Thus, far from being rent asunder the Meeting arrived at conclusions on major questions confronting mankind, and in the course of doing so created conditions for strengthening the unity of Communist and Workers' Parties on the firm foundations of Marxism-Leninism and proletarian internationalism.

The methods and procedures pursued by the Meeting did much to facilitate its positive outcome. The Meeting was an open one, conducted in a highly democratic fashion. No time limits were set for contributions to the discussion. All delegations could and did express their views openly and sharply.

In addition, a press center was established so that the press of the world could ask any questions they wished of those parties that participated in the press conferences. There were no secrets and no secret sessions. It is interesting to note that although the advocates of "freedom of the press" chose to play up those remarks which suited their aims while suppressing others, the press of the Soviet Union and of other socialist countries published all contributions, including those critical of some aspects of policy of the socialist countries. So much for "freedom of the press".

The wide-open character of the Meeting was coupled with collective hammering out of agreements. No votes were taken. There were no minority and majority positions. All agreements were arrived at through debate and exchange of views. The capitalist mass media chose to characterize the wide-ranging and critical debate as an expression of "the crisis of world communism," when in fact it attested in large measure to the strength and maturity of the communist movement, to the different conditions under which parties are compelled to work which often necessitate different tactical approaches to this or that phenomenon. In this sense, what the Meeting brought forward was not the differences, many of which still need to be resolved, but the basic agreements and unity. This is why the capitalist mass media have been rather silent since the Meeting. Their hopes and those of their mentors of a fragmented and splintered communist movement, unable to meet the challenge of the times, have not been realized. Indeed, if the Meeting did nothing else, it halted the trend toward fragmentation and splits and charted a course leading toward greater unity and cohesion of the international communist movement. It did this not by "diktat", not by "orders from Moscow", not through the creation of a new international center, but by a correct blending of national and international tasks as expressed in the documents of the Meeting which on the one hand uphold the sovereignty, independence and equality of each Party, and on the other, strengthen international solidarity and unity of action against imperialism. It is a great gain for the international working class that this task was accomplished. In this lies the historical significance of the International Meeting. The groundwork has been laid for a new upsurge of the world communist movement and for uniting all the anti-imperialist forces of the world in common struggle against reaction and war, and for strengthening the fight for peace, democracy, national liberation and socialism on a world scale.

ROAD AHEAD

Essentially the Meeting had the task of summing up the events of the nine years since the 1960 Conference, and on the basis of a sober, scientific and rounded-out analysis of world developments, to indicate the prospects ahead. Some parties took the position that the situation was not ripe for such a summing-up, that the Meeting should limit itself to adopting a program of anti-imperialist action. The majority of parties, however, maintained that without such an analysis of new phenomena, a sober estimation of class forces on a world scale, the strategy and tactics of imperialism at this stage, there would be a lack of perspective and direction without which an effective joint offensive of all the revolutionary forces of our day against the positions of world imperialism could not be mounted.

This also had to do with estimates of events over the past nine years. During that period the forces of imperialism did everything possible to weaken the socialist camp, the national-liberation movement and the working-class movement in the capitalist world as part of its efforts to maintain its world positions. Imperialism instigated wars and crises in various parts of the world and even took the world to the brink of nuclear war. During this period U.S. imperialism undertook aggression against Vietnam and provoked the Middle East crisis, while Bonn stepped up its revenge-seeking plans in Europe. During this period some setbacks and retreats for the anti-imperialist forces took place, as in Indonesia, Ghana and Greece.

In the face of the increased aggressiveness of imperialism there was need to achieve stronger bonds of unity of the international communist movement. The global strategy of imperialism required a strategy of unity of the entire communist movement and of all anti-imperialist forces.

New phenomena requiring serious analysis had shaped up in the capitalist world particularly in relation to the scientific and technological revolution. Moreover, in the past period the leadership of the Communist Party of China undertook an open attack against Marxism-Leninism, including a policy of splitting the communist and anti-imperialist movement. Imperialism used the divisions in the communist movement and deviations from Marxism-Leninism of a right and left character to weaken socialism, the working class and national liberation movement.

In these conditions the International Meeting had a dual task: drawing political conclusions from past events, to outline a clear perspective for the period ahead, and on that basis to strengthen the unity and cohesion of the international communist movement.

As a result of looking at the situation in a one-sided way tendencies had arisen among some Communists to view temporary setbacks and retreats as evidence of a basic shift in the balance of power in favor of imperialism. Without minimizing these temporary retreats and setbacks, the main document stressed that "the contradiction between the imperialist 'policy of strength' and the real possibilities of imperialism is becoming ever more evident. *Imperialism can neither regain its lost historical initiative nor reverse world development.* The main direction of mankind's development is determined by the world socialist system, the international working class, all revolutionary forces." The truth of this is to be seen in the marked successes of the world socialist system in the economic and political spheres, no less than in the military sphere. In the continued growth and development of the national-liberation movement, which in some areas is beginning to take on more directly anti-capitalist positions. In the upsurge of working-class action against monopoly alongside the entry of new forces into the anti-imperialist struggle, particularly the youth. The truth of this is particularly evident in the military defeat U.S. imperialism has suffered in Vietnam.

These developments — on the background of the deepening of the general crisis of imperialism; the aggravation of inter-imperialist contradictions and rivalry, expressed in a sharpened struggle for markets and spheres of influence; growing economic instability in the capitalist world, expressed in the currency crisis — indicate that as a world system imperialism has not become stronger; that socialism and the forces of peace and progress, and not imperialism are on the offensive. From this the main document concludes that "at present there are real possibilities for resolving the key problems of our times in the interests of peace, democracy and socialism, to deal imperialism new blows."

At the same time the main document cautions against any

tendency to underestimate imperialism's strength and its capacity to inflict terrible harm on mankind. Imperialism, although it has not grown stronger, remains a serious and dangerous foe. The USA, the chief imperialist power, has grown more aggressive and dangerous. While imperialism has been compelled to adapt itself to the new relationship of forces on a world scale, it has not given up its basic aims: to stimulate tension, provoke local wars, weaken socialism from within, split the international communist movement, and halt "the irreversible decline in capitalism."

PEACEFUL CO-EXISTENCE AND SOCIAL ADVANCE

The question of peace and war was therefore at the center of attention of the Meeting. As comrade Brezhnev correctly stressed in his remarks, "One of the cardinal tasks of the international communist movement is to head the struggle of the people for a lasting peace, and today, far from diminishing, the importance of this task constantly grows. It would be wrong to underestimate the threat of war created by imperialism, above all, U.S. imperialism, the main force of world reaction."

It is in this spirit and conscious of its reponsibility to deliver mankind from the threat of world nuclear war that issue was taken with the Maoist thesis on the inevitability of war. In his contribution comrade Gomulka took issue with the Maoist position, stating that "the thesis that world war is inevitable is theoretically false and politically sterile. To accept that thesis means to abandon the struggle for achieving the most advantageous conditions for settling the basic conflict of this era — the conflict between socialism and capitalism. The alternative to passive reconciliation with the prospects of world war is the struggle for peaceful co-existence. To oppose the prospects of peaceful co-existence with the thesis that there are only two possibilities on the question of world war, 'either war will lead to revolution or revolution will prevent war',* means to shy away from the actual problems of our times."

*From Lin Piao's report to the Ninth Congress of the Communist Party of China.

It is useful to note that the above statement of Lin Piao veers closely to that of Trotsky during the Brest-Livotsk negotiations — "neither peace nor war." Under cover of a "revolutionary phrase" the Maoist line offers war rather than the struggle for peace as the way to socialism.

In rejecting this dangerous line the Meeting restated its basic support for the struggle for peaceful co-existence between countries of different social systems whose aim is to secure the renunciation of war as a method of settling conflicts between states. While the danger of military conflicts remains as long as imperialism exists, the growing strength of the international communist and workers' movement, and of the world peace movement, makes the struggle for peaceful co-existence a realistic task. At the same time the Meeting emphasized that the class struggle, of which the ideological struggle is a part, continues on an international and national scale, that the struggle for working-class power and of the former colonies for complete independence, develops within the framework of peaceful co-existence. In short, the aim of the struggle for peaceful co-existence is to create the best possible conditions for resolving basic class conflicts without another world war.

The Meeting did not only affirm the aims of peaceful co-existence. It laid particular stress on the fact it could only be won in the course of many-sided struggles against imperialism. As the main document emphasizes: "The defence of peace is inseparably linked up with the struggle to compel the imperialists to accept peaceful co-existence of states with different social systems. *Mass action against imperialism is a condition for implementing the policy of peaceful co-existence.*"

The Meeting not only dealt with imperialism as a system but with its aggressive aims and actions. These were spelled out in the comprehensive program of anti-imperialist actions which is part of the main document. It focussed on the main danger spots in the world today: Vietnam, the Middle East, Bonn revanchism, the struggle against colonialism and neo-colonialism, racism and neo-fascism, the struggle for nuclear disarmament. As distinct from the reservations some parties held with respect to other parts of the main document, there was virtually unanimous agreement with this section dealing with anti-imperialist actions.

By focussing its main fire on imperialism as the main enemy of peace, freedom, independence and social progress, the Meeting opened the door to uniting the main streams of the world revolutionary process, the socialist world system, the working class in the capitalist countries and the national-liberation movement into a mighty force for peace and social progress. As the main document states: "The main link of united action of the anti-imperialist forces remains the struggle for world peace, the menace of thermonuclear war and mass extermination which continues to hang over mankind."

It is with this in mind that the Meeting concentrated its attention on co-ordinating the efforts of all anti-imperialist forces, first of all the Communist and Workers' Parties, all directed to strengthening the alliance of the socialist world system with the working-class and national-liberation movements.

It goes without saying that the socialist world system is the decisive factor in the struggle against imperialism. This was underscored in the main document. Therefore the strengthening of the unity of the socialist system based on socialist internationalism is of profound significance to the outcome of the struggle against imperialism. Moreover, precisely because the socialist system is the principal obstacle to imperialism and its drive to reaction and war, defence of socialism is the internationalist duty of all Communists. This too was underscored in the main document.

The events in Czechoslovakia brought this out clearly. While some parties expressed disagreement with the action taken by the Warsaw Treaty countries in coming to the defence of socialism in Czechoslovakia, the great majority who spoke on the question expressed approval of that action of socialist internationalism as being in the interests of European security and the socialist gains of Czechoslovakia. Their positions were further buttressed by the delegation of the Communist Party of Czechoslovakia which drew attention to the tactics used by imperialism to undermine socialism from within, to the necessity for firm action against the anti-socialist and right-opportunist forces within Czechoslovakia and the Communist Party of Czechoslovakia.

The overwhelming majority of delegations sharply condemned the divisive actions of the leadership of the Communist Party of China, its efforts at substituting Maoism for Marxism-Leninism, its break with its international commitments, its anti-Leninist course. What stood out is the fact that the efforts of the Maoists to impose their particular line on the international communist movement had suffered virtual defeat.

STATE-MONOPOLY CAPITALISM AND
THE ROLE OF THE WORKING CLASS

Particular attention was paid to developments shaping up in the capitalist countries. This had to do not only with an examination of the role of state-monopoly capitalism, the emergence of multi-national corporations, the scientific and technological revolution, the old and new contradictions within capitalism. It had to do particularly with the growing upsurge of democratic, anti-imperialist and working-class action in the capitalist countries generally. In this process the role of the working class as the main motive and mobilizing force of the present stage of the revolutionary struggle was given particular emphasis. Attention was drawn to the growing consciousness of the working class which by its struggle is helping to bring new forces into the struggle against imperialism and capitalism. At the same time the course of the struggle is compelling the working class to advance larger aims and to come into direct conflict with the political power of state-monopoly capitalism. The scientific and technological revolution under state-monopoly capitalist rule will accelerate this process and strengthen the trend toward unity in the working class and trade union movement. The prospect is one of new class battles in some countries that could lead to fundamental social change.

The Meeting also noted the revolutionary potential of the working farmers, the progressive intellectuals and the youth, all adding up to a sharp increase of mass popular pressure for social change.

Drawing upon international experience the Meeting emphasized that the working farmers remain the chief allies of the working class despite the fact that there has been a considerable diminution of their numerical strength in all advanced capitalist countries. This was important, to avoid using the term alliance too loosely as in the case of the worker-student alliance. Alliances refer to classes and the youth do not constitute a separate class. Emphasis was therefore placed on the *unity* of workers, students and intellectuals, as distinct from the worker-farmer alliance.

The radical upsurge which mirrors the growing crisis of imperialism is to be seen in the fact that millions of hitherto politically passive individuals have been drawn into active political struggle and joined the battle against imperialist policies of reaction and war. The inclusion of a large petty-bourgeois mass in the arena of social and political struggle presents new problems for the revolutionary movement. These forces are impatient at the injustices of the system but have not yet accepted the discipline nor acquired the experience of revolutionary struggle against it. This explains why they tend to be susceptible to various theories, particularly those critical of Marxism-Leninism and of the Communist and Workers' Parties.

These new forces, which are anti-imperialist in the main, need to be brought into the revolutionary struggle. But to do so requires the defeat of these basically petty-bourgeois theories, bringing socialist consciousness and organization into these movements and winning acceptance of the leading role of the working class among them. Only close unity with the working-class movement and its communist vanguard can give the youth a genuinely revolutionary perspective.

To implement such an approach requires two things — a broad, flexible approach to all potential allies, on the one hand; a firm Marxist-Leninist position, an independent class position, the ability to advance and defend that position among these potential allies, on the other.

As the Meeting emphasized, the sharpening contradictions

between labor and capital are developing into a deepening antagonism between monopoly and the majority of the nation. Objectively and subjectively the basis is being laid for uniting all those forces into a powerful anti-monopoly and anti-imperialist alliance.

The basis for such a development lies in unity of the working-class movement, more particularly the unity of Communists and social democrats. Experience showed that the struggle for unity of action had helped stimulate a genuine left. Unity, however, could not succeed without a consistent struggle against right-wing social democracy, from the firm principled positions of Marxism-Leninism. It is the sharp criticism of opportunism which will, as the main document states, "deepen the crisis of reformist concepts." The Communists were called upon to strive for co-operation and joint action with all those genuinely prepared to fight imperialism, for peace, for democracy and the interests of the working people, for full co-operation with social democrats, for the larger aim of establishing an advanced democratic government leading toward the building of a socialist society.

It is the policy of unity and the fight for it that can make it possible to bring unorganized workers and those still under the influence of capitalist parties into the anti-imperialist struggle and widen its base.

As the main document states: "In the course of anti-monopolist and anti-imperialist united action, favorable conditions are created for uniting all democratic trends into a political alliance capable of decisively limiting the role played by the monopolies in the economies of the countries concerned, of putting an end to the power of big capital and of bringing about such radical political and economic changes as would ensure the most favorable conditions for continuing the struggle for socialism. The main force in this democratic alliance is the working class. The objectives can be achieved, above all, by diverse forms of powerful mass action by the working class and the broadest sections of the population. While making use of all possibilities of parliamentary activity, communists emphasize that the mass movement of the working class and of all working people is the decisive factor in the struggle for democracy and socialism."

The Meeting devoted particular attention to the urgent task of strengthening the unity of Communist and Workers' Parties without which no effective offensive could be mounted against imperialism. As the main document declared: "Cohesion of Communist and Workers' Parties is the most important factor in rallying together all the anti-imperialist forces."

Emphasis on this question was not accidental. Divergencies have arisen among some parties in the socialist states which imperialism uses to separate and weaken them.

Referring to the difficult period of development of the communist movement, the fact that unity has been disrupted, comrade Brezhnev expressed the view that it had been largely caused by "the penetration of revisionist influences of a right and left nature in the communist movement. Revisionism in theory leads to opportunism in practice. Revisionism is a departure from proletarian class positions, a substitution for Marxism-Leninism of all sorts of bourgeois and petty-bourgeois concepts, new and old. The unity of the Party, the interests of the anti-imperialist movement, demand intensification of the struggle against revisionism, both right and left opportunism. A principled stand on this issue has always been a most important condition for strengthening a party's political position. Right-wing opportunism means a slide down to liquidationist positions and to conciliation with social democracy in policy and ideology. Left-wing opportunism under cover of ultra-left verbiage pushes the masses to adventurist actions and the Party into a sectarian path."

It is in this light that the main document stressed the need for a consistent struggle against bourgeois ideology and its offshoot, anti-communism, which have become the main weapons of imperialism against Marxism-Leninism, the revolutionary movement and socialism.

Indeed, in conditions of a revolutionary upsurge, failure to fight revisionism and opportunism could lead to serious setbacks. The struggle against right and left opportunism is of decisive importance. Both undermine the revolutionary character of the Party, its vanguard role, and thereby weaken the working class and the unity of the anti-imperialist forces.

The main document spells out the ways and means of overcoming divergencies and strengthening unity, based on the independence and equality of every Party, the fact that each Party develops its own policies in keeping with national conditions, always guided by the principles of Marxism-Leninism, but based also on the principles of proletarian internationalism, solidarity and mutual support. Thus the national and international responsibilities of the parties are one and indivisible. This is so because Marxist-Leninists are both patriots and internationalists. At the same time, mindful of the fact that differences do exist on some questions, the Meeting agreed with the proposal to convene international theoretical conferences which could come to grips with them and generalize new phenomena arising from the contemporary scene. There is no doubt that such international theoretical conferences, combined with the strengthening of fraternal relations between parties through bilateral or wider conferences, will strengthen unity and be of inestimable value for all Communist and Workers' Parties.

It is impossible in this brief article to deal with all the questions encompassed in the documents of the Meeting. The documents and the rich contributions made by many delegations should be read and studied by Communists and all anti-imperialist forces in our country. In many respects the conclusions drawn are similar to those arrived at by the 20th Convention of the Communist Party of Canada. Our Party signed the main document, seeing in it a correct line of march for the period ahead. Some parties had reservations on this or that point. A few agreed only to sign the section on anti-imperialist action. Only one party, the Dominican Party, did not sign it. Events will prove the main document to be a truly living document, the inspirer of ever-widening anti-imperialist action based on stronger unity of the international communist movement, a document that correctly outlines the strategy and tactics of our epoch.

The results of the Meeting clearly demonstrated that the international communist movement has emerged after many trials, difficulties and some partial setbacks, as the greatest single political force in the world. Its cohesion and unity flowing from joint anti-imperialist action will become a powerful point of attraction for all anti-imperialist forces on a world scale and enable it to broaden and deepen the worldwide offensive against imperialism.

The Meeting demonstrated above all that the three main revolutionary streams of our time — the socialist system, the national-liberation movement and the working-class and democratic movements in the imperialist countries — can not only prevent a third world war but will bring an end to imperialism as a system. The Meeting correctly emphasized that on the activity of Communist and Workers' Parties will largely depend world development in the closing third of the 20th century.

The conclusion of the main document places the tasks fairly and squarely:

"Tense battles lie ahead and they cannot be avoided. Let us step up the offensive against imperialism and internal reaction. The revolutionary and progressive forces are certain to triumph.

"Peoples of the socialist countries, workers, democratic forces in the capitalist countries, newly free peoples and those who are oppressed, unite in a common struggle against imperialism, for peace, national liberation, social progress, democracy and socialism!"

There is no doubt that this appeal and all the documents of the Meeting will find an ever-widening response in our country.

Communist Viewpoint,
September-October 1969.

VI

Lenin and contemporary imperialism

Lenin made a signal contribution to Marxism in his monumental work, *Imperialism, the Highest Stage of Capitalism*. With characteristic modesty, he called it a "popular outline". In actual fact it was a direct continuation of Marx's theory of capitalism. Marx brought to light the fundamental economic and class contradictions of capitalism, the laws of its development, the scientific basis for the theory of proletarian revolution and the dictatorship of the proletariat. However, neither Marx nor Engels lived to see the new epoch of monopoly capitalism in its full development — imperialism. It remained for Lenin to bring to light the new features, the new and more acute forms of economic and class contradictions of capitalism which arose in the epoch of imperialism. From a study of these features Lenin drew the conclusion that capitalist society had entered a new stage of development.

"Capitalism," he pointed out, "became capitalist imperialism at a definite and very high stage of its development, when certain of its fundamental attributes began to be transformed into their opposites, when the features of transition from capitalism to a higher social order and economic system began to take shape and reveal themselves all along the line. The fundamental economic factor in this process is the substitution of capitalist monopolies for capitalist competition." Lenin then goes on to say, "at the same time monopoly which has grown out of free çompetition does not abolish the latter but exists alongside it, and hovers over it, as it were, and as a result gives rise to a number of very acute antagonisms, frictions and conflicts" (*Selected Works,* Vol. 5, Chapter VII, p. 80).

Lenin returned to this position in discussing the revision of the Party Program, stating, "It is in fact this combination of antagonistic principles, viz., *competition and monopoly,* that is the essence of imperialism, it is this that is making for the final crash, i.e., the socialist revolution" (*Selected Works,* Vol. VI, p. 110).

In his definition of imperialism Lenin drew attention to the following five main characteristic features:

(a) the concentration of production and capital developed to such a stage that its creates monopolies which play a decisive role in economic life.

(b) the merging of bank capital with industrial capital, and the creation, on the basis of finance capital, of a financial oligarchy.

(c) the export of capital, which has become extremely important, as distinguished from the export of commodities.

(d) the formation of international capitalist monopolies which share the world among themselves.

(e) territorial division of the whole world among the great capitalist powers is completed.

VALIDITY OF LENINISM

These economic, social and political features of imperialism determined the course of events in the capitalist world until the October Socialist Revolution brought to an end its undivided world domination. They are still valid. Indeed, they provide the only sound basis for an analysis of contemporary imperialism.

Lenin showed that imperialism is the last stage in the development of the capitalist mode of production and the beginning of the era of socialist revolution. This view was borne out by the October Revolution; the emergence of the world socialist system; the break-up of the colonial system; the deepening crisis of imperialism and the accentuation of all its contradictions.

It is strange indeed that in spite of history and experience there are those who argue against the validity of Lenin's theory of imperialism. They claim that contemporary capitalism is basically different from the characterization made by Lenin. The claims are made that the contradictions of the capitalist world have either been eliminated, or at least greatly lessened, that the contradictions between the imperialist states and those plundered by them no longer exist, that monopoly means "efficiency and public good", and therefore, "socialist revolution is no longer necessary". Life does not substantiate these claims.

This whitewashing and embellishment of capitalism is done to hide the real *economic foundation of imperialist expansion,* which determines its predatory and aggressive nature, its drive to domination, reaction, fascism and war.

This is not to deny that monopoly capitalism has acquired some new features, typical of the present stage of the development of the general crisis of capitalism. Referring to this, the main document of the International Conference of Communist and Workers' Parties pointed out that "present-day imperialism, which is trying to adapt itself to the conditions of the struggle between the two systems and to the demands of the scientific and technological revolution, has some new features. Its state-monopoly character has become more pronounced. It resorts ever more extensively to such instruments as state-stimulated monopolistic concentration of production and capital, redistribution by the state of an increasing proportion of the national income, allocation of war contracts to the monopolies, government financing of industrial development and research programs on a countrywide scale, the policy of imperialist integration and new forms of capital exports."

State-monopoly capitalism, however, has not altered the nature of imperialism. Indeed, since Lenin wrote *Imperialism* there has taken place a further leap in the process of concentration and centralization of production and capital. This has found expression in the growing process of mergers, the emergence and further development of multi-national corporations, and alongside them, the emergence of conglomerates. This has led to a further strengthening of monopoly's positions in the economy and politics of the capitalist world, to a merging of monopoly capital with the state and the further subordination of the state to it. Lenin foresaw this development, pointing out that imperialism was at the same time the era of gigantic capitalist monopolies, of the development of monopoly capitalism into state-monopoly capitalism. "Monopoly in general," he stated, "has evolved into state-monopoly capital" (*Selected Works*, Vol. VII, p. 99).

CONTRADICTIONS SHARPEN

The measures undertaken by state-monopoly capitalism to bolster capitalism result in the further sharpening of its contradictions and undermine its foundation. Despite its efforts to regulate the economy, anarchy of production is increasing, economic inequality is growing, market problems are becoming more acute, general economic instability and polarization of wealth are increasing. The antagonism between labor and capital and between monopoly and the people is growing, and so are the contradictions among the imperialist powers and between imperialism and the less-developed countries.

Lenin spoke of imperialism as "moribund capitalism", as decaying and dying capitalism. Some bourgeois ideologists have endeavored to distort this to mean that Lenin advanced the theory of the constant stagnation and complete paralysis of the productive forces under imperialism. Lenin never advanced such a viewpoint. What he drew attention to in *Imperialism* was the "*tendency* to stagnation and decay which is a feature of monopoly", that "for certain branches of industry, in certain countries, for certain periods of times, becomes predominant" (*Selected Works*, Vol. 5, Chapter VIII, p. 91). But he added to this the following: "It would be a mistake to believe that the *tendency* to decay precludes the possibility of the rapid growth of capitalism. It does not. In the epoch of imperialism, certain countries betray, to a greater or lesser degree, one or other of these *tendencies*. On the whole capitalism is growing far more rapidly than before, but it is not only that this growth is becoming more and more uneven; this unevenness manifests itself also, in particular, in the decay of the countries which are richest in capital (such as England)" (*Selected Works,* Vol. 5, Chapter X, p. 116).

Developments in modern-day imperialism, rather than invalidating Lenin's characterization of imperialism, underscore it. We witness both tendencies, decay and rapid growth, within various capitalist countries and on a world scale. The simultaneous operation of both tendencies undermines the very foundations upon which capitalist society rests. Marxism-Leninism maintains that the productive forces are the most revolutionary factors in society.

Lenin saw the totality of all the processes at work in developing the theory of imperialism. From this he drew the conclusion that "state-monopoly capitalism is the fullest material preparation for socialism, it is its *threshold,* it is that rung in the historical ladder between which and the rung called socialism, *there are no intervening rungs"* (*Selected Works,* Vol. VII, p. 367). He saw how acute the contradiction between social production and private appropriation becomes under imperialism.

NEO-COLONIALISM AND ECONOMIC DOMINATION

In his analysis of imperialism Lenin showed that the development of monopoly capitalism is at the same time the history of its territorial expansion, of its drive to subjugate other peoples and for world domination. He drew attention to the export of capital as one of the essential forms of this process. This characterization of imperialism holds true today as one of the principal means through which it exercises its policy of neo-colonialism. The main aim of neo-colonialism is to keep the newly-emerging countries within the capitalist orbit and undermine the national and social liberation movements. The export of capital is used as an instrument in the competitive struggle between the monopolies of different countries for spheres of influence, within the narrowing bounds of the imperialist system.

Capital export in the guise of investments and loans is one

of the ways through which U.S. imperialism has extended its control over the Canadian economy, not to speak of other capitalist countries, with the aim of subordinating them to U.S. imperialist aims.

Despite this drive toward domination, inherent in imperialism, the claim is made that because most colonial countries have achieved their political independence, imperialism has changed its nature and is a thing of the past.

Those who advance this erroneous position make the question of colonies the *main* or sole attribute of imperialism. What they choose to ignore is the *economic foundation of imperialist expansion.* As Lenin stated in his *Imperialism,* "The economic quintessence of imperialism is monopoly capitalism" *(Selected Works,* Vol. 5, Chapter X, p. 114). What is also ignored is Lenin's position that under imperialism "economic annexation is fully 'achieveable' without political annexation." Canada illustrates this perfectly, *vis-à-vis* U.S. imperialism. U.S. imperialism "prefers" maintaining the façade of an independent Canada, in a formal sense, while striving to control it economically. This provides U.S. imperialism with certain advantages, not least having Canadian monopoly as its junior partner to facilitate the process of "peaceful" takeover. It provided U.S. imperialism with the possibility of penetrating the British imperialist market in Canada. In the more recent period it is striving to accelerate the process of takeover through integration and continentalism, through a form of partnership with Canadian monopoly. This uneasy and unequal partnership, which has accelerated the process of U.S. domination, has in turn given a new impetus to and broadened the opposition of Canadians to the sell-out.

The predatory nature of imperialism is to be seen most vividly in Vietnam and the Middle East, and also in the sharpening contradictions within the imperialist camp. The ceaseless struggle for markets and raw materials sharpens this conflict and finds expression in the formation of opposing trade blocs. These trade blocs represent the partitioning of spheres of influence by the international trusts. This is a sort of "uneasy peace" that changes with the changes in the relative strength of the various imperialist powers. Despite the attempts of these powers to resolve the contradictions of imperialism, objective developments upset their efforts.

LAW OF UNEVEN DEVELOPMENT

The law of uneven economic and political development of capitalism, which Lenin brought to light and characterized as "an absolute law of capitalism" (*Selected Works*, Vol. 5, p. 141), is the objective source giving rise to inter-imperialist conflicts.

The law of uneven economic and political development of capitalism operates with full force today. It is illustrated in the sharpening of imperialist contradictions, the growing rivalry of imperialist powers, the changing relationship of forces within the imperialist camp, the emergence of West German and Japanese imperialisms as major competitors of U.S. and other imperialist powers. It is illustrated further by the financial and currency wars within the capitalist world.

Imperialism strives to mitigate these contradictions and prevent them from reaching the stage of open conflict and inter-imperialist war. U.S. global strategy is directed to unite the imperialist states against socialism. In Europe it has established a U.S.-West German axis, in the Far East a U.S.-Japanese axis, in the Middle East a U.S.-Israeli axis. However, these efforts on the political and military planes constantly collide with the contradictions within the imperialist camp, arising from the differing economic interests of the various monopoly groupings. The tendencies to come together and to fall apart operate simultaneously in the capitalist system expressing the antagonistic partnership typical of imperialism. These tendencies are influenced by the main contradiction of our time — that between capitalism and socialism.

IMPERIALISM AND OPPORTUNISM

Lenin's theory of imperialism is not based on passive waiting for the rule of the monopolies to collapse under the weight of their contradictions. It is based on the principle that the driving force of historical progress is the revolutionary struggle of the working people against their exploiters. Lenin sharply condemned those who advanced the theory of the automatic collapse, who tried to embellish capitalism and make it appear attractive, or who substituted reformism for the fundamental change of capitalism.

"The most dangerous people of all in this regard," Lenin stated, "are those who do not wish to understand that the fight against imperialism is a sham and a humbug unless it is inseparably bound up with the fight against opportunism" (*Selected Works*, Vol. 5, Chapter X, p. 117).

This too is valid today when opportunism and revisionism try to embellish contemporary capitalism. Opportunism today finds its expression in denying that imperialism exists or that it is predatory in nature. It rejects the importance of the struggle to *impose* peaceful co-existence on imperialism. Right opportunism rejects the revolutionary transformation of society and the need of the working class to assume state power — the dictatorship of the proletariat. It advocates the gradual, evolutionary reform of capitalism, calling this socialism. It advances utopian non-class concepts of so-called new models of socialism. There can be no reconciliation with opportunism, reformism and revisionism.

Lenin's theory of imperialism has stood the test of time. It finds its expression today in the growing anti-imperialist struggle of all the peoples, a struggle in which the three revolutionary currents of our time are increasingly in the ascendancy. Imperialism remains a strong and treacherous foe of progress. As Lenin correctly emphasized: "politically imperialism is in general a striving toward violence and reaction" (*Selected Works*, Vol. 5, Chapter VII, p. 83). Therefore, there are no grounds for complacency or lack of vigilance by the people. On the contrary, unity and vigilance are needed more than ever to curb the power of imperialism and finally destroy it.

Communist Viewpoint,
March-April, 1970.

VII

A new phase in the struggle
for Canadian independence

The debate over Canadian sovereignty in the Arctic as well as over energy policy shows that the issue of Canadian independence is very much alive. Underneath a seemingly calm atmosphere powerful forces are shaping up in opposition to U.S. domination of our country.

U.S. aims on these two questions are fairly clear. U.S. imperialism is opposed to Canada asserting its sovereignty over the Arctic. It takes the position that the Arctic is "open seas", that the U.S. should therefore have the freedom of passage through the Northwest Passage. This is in the tradition of U.S. imperialism which fought for an "open door" policy to pry open doors closed to it by other imperialist powers in the past. In this case, with huge supplies of oil and minerals in Alaska, it is seeking a route through which to transport these riches. The Canadian Arctic and the Northwest Passage are that route.

But there are also military considerations involved in the position taken by U.S. imperialism. This was put rather bluntly in *Military Review,* a magazine issued by the U.S. Army from its command and general staff college at Fort Leavenworth.

"Over the past quarter-century," it begins, "U.S. defense authorities have had to be concerned with many regions of the world, including the rice paddies and swamps of Southeast Asia, the jungles and grasslands of Africa, the sandy wastes of the Middle East. If the mining potential of the North should be tapped, if harbor facilities and storage areas should be constructed, and if great vessels regularly ply the Northwest Passage, then the Northern region would suddently become rich in military targets. The U.S. defense posture — for the first time in history — would have to become northern-oriented."

Knowing what U.S. imperialism is doing in Southeast Asia, Africa and the Middle East, despite its poetic and flowery language about "rice paddies and swamps, jungles and grasslands and the sandy wastes", it requires no stretch of the imagination to understand its aims and ambitions in Canada's North and Arctic.

INTEGRATION AND SHARING

President Nixon, and Mr. Hickel before him, also put the squeeze on Canadian sovereignty with respect to energy policy. They both called for the adoption of an integrated North American energy policy. They proposed the pooling of uranium, coal, gas, oil, hydro-electrical power and water resources. Pressure on Canada to agree to such integration has been doctored up with the high-sounding phrase of "jointly sharing the North American market". In fact, however, there would be no "joint sharing". The energy resources U.S. imperialism wants to integrate are on Canadian territory. What it is striving for is the taking over of these energy resources to feed its vast industrial and military machine.

In pursuit of these aims U.S. imperialism, through President Nixon, has undertaken a pressure campaign on the Canadian government. Its first step was the decision to reduce imports of oil from Canada into the USA and that this may be followed by other measures. Most Canadians grasped the meaning of this decision as a blatant form of blackmail of Canada, aimed at getting an agreement on a continental energy policy including water and an open line through the Arctic and the Northwest Passage to Alaska.

The question of energy resources is of vital importance to Canada. Indeed, it will determine both the present and future development of Canada's economy. Energy resources are the basis upon which secondary industry can be developed on an independent basis. Whoever controls and owns these resources decides the future of the country and, in fact, whether it has a future at all.

In these circumstances a continental energy policy can have only one meaning and one result. It means placing these resources at the disposal of U.S. monopoly interests, to be used for their benefit and profit at the expense of both the immediate and future development of Canada. It means transforming Canada more and more into a supplier of raw material resources for U.S. imperialism and further undermining Canada's sovereignty and independence.

CANADIAN INDEPENDENCE

The pressures of U.S. imperialism on Canada's sovereignty in the Arctic along with its efforts for a continental energy policy are part of the larger drive of U.S. imperialism against Canadian independence.

This is to be seen in the increasing takeover of Canadian-owned companies by the multi-national corporations and conglomerates. In the past few years over 600 such companies have been swallowed up and this process is continuing.

It is to be seen in the continued growth of U.S. investments in Canada. The extent of these U.S. investments rose by 400 per cent in the period 1945 to 1966 — from $5 billion to $25 billion, most of it going into plant and equipment, with a large portion of it coming out of the surplus values extracted from Canadian workers.

It is to be seen in the increasing Americanization of Canadian universities, as well as in the continuing efforts of U.S. imperialism to penetrate the banking and communications systems.

Not least, it is to be seen in the constant pressures on the Canadian government to subordinate Canadian foreign policy to the aims of U.S. imperialism and prevent Canada from pursuing an independent course in foreign affairs.

These are the fruits of the policy of integration pursued by Liberal as well as Tory governments over the postwar years — policies that have opened the dikes for the U.S. takeover.

In these developments one sees how correct Lenin was when in his book, *Imperialism, the Highest Stage of Capitalism,* he drew attention to the fact that "Finance capital is such a great, it may be said, such a decisive force in all economic and international relations that it is capable of subordinating to itself and actually does subordinate to itself even states enjoying complete political independence" (*Selected Works,* Vol. 2, p. 74).

This aptly describes the relationship between U.S. imperialism and Canada, itself a secondary imperialist power.

To some people imperialism is limited to colonial possessions, forcibly obtained. U.S. imperialism in its relation to Canada has so far not exercised direct military aggression. It has instead pursued a policy of buying the dominant sections of Canadian monopoly and making Canada a junior partner in pursuit of its imperialist aims, in return for which it makes available some of the crumbs of its profit. For U.S. imperialism, Canada is of great strategic importance as a secure and stable source of raw materials. Its aim is the "peaceful" takeover of the country, its annexation by dollars, not arms. This is the main form of U.S. imperialist aggression against Canada.

U.S. imperialism would not have succeeded in undermining the sovereignty and independence of Canada without the connivance and agreement of the main Canadian monopoly interests and their governments.

Now that the pressures of U.S. imperialism are mounting and facing growing resistance on the part of wide sections of the Canadian people, particularly from the young people, the government is being compelled to manoeuvre and create the pretence that it is standing up in defence of Canadian sovereignty and independence. Reality, however, does not bear this out.

The government has so far refused to assert Canadian sovereignty over the Arctic. Instead of asserting Canadian sovereignty it is diverting attention to pollution control, something the U.S. government does not object to, particularly when Canadian taxpayers will be paying the shot while U.S. ships will be escorted safely through the Arctic waters.

This supine attitude is similarly displayed with respect to energy policy. The main burden of attention is not directed to formulating an all-Canadian energy policy based on public ownership of energy resources and Canadian development. Instead, it is directed to bargaining, that is, to the sale of these resources to the U.S. corporations for maximum profits for monopoly interests in Canada. As part of the bargaining, the government is not averse to stimulating various forms of pressure on the U.S. government so as to get the best possible deal. However, the Canadian government wants to contain this pressure so that it does not go too far, because it is orientating on arriving at an agreement with the U.S. on energy policy, one that will be profitable to Canadian monopoly even though it results in undermining the very base for independence economic development and further erodes Canadian sovereignty and independence.

INTER-IMPERIALIST CONTRADICTIONS

This is not to deny that there are differences between Canadian monopoly and U.S. imperialism, or that differences may exist in government circles on what course to take. Indeed, inter-imperialist contradictions are growing between the U.S. and Canada. There is ample evidence that the relationship between Canadian monopoly and U.S. imperialism is not an idyllic one, but rather that it takes the form of an "antagonistic partnership". To achieve this it is seeking to counterbalance the pressures of U.S. imperialism by establishing relations with other countries. What is involved here is not only trade but more "elbow room" with which to bargain with U.S. imperialism.

However, the general direction of policy is not independent Canadian development but continentalism. The dominant sections of monopoly are tied by a thousand strings to U.S. imperialism and cannot be counted upon as a factor in the struggle for Canadian sovereignty and independence.

The Trudeau government position is that of continentalism. It is the continuation of the fatal policy of integration pursued by previous Liberal and Tory governments. If there is a difference, it lies in the direction of trying to become an equal rather than a junior partner of U.S. imperialism. At the same time public pressure compels it to take action, as on uranium.

PEOPLE'S OPPOSITION

The argument is advanced in some quarters that there is no other road open for Canada than that of integration, in light of the emergence of various world trade blocs from which Canada is excluded. The apologists of integration claim it is an objective process and that nothing can stop it. With a wave of the hand they throw overboard the necessity of policies, including nationalization, which could ensure genuine independent economic development and an independent foreign policy for Canada.

The adverse effects of integration can already be seen in the results of the auto pact. They can be seen in the way inflation has been aggravated in Canada, and in the rise in unemployment.

In noting these developments it is necessary to draw attention to the considerable upsurge of people's opposition to U.S. imperialist pressures and the growing demand on the Trudeau government to uphold Canadian sovereignty. Indeed, the further the process of integration goes the more widespread the opposition becomes, reflecting the rise of Canadian consciousness, awareness and resentment. This is to be seen in the demand within Liberal Party ranks that the Trudeau government take a firm position on Arctic sovereignty, energy policy and foreign investments. It is particularly to be seen in the NDP, which at its last convention was compelled under pressure of its left wing to come out more clearly for a set of policies which in effect constitutes a break with its previous position of support for policies of Canadian-U.S. integration. This went together with the adoption of resolutions calling for Canada's withdrawal from NATO and NORAD, for Canada to stay out of OAS, and for support to the struggle of the Vietnamese people against U.S. imperialist aggression.

This is a significant development that undoubtedly reflects rising Canadian consciousness and resistance to U.S. domination. Tied as it is to an international (USA-Canada) trade union base, however, it remains to be seen how energetically the right wing within the NDP will heed and respect NDP convention policy.

The position the left wing fought for at the NDP convention was in many respects similar to the program the Communist Party has been fighting for over many years. However, an essential difference needs to be noted. The Communist Party proposed and still proposes measures *directed primarily against U.S. and Canadian monopoly,* the forces standing in the way of the genuine independence of Canada. The struggle against these forces and their defeat is an essential part of the struggle for socialism. The NDP left wing, on the other hand, leaps over that necessary stage of the struggle, equates Canadian independence with socialism, as exemplified in its slogan "an independent socialist Canada", and thus closes the door to winning allies who are not yet ready to struggle for socialism but are prepared to battle for Canadian independence.

The argument it advances for its position is that the Canadian capitalist class in general has gone over, hook, line and sinker, to U.S. imperialism. Here, however, the NDP left wing tends to mix up monopoly with the non-monopoly bourgeoisie. Canadian monopoly is the force that has allied itself with U.S. imperialism. It constitutes the main force to be defeated. The non-monopoly bourgeoisie are not so integrated, and can be won as allies in the struggle for Canadian independence. This is particularly true of important sections of the middle class. Indeed, that section of the population is at this stage most vocal in opposition to the U.S. takeover. This is reflected to some degree in the manoeuvres of the Trudeau government.

There is a tendency toward impatience in the position of the left wing of the NDP. But impatience is no substitute for the many-sided struggle and the winning of allies required to regain Canadian independence — a struggle requiring the unity of all forces that can be united against monopoly-capitalist interests in Canada and their government, as well as against U.S. imperialism.

It should be pointed out that while calling for an "independent socialist Canada", the actual proposals advanced by the left in the NDP are not basically socialist measures. The nationalization proposals, the essence of their program, are of a state-capitalist character. This does not deny their significance. The fact is that the Communist Party has been calling for such measures for some time, and calls for them now with regard to energy policy. Nationalization under democratic control would limit monopoly to some degree, although it would still be nationalization within the limits of the capitalist system. And as we see, with respect to hydro, CNR, CBC, etc., capitalist governments will enact such measures when it suits the interests of the capitalist class as a whole to do so.

Nationalization as a state-capitalist measure is not the same as socialist nationalization carried out on the basis of the political rule of the working class that has undertaken to build a socialist society and put an end to private ownership of the basic means of production. The program of the left wing of the NDP avoids this question, as it ignores the fundamental question of the role of the state.

A clear distinction needs to be made between nationalization and socialist nationalization to avoid confusion and to sharply delineate the stage of the struggle we are at. It is no less important because the issue of nationalization is today becoming a central part of the struggle for Canadian control. Some sections of monopoly and the government want to limit the issue of Canadian control to *Canadian monopoly ownership* — be it in uranium, perhaps other aspects of energy policy and natural resources — and to the matter of foreign investments.

The working-class and democratic forces cannot limit themselves to this, but should fight for democratic control through nationalization as a first step toward undermining the power of Canadian monopoly interests and of U.S. imperialism. All sources of energy should come under public ownership. Other measures short of nationalization could also be considered, providing they really curb and limit the power of monopoly.

In any case, around the issue of nationalization there is a fruitful basis for co-operation on parallel action with the left in the NDP and with others who are now beginning to see the necessity of a fundamental reversal of the fatal policy of continentalism, a reversal that can be effective only in so far as monopoly power is curbed.

It goes without saying that such co-operation would be useful and could be facilitated by friendly polemics and debate with the left wing in the NDP on the platform and program of struggle for Canadian independence, as well as around the path to socialism in Canada.

To be effective, such struggle cannot but take into account the key role of the working class. In fact, to be successful it must be headed by a united working class.

Unfortunately, the working class is not yet at the center of this struggle. Much effort will be required to change that situation, a process which will be facilitated to the extent that the left in the trade union movement together with the Communists wage the struggle for Canadian independence on every issue, tying in the economic and social issues with the battle for autonomy and independence. The battle for a truly united, independent and sovereign trade union movement is thus an essential part of the struggle for Canadian independence.

The battle for Canadian sovereignty and independence has reached a new stage of intensity, centered increasingly on limiting the existing power structure. There is no doubt that this battle is going to shake up Canadian politics and create various types of polarization, thus bearing out the contention of the Communist Party that the struggle to regain Canadian independence constitutes a main lever to transform Canadian politics and open the door to the struggle for socialism. Indeed, the struggle for Canadian independence, peace and democracy merges with the struggle for socialism.

Communist Viewpoint,
May-June, 1970.

VIII

Canadian foreign policy
and foreign investment

In estimating the government's review on foreign policy it would be well to recall that it was undertaken as a result of widespread opinion that Canada needs an independent foreign policy, one free from U.S. domination and more in tune with the realities of a changing world.

What gave impetus to this opinion was the growing realization by Canadians of the implications of U.S. aggression in Vietnam and of its sinister role in world affairs, as well as of Canada's membership in NATO and NORAD which could turn Canada into a no-man's land in the event of nuclear war. What stimulated this opinion was the growing recognition of the failure of U.S. imperialist policy in Vietnam and elsewhere, the bankruptcy of its "containment" policy, its inability to change the course of history despite its desperate efforts to do so — all the evidence indicating that the changing relationship of forces between socialism and imperialism on a world scale is continuing in favor of socialism. In its contest with socialism, the national-liberation movement, the forces of peace and the international working-class movement, imperialism is losing ground and will continue to do so. U.S. foreign policy is in crisis. Canada's foreign policy is in crisis as well, and will continue in crisis as long as it remains an echo of U.S. imperialist policy.

All these factors combined have stimulated the demand that Canada, rather than following U.S. foreign policy, should take an independent position in foreign affairs, work for a relaxation of international tensions, for the expansion of relations between countries with different social and economic systems and for the strengthening of the forces working for world peace.

The debates on foreign policy within the Liberal Party, Conservative Party, and the NDP last year reflected this demand for a Canadian foreign policy independent of the United States.

In light of these factors it was generally expected that the review of foreign policy would mark a break with the past. This is not the case at all. The review provides further evidence of the extent to which the industrial-military complex and the multi-national corporations, through their ties with monopoly in Canada and with U.S. imperialism, not only dominate the Canadian economy but determine Canadian foreign policy.

The review, in fact, indulges in generalities *but proposes to leave U.S.-Canadian relations as they are.* This reflects the inability of the Canadian bourgeoisie to defend the real national interests. True enough, an effort is made, in words, to reflect the demand for an independent foreign policy. In the realm of foreign investment a similar effort is made to reflect the demand for Canadian control over the economy.

That the government is compelled to do this is in itself important. First of all, it attests to an effort by sections of Canadian monopoly to spread their wings and strengthen their positions at the expense of other imperialist powers, including the USA. Secondly, it pinpoints the fact that the rising tide of Canadian consciousness or national sentiment is sufficiently strong that it cannot be ignored by the parties of monopoly. Indeed, it is not too much to suggest that this sentiment is stimulated in part by the government, through which and with which Canadian monopoly seeks to get more "elbow room" in its bargaining and struggle for markets and investments, although it is always careful not to go too far. Thirdly, it shows that the alliance between U.S. and Canadian imperialism is beset with growing *contradictions and tactical differences,* even though *unity exists on strategic aims,* i.e., the class alliance against socialism, the working-class and national-liberation movements. These contradictions and tactical differences need to be noted and made use of by the working-class and progressive movement — not to tail behind Canadian monopoly, but to advance its own independent position and strengthen the movement for genuine Canadian independence.

It may be useful here to deal separately with each of these papers and the proposals advanced in them.

I.   THE WHITE PAPER ON FOREIGN POLICY

The paper virtually covers the whole world and is written with an eye to the maintenance of imperialism, capitalist rule and the global strategy of imperialism. *At the same time it is written with an eye to advancing the specific interests of Canadian monopoly and the fulfilment of its economic aims.* It reflects the inter-imperialist struggle for trade, markets and investment. Indeed, trade and investment run right through the review. In saying this, it must also be said that the effort to secure wider markets and to establish or extend relationships with other countries mirrors an intention by monopoly interests to ease U.S. pressures on the Canadian economy and resist the efforts of U.S. imperialism to use its economic weight in Canada as a means of exerting political pressure on it.

CANADA AND THE PACIFIC

This explains in part the emphasis given in the review to Canada's diplomatic and trade ties with the Pacific nations, which it relates to the economic needs of the western provinces and to national unity.

In relation to establishing diplomatic and trade ties with the Pacific nations, the review makes the point that "however much Canada has in common with the U.S., the Canadian outlook is often fundamentally different." The difference, of course, lies in the fact that, while U.S. imperialism has made the Pacific its monopoly, Canadian monopoly is trying to break in and get some of the crumbs from the disappearance of the old empires. Trudeau's recent visit to the Pacific was part of Canadian monopoly's assertion that Canada has an interest in the Pacific both with respect to trade and to investment.

The establishment of diplomatic relations with the People's Republic of China reflects both Canadian-U.S. differences and a division of their roles. It is hard to conceive that Canada's recognition of the People's Republic of China could fundamentally contradict U.S. overall imperialist aims.

CANADA AND EUROPE

The review states that Canada's continued participation in NATO is in the interests of its national security and that the alliance affords possibilities to resolve basic causes of tension in Europe. At the same time the review indicates that Canada will go beyond the NATO framework to place special emphasis on building stronger relationships with the "dynamic new Europe", in the economic, scientific and cultural fields. What is referred to as the "dynamic new Europe" is the European Economic Community, not the socialist countries of Europe.

The review further declares that it is opposed to Canada assuming a non-aligned or neutral role in the world. "Canada," it states, "will continue to participate in an appropriate way in collective security arrangements with other members of NATO. It will promote European detente and progress toward an East-West political solution. Canada will also use NATO and other international bodies to promote mutual and balanced reductions in Europe and to encourage arms control and disarmament efforts within eventual Conferences on European Security when the time is ripe."

The review goes on to say that although Canadian interests are expanding elsewhere, Europe remains of special importance to Canada. "The bulk of Canada's business abroad is centered in the North Atlantic area where are to be found Canada's major trading partners, its main security problems, its most important source of investment and manpower."

With respect to the socialist countries the review speaks of the need to promote efforts to enable Canada to obtain a larger share of the East European markets, and in support of cultural and scientific exchange agreements with the Soviet Union and other East European countries.

CANADA AND LATIN AMERICA

The review stresses the need to strengthen Canada's links with Latin American countries and to expand trade and investment in that continent. As we know, a government mission recently visited a number of Latin American countries with this in mind. Of interest here is the fact that the review opposes Canada's joining the OAS, based on the viewpoint that "Canadian and U.S. views on hemispheric security issues do not always coincide." Presumably this is with reference to Canadian recognition of Cuba and to U.S. armed intervention in some Latin American countries. While the review's position with respect to OAS is to be welcomed, it is somewhat watered down by the proposal that Canada might be prepared to sit in as an observer at OAS meetings.

It should be noted that Canadian monopoly and its governments have for some years tried in Latin America to build up an image of Canada as a non-imperialist country, distinct from Yankee imperialism. It has made use of the deep-seated opposition to U.S. imperialism in Latin America to advance its own trade, investment and political positions in the Caribbean and other Latin American countries. The events in Trinidad recently showed the extent to which Canadian imperialism has extended its penetration of the West Indies.

CANADA AND AFRICA

The review emphasizes an orientation to Southern Africa because there is an unusual opportunity for trade and investment in the growing economy of that region. In line with this it proposes to open a diplomatic mission in Zambia. The review condemns the racist policies of South Africa, but this is coupled with opposition to unilateral trade sanctions by Canada against South Africa, and silence with respect to the struggles of the peoples of Angola and Mozambique for their independence from Portuguese colonial rule.

From the foregoing, what conclusions can be drawn about the White Paper on foreign policy? Are there any new features in it?

On the surface the review creates the impression of being a declaration of Canadian identity and of Canadian independence. Basically, however, there is very little concrete substance to the assertion of Canadian independence. Canadian foreign policy, according to the review's proposals, will remain as is. Canada will remain in NATO and NORAD, the mechanisms through which the U.S. dominates Canadian foreign and military policy, as well as its arms spending. The paper does not propose that Canada dissociate itself from U.S. aggression in Vietnam. It does not come out clearly and distinctly for a European Security Conference, nor does it condemn Israeli aggression against its Arab neighbors in the Middle East. There is no proposal that Canada dissociate itself from neo-colonialist policies and assert its solidarity with Black Africa by imposing trade sanctions on South Africa, nor that it give support to the national-liberation movements in Angola and Mozambique in their struggle for independence.

It does not propose the exclusion of fascist Greece and Portugal from NATO. While the White Paper speaks in general of a detente, it still refuses to recognize the Democratic Republic of Vietnam, the Democratic Republic of Korea and the German Democratic Republic; nor does it call for their inclusion in the United Nations so as to make that body both universal and more effective. While it speaks in general about reducing arms, it says nothing about the sale to the U.S. of arms, including raw material for napalm bombs for U.S. aggression against the Vietnamese people — nor does it say anything about Canadian participation, together with the U.S. and Great Britain, in research work on chemical and biological warfare.

We need to reiterate what we have stated continually: As long as the decisive sectors of the Canadian economy are foreign-owned and monopoly-dominated, roadblocks will be placed in the way of asserting a truly independent foreign policy for Canada. Canadian independence, independent economic development based on nationalization, and an independent foreign policy are inextricably bound together.

This is not to say that one must await an end to U.S. economic domination before the fight for an independent foreign policy can be waged. That fight is at the same time an important contribution to an an integral part of the struggle for Canadian sovereignty and independence. As we know, the fight for an independent foreign policy is a continuing one. It has many concrete aspects to it, the crux of which is Canadian withdrawal from NATO and NORAD. Such a struggle also finds expression around the issues of European security, a political settlement of the Middle East crisis and the withdrawal of U.S. troops from Indochina, issues which today are at the center of the struggle against imperialism.

CANADA AND EUROPEAN SECURITY

Here we are faced with a two-sided approach. On one hand, we should continue stimulating the movement for Canada's withdrawal from NATO and NORAD, including the demand that Canada should end the defence production agreement with the U.S., one of the means through which the industrial-military complex exercises a baneful influence on Canadian foreign policy. On the other hand, we should press for Canada to play a constructive role in the forthcoming Conference on European Co-operation and Security. On the surface these may appear to be contradictory proposals. In reality, they complement each other and should be fought for simultaneously. The fact that the NDP at its last convention came out for withdrawal from NATO and NORAD and for support of a European Security Conference should help open the door in the broad labor and democratic movement for such a two-pronged fight, *to which should be added the demand for recognition of the GDR in international law.*

We should popularize the European People's Congress planned for next year and explore possibilities for participation in it by various forces in Canada.

The treaty between West Germany and the Soviet Union, which has yet to be ratified in West Germany, is of great international significance. It creates better possibilities for consolidating European security, stabilizing relations in Europe and laying the basis for a durable peace. The essence of the treaty, as we know, is the recognition of the territorial status quo in Europe arising from the Second World War; the recognition of the inviolability of European frontiers and, above all, of the borders between the GDR and West Germany, as well as of the Oder-Neisse line bordering on Poland. It thus registers a recognition of the political and territorial realities in Europe and of the balance of forces between socialism and imperialism.

The treaty marks a defeat for the revanchists and militarists in West Germany and their allies abroad who want a revision of the results of the Second World War by "peaceful" means or through war, and it points to the political realism of those in West Germany who support the treaty. By the same token, it registers the victory of the principles of peaceful co-existence between states with different social systems, a policy fought for persistently by the Soviet Union and the socialist states allied with it. The treaty — a victory for the forces of peace on a world scale — should have an important influence on international affairs, facilitating both the convening of the European Security Conference and the recognition in international law of the GDR. We need to apply ourselves to these matters with great vigor, because the revenge-seeking forces in West Germany and their supporters abroad will do everything possible to delay or prevent the ratification of the treaty.

CANADA AND THE MIDDLE EAST

The ceasefire, to be followed by negotiations, opens up possibilities for a political settlement based on the UN Security Council resolution of November 22, 1967.

Why did U.S. Secretary of State, Mr. Rogers, propose the ceasefire?

It may be recalled that up to the point of the ceasefire, U.S.

imperialism, contrary to the proposals of the UN Security Council resolution, took the position that direct talks between Israel and the Arab states be conducted in conditions of the continued occupation of Arab lands by the Israeli troops.

The Arab resistance to the Israeli aggressors, first of all the resistance of the United Arab Republic, a resistance made possible by the considerable material assistance of the Soviet Union and other socialist states; the growing international isolation of Israel; the collapse of the hopes for the overthrow of progressive Arab governments and the emergence of progressive regimes as in Libya and Sudan; the development of widespread democratic actions for peace in Israel — all of these have compelled U.S. imperialism either to continue its unconditional support of the annexationist aims of the Israeli ruling class, with all the attendant consequences for the U.S. in the Arab countries, or to shift its tactics. *It has shifted its tactics to a more disguised support* of Israeli aggression and advanced the proposal for a ceasefire.

As is known, the UAR immediately agreed to the terms of the ceasefire, as it had previously agreed to the terms of the UN Security Council resolution, thereby showing the whole world that Egypt is for a political settlement of the Middle East conflict and for a just and stable peace. This position, it should be noted, followed the conclusion of Soviet-Egyptian talks in which both sides agreed to work for a political settlement of the Middle East conflict, on the basis of the complete fulfilment of the UN Security Council resolution and of United Nations decisions concerning Palestine refugees.

As against this constructive approach, an opposite approach has been taken by the Israeli aggressors. Compelled to agree to a ceasefire, the war hawks have moved heaven and earth to prevent negotiations from taking place and to prevent achievement of a political settlement based on the UN resolution. By their actions they have shown the world who wants a political settlement and who orientates on expansionism.

Within the Arab national-liberation movement there is also no full agreement on a political settlement. This has resulted from different approaches to the conflict and the reasons that gave rise to it.

Those who fight for a political settlement base themselves on a *class* approach which sees the Israeli aggression as an attempt by imperialism, headed by the USA, to use the Israeli ruling class to crush the progressive regimes in the Arab countries, suppress the Arab liberation movement and restore imperialism's positions in the Middle East. Such an approach draws a distinction between the Israeli ruling class as a tool of international imperialism, and the Israeli working people, whose vital interests lie in living in peace with their Arab neighbors.

As against this *class* approach, one fought for by Arab and Israeli Communists, the Soviet Union and other socialist countries, as well as by many other anti-imperialist forces, another approach is being advocated. Its essence lies in proposing a bourgeois-nationalist approach to the solution of the conflict, an approach that pits all Arabs against all Jews in a struggle for the liquidation of the Israeli state.

Such a position is incorrect in theory and practice. Marxists never advocate the destruction of states or peoples. Their struggle is directed to the elimination of national and social oppression. They do not propose that the right to national self-determination of one nation be at the expense of the same right of another nation.

The struggle of the Palestinian Arab people against the occupation and for its homeland, a struggle that has led to the emergence of a mass Palestinian Arab national movement, is a just struggle which has won the sympathy and support of all progressive mankind. The essence of that struggle is the right to national self-determination.

A correct and realistic solution to the national question is the right to national self-determination of the two peoples, the Israeli people and the Palestinian Arab people.

However, the form of the solution of a national question is always concrete, taking as its starting point the interests of the anti-imperialist struggle, the interests of the independence of peoples and of international peace and security.

In the prevailing circumstances, taking into account the

real balance of forces in the world and in the Middle East, the proposed solution of the Palestinian problem at the expense of the existence of the State of Israel is neither correct nor acceptable. It can only do harm to the cause of the Palestinian Arab people and the Israeli people, and play into the hands of imperialism which strives to divide peoples and nations in order to rule them.

The fact is that a political settlement based on the UN Security Council resolution creates the basic conditions for winning peace in the Middle East and simultaneously winning the just national rights, the right to self-determination, of the Arab people of Palestine, without infringing upon the rights of the Israeli people.

The struggle for a political settlement of the Middle East conflict is not only a part of the anti-imperialist struggle directed against U.S. imperialism and its tool, the Israeli ruling class. It is also part of a sharp class struggle in the Arab countries, no less than it is part of the sharp struggle we need to wage in our country against those in the Jewish community and outside it who oppose a just political settlement and stand for Israeli expansionism.

Conditions are now more favorable for waging such a struggle despite the continuing complexity of the situation and the danger of a collapse of negotiations as a consequence of recent Israeli ruling-class actions and U.S. abandonment of its own initiative.

The canard that the Soviet Union and other socialist states were for the destruction of the Israeli state has been completely refuted. The fact is that it is precisely the Soviet Union which has consistently fought against aggression, against political Zionism and imperialism, as well as against Arab chauvinism, and for a just political settlement which alone guarantees the security of all states in the Middle East. This principled position was recently reiterated by the Supreme Soviet when it stated that "Every country in the Middle East has the right to an independent, national existence, to independence and security."

The Communist Party of Canada stands forthrightly for a political settlement based on the UN Security Council resolution and UN decisions on the Palestine refugees, and *against political Zionism, the annexationists and imperialists.* It is all the more urgent to emphasize this in light of the Israeli and U.S. governments' sabotage of the negotiations.

All this should go together with systematic pressure on Parliament and the government to give all-out support to a political settlement based on the UN Security Council resolution, and to repudiate those who try to scuttle the ceasefire and the implementation of the UN resolution.

CANADA AND INDOCHINA

There is need to emphasize again the necessity to step up the OUT NOW petition campaign and the demand on Parliament to stop the shipment of arms to the USA. We need to contrast Trudeau's opposition to the proposed sale of British arms to South Africa with the continued sale by Canada of arms to the U.S. for its aggression in Indochina — not only to expose the hypocrisy, double-dealing and complicity of the Canadian government in U.S. aggression, but also to pinpoint the dangerous role of the industrial-military complex in determining and shaping Canadian foreign policy. We should demand, not only an end to the defence production agreement with the USA, but that *Canada call on the USA to get out of Indochina and back this up by recognizing the DRV and with a pledge to help in the reconstruction of Vietnam.*

CONCLUSIONS

These concrete questions, as well as active support and stimulation of movements of solidarity in support of Greek democracy, against racism, colonialism, apartheid, and other manifestations of colonial and neo-colonial rule, conform with the real needs of Canada, its security, and the cause of world peace. In this connection we should demand that Canada not only call for the withdrawal of Greece and Portugal from NATO. It should itself break off trade and diplomatic relations with these countries. All these are an integral part of the fight for an independent Canadian foreign policy and of the struggle against imperialism.

Parliament has yet to discuss the review of foreign policy and our intervention at an appropriate time should serve a useful purpose. The main thing, of course, is the continuing task of broadening and extending the peace movement and other movements in the struggle for an independent foreign policy. It is obvious that much deeper and more extensive struggles are required to win it.

II.   FOREIGN INVESTMENT

With respect to the proposals on foreign investment put forward by the Commons Committee on External Affairs and National Defence: As we know, these proposals include the demand for 51 per cent Canadian ownership of the stock of all companies doing business in Canada; the placing in trusteeship of foreign-controlled firms forbidden by U.S. law to sell products manufactured in Canada to nations which the U.S. government considers enemies; the prevention of takeovers of Canadian-owned companies without a permit from the government; the percentage of debt capital that foreign-controlled companies be permitted to raise in Canada be limited to the percentage of Canadian participation in the ownership of these companies; the creation of a new government agency called the "Canadian Ownership and Control Bureau."

According to the proposals of the Commons Committee this bureau would have fairly wide powers to investigate and regulate foreign-controlled companies. It would determine whether a takeover of a Canadian industry would be allowed. It would decide whether to permit foreign investment and what action to take against a U.S.-owned company refusing to trade with other countries.

The central feature of the proposals is that of 51 per cent Canadian ownership.

It should be borne in mind that along with these recommendations, which go to the cabinet, the cabinet has also asked for a report on foreign ownership of the Canadian economy from Mr. Gray, Minister of National Revenue.

Such a report presumably will coincide more closely with what the government wants or may intend to do.

Here, as on the question of foreign policy, the report is forced to reflect the fairly widespread opposition to U.S. control of the Canadian economy. It is interesting to note that in a mini-poll conducted in his own riding by Mr. Ian Wahn (the chairman of the Committee) on the question: "Do you oppose the present level of American influence in Canada?", 58 per cent said yes, 37 per cent said no. This probably is typical of the country as a whole.

The *Globe and Mail,* in an August 9 editorial, underscored the mood of Canadians when it stated, "It is tempting to suspect that the Commons Committee on External Affairs and National Defence, *sensing the rising tide of nationalism among Canadians, felt impelled to produce a very nationalist report* on foreign ownership of Canadian industry ..."

Some of the proposals are a reflection of the Watkins Report, and of the Communist Party's consistent fight over the years for Canadian independence. They may also have been advanced as a means of taking the ground from under the feet of the NDP's position as exemplified at its last convention, or as part of the "hard bargaining" with the U.S. government over energy resources and other issues. *Not least, the proposals reflect the growing conflict of interest between Canadian and U.S. capital for influence and control over the Canadian economy.*

It should not be overlooked that while the Canadian capitalist class has shared with U.S. monopolies the profits from the development of Canada's raw material export industries, they also have their own interests which they constantly strive to advance. The growing financial strength of Canadian capital, and of a much stronger Canadian financial oligarchy, has made it possible for the Canadian capitalist class to become the *main force* confronting the U.S. monopolies in the competitive imperialist struggle for Canada's resources. *Today, the conflict between Canadian and U.S. capital for influence and control over the Canadian economy is the most important element of imperialist contradictions in Canada,* with British-U.S. rivalry in Canada taking second place in importance. This struggle is directed to achieve maximum profits for Canadian monopoly, not to regain Canadian independence.

The growing control of U.S. capital in Canada's key industries has led to strong resentment among sections of the Canadian capitalist class, not only because a sizeable part of the profits from the development of Canada's natural resources goes into U.S. hands and in turn further strengthens its control over the Canadian economy. The fact is that U.S. and British subsidiaries have been pursuing policies directed to safeguarding the interests of their parent monopolies, interests that frequently do not coincide with those of the Canadian capitalist class. What is strongly attacked is the unwillingness of these subsidiaries to seat Canadians on their boards, the blocking of purchases by Canadians of the shares of foreign-controlled companies on the stock exchanges, the attempts to squeeze out Canadian companies from industries monopolized by U.S. corporations, or to take them over. There is also strong resentment over the research policies of U.S.-owned subsidiaries, policies which tend to slow down progress in Canada and narrow down the field of activity for Canadian scientists.

Contradictions also exist over the export policy of U.S.-owned companies operating in Canada. These subsidiaries operate only in markets where their products do not compete with those of the parent companies. Many of them have their production geared only to the Canadian and Commonwealth market. Such policies do not always coincide with the foreign policy aims of the Canadian capitalist class. Moreover, they aggravate Canada's chronic balance-of-payments deficit.

On the other hand, other sections of the Canadian capitalist class, under cover of provincial rights, press for the sale of natural resources, including energy resources, to the USA, based on the argument that this is necessary for further economic development. This continuing alienation of Canada's natural resources under cover of constitutional rights emphasizes the need for a policy of independent Canadian development and for a new Canadian constitution which could include the prohibition of ownership of these natural resources by foreign monopoly interests.

The sharp competitive struggle between Canadian and U.S. capital for dominant influence in Canada reflects the growing rivalry between them over who will get a bigger share of the profits at the expense of intensified exploitation of the working class.

Canadian monopoly is not a weak force. The fact is that it is more than a junior partner of U.S. imperialism: it is an integral part of the world imperialist system with its interests interwoven with those of U.S. and British finance capital. *What it now finds increasingly important is external expansion in the spheres of both trade and capital exports.* Of primary concern to it is the struggle to secure market outlets for raw materials, manufactured goods, and investments. This explains the increased activity of the capitalist class and its government in the sphere of trade, its efforts to rationalize and modernize industry and stimulate multi-national corporations in Canada able to compete in the capitalist world market. This may well be one of the main purposes of the Canadian Development Corporation, if and when it is set up by the government.

These aims of Canadian monopoly find their reflection in the White Paper on Foreign Policy, as they do in the proposals on foreign investment.

What should our position be toward these proposals?

In general, proposals which weaken U.S. control, such as measures to prevent further U.S. takeovers and to compel foreign-owned companies in Canada to trade with other countries, are to be welcomed and supported even though they fall short of what we advocate, that is, democratic nationalization of U.S.-owned companies in Canada. These two questions — takeovers and trade — are of considerable importance in the struggle for Canadian independence. The fact is that if the Canadian people are not aroused against such takeovers and in defence of Canadian sovereignty with respect to trade, economic factors will lead the bourgeoisie to strike a bargain with the USA at the expense of the sovereignty and independence of Canada. We should link up the struggle for such measures with the overall struggle for democratic nationalization and, more immediately and concretely, with the battle for public ownership of key natural resources, starting with energy resources. It is here the issue is most pressing. It is here U.S. pressures are mounting. It is here so-called bargaining is taking place and where, behind the scenes, a deal is being worked out between the Canadian and U.S. governments at the expense of the real interests of the Canadian people.

We can already see some of the results of the "hard bargaining". The Nixon government, as we know, imposed import quotas on oil which it recently revised coincident with a story that a pipeline was going to be built. The "hard bargaining" is seen in the demand for a change in the terms of the auto trade pact. Other pressures may be exerted in the coming period.

Mr. Greene and the government reflect the weaving from a policy of continentalism to a national policy on energy resources, a reflection of the inconsistent policy of compromises by the Canadian bourgeoisie on the question of growing U.S. penetration of the Canadian economy, arising from its cosmopolitan character and its primary concern with making a fast buck. This finds expression in apparent agreement on the construction of a pipeline and the sale of nine trillion cubic feet of natural gas worth three billion dollars to the USA over the next 20 years, a proposal presently before the cabinet. The *Globe and Mail* recently asked whether the agreement on a pipeline had not in fact been *secretly agreed to,* a good question indeed.

Behind the smokescreen of so-called hard bargaining, therefore, the door is being opened to effect an energy deal with the USA before the needs of Canada are clearly established. In support of the sale of natural gas and other energy resources, the argument is being advanced that a 30-year reserve is assured for Canada, so as to condition Canadians to acceptance of such a deal. Such an argument is false and misleading. What is requires is not a 30-year reserve but an unlimited reserve, based on the perspective of growth and expansion of the population, of the economy, and the needs of the Canadian people. Canada's life expectancy goes beyond 30 years.

The present deal is bound to have adverse effects on Canadian development, push up prices for natural gas in Canada, and limit the extent of new job opportunities. *Moreover, the sale of natural gas, if it goes through, is but the prelude to agreement on an overall energy deal.*

From this standpoint the Communist Party should focus major attention on the battle for public ownership of energy resources and work to unite with all other forces that can be united around this demand. Here there may be a basis for fruitful co-operation with the Waffle and the NDP generally. As part of this struggle we should advance demands such as "No sale until the long-term needs of Canada are known", "Canadian resources for independent development and jobs", etc. We, of course, are not opposed to the sale of surplus energy, other than water, but it should be under government licence and only after the long-term needs of Canada are clearly established.

What should our attitude be toward the proposal for 51 per cent Canadian ownership of foreign-owned plants in Canada?

As we know, some capitalist countries have such provisions in their laws which to some degree limit the extent of foreign ownership. Such a measure here could also be a *limiting factor* over U.S. investments and ownership. In general we should not oppose the proposal but emphasize that Canadian control, to be really effective, must be based on public ownership. However, the immediate and urgent task today is the application of effective measures to prevent further take-overs, a process which is going on daily and which the government has done nothing to stop except in uranium. All the evidence shows that neither the Liberal nor the Conservative governments are capable of doing anything of a decisive nature to reduce U.S. influence over the Canadian economy or at least prevent it from growing. This is also borne out by the statement of Mr. Ian Wahn, the Commons Committee chairman, regarding 51 per cent Canadian ownership: "It may never be enacted — perhaps it wouldn't even be practical." In any case, if the government were really serious about preventing further takeovers the place to start is by public ownership of the key natural resources and, in the first place, of energy resources. This could be the first in a series of steps including nationalization of the CPR, the restriction of foreign investments to loan capital only, directed to regaining Canadian control through public ownership of the decisive sectors of the economy and over foreign policy. In the battle for nationalization we should constantly seek out those intermediate steps, those links which lead toward nationalization.

The struggle for these aims and for the regaining of Canadian independence can only be effective in so far as it is directed against Canadian monopoly and U.S. imperialism, with the working class playing a leading role in this all-out effort.

As part of this struggle there may be some value in supporting the proposal for the establishment of a Canadian Ownership and Control Bureau on the basis of clearly defined terms of reference, that is, with respect to the prevention of further takeovers and the elimination of U.S. controls regarding foreign trade. Such a regulatory body could, under certain circumstances, be a useful instrument in the struggle for public ownership.

CONCLUSION

The various White Papers prepared by government agencies, some of which are compelled to reflect the rising demand for Canadian independence and peace, may well be at the center of the federal election in 1972. The fight we wage now on these two related questions of economic and foreign policy, both in general and in their concreteness, taking due account of divisions in the capitalist class, is part of our preparations for it, and in helping to bring about a new political alignment in the country, directed to winning new policies for Canada.

The Communist Party calls for a foreign policy for peaceful co-existence; the withdrawal of Canada from NATO and

NORAD; for trade with all countries on a mutually advantageous basis; the recognition of the GDR, the Democratic Republic of Vietnam and the Republic of North Korea; an end to the defence production agreement with the USA; an agreement with the USA and Great Britain against chemical and biological warfare; active support for a European Security Conference; for a political settlement of the Middle East crisis based on the UN Security Council resolution; for unconditional and immediate withdrawal of U.S. troops from Indochina; for active support to the national-liberation movement and against neo-colonialism.

Such an independent foreign policy — buttressed by nationalization of key natural resources, and more immediately of energy resources, the regaining of Canadian control through public ownership of the decisive sectors of the economy — is an integral part of the struggle to regain Canadian independence, to defeat Canadian monopoly and U.S. imperialism and take Canada on the path to socialism. The working class must become the leading force in this struggle.

Communist Viewpoint,
November-December, 1970.

IX

Tim Buck's 80th Birthday

January 6, 1971, marks Tim's birthday. All who know him, and they are legion, will wish him many happy returns of the day and pay tribute to an outstanding revolutionary and internationalist, a man who throughout his life has devoted all his talents and strength to the cause of the working class and the struggle for socialism.

When one thinks of Tim, one thinks of an outstanding political leader and organizer, a creative Marxist and writer, of his warmth and closeness to people, his personal magnetism which immediately attracts others to him.

He has that quality of speaking which has always enabled him to explain in simple terms, clear to everyone who hears him, the most complicated problems calling for solution. Tim indeed embodies in him what Lenin called· a "public tribune", an outstanding propagandist and agitator, the Party's greatest popularizer of socialism and of the achievements of the first socialist land — the Soviet Union.

Tim is one of those rare men — a worker intellectual. It is often assumed that it is only the intellectuals coming from the bourgeoisie who bring the science of socialism into the working class. The working class, however, advances its own intellectuals. Tim is one of those among others who come from the working class and use their talents as organizers, speakers and writers not to separate themselves from their class, but to help the working class become conscious of itself as a class so that it can perform its historic mission, the replacement of capitalism by socialism.

Tim's entire life has been devoted to this lofty aim.

Tim's name is bound up with every stage of the struggle of the working class in Canada, to which he made a signal contribution.

He helped found a new type of party of the working class, the Communist Party, so that the working class would have a political instrument with which and through which to advance its immediate and long-term aims.

Tim always saw the Party not as a debating society or as a propaganda sect divorced from the real life of the working people, but as *a party of action.* He used his talents to integrate Marxism-Leninism with the working-class struggle and thereby raise the political consciousness of the working class.

As a machinist and later as Labor Secretary of the Communist Party, Tim fought against narrow craft unionism and class collaborationism, and for the organization of the unorganized in the mass-production industries. He linked this up with the struggle for one union in every industry and for the autonomy of the trade union movement. It was this which laid the groundwork for the eventual emergence of the industrial unions, the organization of the mass-production industries, the merger of the two trade union centers and the upsurge in the demand for a fully autonomous, sovereign and independent trade union movement in Canada.

In the late 20's when growing signs of an impending economic crisis appeared on the horizon Tim fought the revisionist and opportunist theory of "American exceptionalism", whose proponents in the Canadian Party claimed that North American capitalism had overcome its inner contradictions and was immune from capitalist crisis. That struggle prepared the Party for the economic crisis when it broke in 1929 and orientated it on a course which helped it become the center of opposition, the leading organizing force of working-class, farm, women and youth action.

At the same time, Tim led the fight of the Party against Trotskyism and defeated its supporters in the Party.

This struggle against opportunism from the right and from the left, the struggle against reformism and bourgeois ideology and for a consistent revolutionary position based on

Marxism-Leninism, has been typical of Tim's work and leadership.

It was precisely the uncompromising and clear-cut class position of Tim in defence of the interests of the working people which made him the main target of the attack of monopoly immediately following the outbreak of the economic crisis. The Ontario Tory government used Section 98 to arrest and imprison him and other leaders of the Party and declare the Party illegal. They even conspired for someone to shoot at him in Kingston Penitentiary. Reaction thought that in this way it would eliminate the main political force opposing its anti-people's policies. The Party, however, grew despite its condition of illegality and emerged as an ever-stronger force in this period of its history.

Tim gave particular attention to the problem of independent labor political action, always seeking for ways in which to help the working class to free itself from the influence of capitalist parties and capitalist ideology. He understood very well that the trade union struggle by itself would not take the working class outside the confines of capitalist politics and would result in the working class tailing the capitalist parties. He therefore devoted considerable time and attention to seeking out the forms through which the working class, through its own experience, would begin to break with the capitalist parties. He fought for the concept of a federated farmer-labor party as an integral part of the process of helping the working class become conscious of itself as a class. In fighting for this approach he at the same time linked it up with the vital task of the Communist Party itself — to bring socialist consciousness into the working-class movement. He did not see any contradiction between one and the other, but rather a dialectical unity. Bringing socialist consciousness into the working class meant establishing firm links between the Communist Party and the working people and, above all, strengthening the Party in the working class as the decisive factor for fundamental social change.

A particular contribution of Tim was his criticism of the Abbott Plan, the first open turn of Canadian monopoly to a policy of continentalism, of integration with U.S. imperialism. This marked a significant change of direction for Canadian capitalism, related to its subordination to the drive of U.S. imperialism for world hegemony from which it hoped to get a few crumbs.

It is to the credit of Tim that he grasped the essential character of this turnabout of Canadian monopoly arising from the general crisis of capitalism and its implication with respect to the sovereignty and independence of Canada; and called upon the Party and working class, indeed all democratic forces, to take up the banner of the nation and fight for Canadian independence and for peace.

This was not fully understood in the Party where tendencies arose to place the working-class struggle in opposition to the struggle in defence of the true national interests of the country. This arose from a narrow, sectarian approach, a failure to understand that a proper placing of the defence of the national interests, properly related to the defence of working-class interests, is in fact an important ingredient around which to build an alliance led by the working class that could open up new prospects of advance to socialism.

Tim's contribution here has been enormous. One can see today how his far-sighted leadership has helped bring into being a movement which is increasingly challenging Canadian monopoly and U.S. imperialism, and is creating favorable conditions for a polarization of political forces on a countrywide scale.

No less significant has been Tim's contribution to the national question as it exists concretely in Canada, expressed around the demand for the right to self-determination of the French-Canadian nation.

Above all, what characterizes Tim's work and leadership is his consistent patriotism and internationalism. Tim never saw them as being opposed to each other, but as integrally related. Tim fully understood the profound significance of the Great October Socialist Revolution and its impact of world politics. He fought consistently and indefatigably to bring knowledge and awareness of the achievements of the Soviet Union to the widest masses of the Canadian people. He fought tirelessly in defence of the Soviet Union against all its attackers from the capitalist and social-reformist world, as he fought against those inside the Communist Party who would denigrate these achievements and failed to understand that the Soviet Union, and later the socialist system of states, was the firm, reliable base upon and around which the future of mankind would be decided.

Defence of the true national interests, defence of internationalism — this has been a major contribution of Tim to the history and the work of the Communist Party, as it has been a contribution to the international communist movement.

Tim, perhaps more than any other Canadian Communist, understood in a deep sense the Marxist-Leninist conception of the Communist Party as the vanguard of the working class, and vigorously fought those who would revise Marxism-Leninism or would stand in the way of its creative development at each new stage of the working-class struggle.

Tim has never underestimated the role of the Communist Party, no matter how small it might be under certain political conditions, and consistently fought to help transform it into a mass party, one able to lead the working class at every stage of the struggle. In this he was always concrete, starting from the reality around us, never giving way to empty phrase-mongering but also never losing sight of the goal of socialism.

In this he has shown himself to be a revolutionary optimist, a model for Communists, young and old.

Tim never tired of saying that one has to keep one's feet on the ground but always look up to the stars. It expresses his outlook, his convictions, his revolutionary optimism, and his ability to inspire Communists and non-Communists alike.

On this his 80th birthday all Communists, all those who know him, wish him a happy birthday and an early return to continued creative work in the cause he has championed all his life.

The Canadian Communist movement is now preparing to celebrate its 50th anniversary in the year 1971. Tim's life, work and contributions are so integrally a part of the Communist and working-class history that it is natural for the 50th anniversary to merge with Tim Buck's 80th birthday.

Communist Viewpoint,
January-February, 1971.

X

On the 50th Anniversary of the
Communist Party of Canada

Comrade chairman, comrades and friends:

This banquet tonight is the first of a series we are holding throughout the country to celebrate the 50th Anniversary of our Party. It is an important occasion and a joyous occasion.

Our Party was founded in June 1921. Since then, in the course of five decades, under conditions of legality and illegality, the Communist Party has consistently defended Marxism-Leninism and proletarian internationalism, and sought to creatively fulfil its role as a revolutionary party of the working class.

In the course of its rich history, it has many achievements to record in defence of the interests of the working class.

Two factors influenced the emergence of the Communist Party on the Canadian scene.

The first was the class struggle in Canada.

The Communist Party grew out of the rich soil of the working-class struggle. Socialist aspirations had a long history in Canada. Indeed, the International Workingmen's Association included supporting groups in Canada. With the growth of the working class as a consequence of the growth of the productive forces of capitalism, trade union organization and socialist ideas spread out to various parts of the country. The Socialist Party of Canada was one expression of this. Later on the Socialist Party of North America was founded. It stressed the importance of merging Marxist theory with the day-to-day struggles of the working class.

In this connection it is necessary to note the active and important role of the immigrant workers from the European continent. Immigrant workers of Ukrainian, Jewish, Finnish and Lettish origin brought the Socialist Democratic Party into being. This party was not the typical social-democratic party, as in Europe. It played a key role in the struggle to spread Marxism in the working-class movement and the ethnic communities of which they were a part. From that source, a substantial number entered the ranks of the Communist Party when it was founded.

Thus, the growing struggles of the working class and the spread of socialist ideas led class-conscious workers and the left wing of these parties to the conclusion that a revolutionary party was needed.

The second factor stimulating the emergence of the Communist Party was the Great October Socialist Revolution, the revolution that ushered in a new stage in history, the epoch of transition from capitalism to socialism on a world scale.

That revolution had a profound effect on the working-class movement in Canada as elsewhere. It inspired the working class, while creating fear in the hearts of the capitalist class. When the 14 armies of intervention, including the Canadian army, invaded the Soviet Union, Canadian workers like their counterparts elsewhere in the capitalist world rallied in their thousands against the intervention. They formed "hands off" committees to signalize their opposition to the efforts of imperialism to crush the young socialist state, and to signalize their solidarity with the Soviet Union, the first socialist state.

The revolution inspired a great upsurge of labor and farmer struggles across Canada. This upsurge found reflection in the election of a farmer-labor government in Ontario, in the election to Parliament of 65 progressive MP's from Manitoba, Saskatchewan and Alberta, and in the 1919 General Strike in Winnipeg. The Winnipeg strike committee became in large measure responsible for the whole community and contained within it the elements of workers' power.

This upsurge raised in all sharpness the question: What kind of party is needed to lead the working class and its allies to socialism?

Inspired by the October Revolution the class-conscious workers turned to Lenin's ideas on the kind of party necessary to bring about the revolutionary transformation of society. These workers saw that opportunism and reformism had led the working class nowhere, while the October Socialist Revolution showed that only a consistent revolutionary policy leads to the victory of the working people and the realization of their aspirations.

Out of this questioning and discussion grew the view that what was now required was the formation of a party of a new type, a party which fights for reforms but rejects reformism as a substitute for social revolution.

In June 1921 such a party was founded in Guelph, a party based on patriotism and internationalism, and solidarity with the Soviet Union. Throughout these 50 years our Party has consistently held high this banner and fought against those who wanted to deflect the Party from this course.

The conditions of illegality of that time — when the War Measures Act was still in operation and prevented revolutionary organizations from functioning legally, and when the working-class upsurge demanded that the Party be able to work publicly — led to the formation of the Workers' Party in 1922. This party continued up to 1924 when it was possible to change its name to the Communist Party of Canada.

The formation of the Communist Party marked a turning point in the development of the working-class movement. It was not just another party which was being formed, but a party of a new type, a revolutionary party, a vanguard party based on Marxist-Leninist principles, and dedicated to the revolutionary transformation of society. The working class now had a party which could give it direction, a perspective, relating its immediate struggles to its longer-term aims of socialism. It was necessary for the Party to conduct a fierce and systematic struggle against bourgeois and reformist influences, and against anarcho-syndicalism which had some influence in the organized labor movement and among some radical French-Canadian circles. The Party learned through bitter experience that without such a firm and principled struggle against bourgeois ideology and reformism the working class could not be won for the aims of revolutionary struggle.

The 20's were difficult years for the Communist Party. Postwar stabilization had set in. The revolutionary wave had ebbed in Europe. A wave of speculation hit North America. A certain expansion of the economy took place. In these conditions illusions were spread about "permanent prosperity" in North America. Fordism, it was claimed, had replaced Marxism. This was the time when the theory of "American exceptionalism" was spread by the ruling class and found its reflection in the working-class movement and among some leaders of the Communist Party. This view held that the laws of capitalism did not apply to North America, that capitalism in North America had overcome its inner contradictions. Superficial, surface manifestations replaced a serious examination of the laws of capitalism and their operation in North America. This led to the spreading of illusions, to the promotion of opportunist views inside the Communist Party. It led likewise to left-sectarian tendencies to turn one's back on the trade unions because they were led by right-wing reformists, and to ignore the fight for the immediate needs of the working people.

These views were fought against and defeated inside the Party under the leadership of comrade Tim Buck. The outcome of that struggle, including the struggle against Trotskyism, was not only important to the Party, it was no less important to the working class. For when the bubble burst and the 1929 crash took place, our Party was in a position to lead the struggles of the working people against the effects of the economic crisis.

Indeed, our Party was the only political force in the country with a clear-cut program of action which it brought before the working people. The Party fought with all its strength to help the workers, the farmers and young people to fight back and prevent themselves from being made to bear the burden of the crisis. As part of this fightback the Party organized the unemployed, fought against evictions of workers from their homes and of farmers from their farms, organized and led demonstrations and marches of young and old around the demand for cash relief, for unemployment insurance, for "work or wages". Many of you here tonight will recall these great demonstrations in Montreal and the role played by French-Canadian and English-speaking Party spokesmen in these events. Many here will also recall that some of them were arrested and served up to a year in jail for their defence of the unemployed.

In contrast to the top leadership of the trade union movement who went along with the employers' wage-cutting drive and argued that "now is not the time to strike", the Communist Party and Communists in industry led the struggle against the employer offensive and showed by their leadership of many strikes that the workers could win gains even in conditions of mass unemployment. This lesson has not been lost on the working class, as we can see in today's struggles.

The Party linked up the struggle against the wage-cutting drive of the employers with the task of organizing the unorganized in the mass production industries. It understood that the strength of the working class lies in its organization. In this spirit the Party together with left wingers in the trade union movement undertook a systematic struggle against narrow craft unionism and the Gompers policy of "reward your friends and punish your enemies", a policy that tied the working class to capitalist parties and capitalist politics. The Party and its members played a significant role in the establishment of industrial unions in virtually all major industries in Canada. There isn't an industry in the country in which Communists did not give of their time and energy, and often their jobs, to lay the groundwork for the powerful unions we have in our country today.

It was the leadership given by our Party to the working class, the farmers and young people, that led reaction to use Section 98 to illegalize our Party. The campaign for the repeal of that piece of repressive legislation and for the release of those arrested merged with the struggle against the economic crisis and grew to such proportions that it led to the defeat of the Tory government.

In the 30's when the dark clouds of war and fascism began to appear on the horizon, the Party waged a systematic struggle for the unity of the working-class and democratic forces against this twin threat and against the appeasement policy of the King government. In this it was helped by the Seventh Congress of the Communist International which marked a new stage of development for the Communist movement in the formulation of its strategy and tactics. That Congress advanced the struggle for working-class and democratic unity in defence of democracy, the struggle for a popular front government. This policy of the united front required a merciless struggle against sectarian attitudes toward social democracy, toward the trade unions, and against obstacles which stood in the way of uniting the widest sections of the people against fascism and war.

During this period the civil war in Spain broke out. One of the proudest chapters in the history of our Party was the role it played in rallying public support in defence of Spanish democracy, threatened as it was by Franco, Hitler and Mussolini. Our Party worked to establish united front movements on this issue throughout the country and took the initiative in helping set up the Blood Transfusion Ambulance Unit headed by Dr. Bethune which played such an outstanding role in Spain.

Nor did our Party limit itself to medical aid. Over 1,200 Canadians joined the International Brigades in Spain. Under the banner of the Mac-Paps, the honor of Canada and the battle for democracy and peace were upheld by these Canadians, half of whom today lie buried in Spain.

The internationalism of our Party found expression in our solidarity with the great struggle of the Chinese people and other peoples fighting against imperialism.

This too was the time of the building of the united front of the young generation. The Canadian Youth Congress, which rallied around itself virtually every youth organization in English and French Canada, played an outstanding role in defence of the needs of the young people, in support of democracy and in defence of peace. The Young Communist

League was a prime force in bringing that movement into being.

With the outbreak of the Second World War — despite all efforts of the democratic and anti-fascist forces, particularly of the Soviet Union, to prevent it — our Party worked might and main for the achievement of an anti-fascist alliance of the Soviet Union and the capitalist countries against Hitler fascism, combining this with efforts to strengthen the role and influence of the working class in the course of that struggle.

The post-war period brought about a new situation in the world. One billion people had turned their backs on capitalism and taken the path of socialist development. The colonial empires were in the process of disintegration. The working class internationally had gained new strength and stature. It was in these conditions that imperialism, headed by U.S. imperialism, unleashed the cold war with the aim of "containing communism" and turning back the wheels of history. Under the smoke screen of anti-Sovietism and anti-communism and with the use of atomic blackmail, U.S. imperialism set itself the course of achieving world domination. The Canadian government under Prime Minister St. Laurent allied itself with the military objectives of U.S. imperialism, seeing in them and in NATO a means of achieving an endless and profitable market for Canada's raw material resources. This found expression in the policy of integration pursued by the Canadian government. This fatal policy opened the door to undermining Canadian independence and sovereignty and tying Canada to U.S. imperialist aims.

In these conditions our Party undertook to rally democratic opinion, above all the working class, in the struggle for Canadian independence — to win an independent foreign policy for Canada by withdrawing from NATO and NORAD and establishing Canada as a nuclear-free zone; to win support for a policy of peaceful co-existence, friendship, trade, cultural and scientific exchanges between Canada and the USSR and all other socialist countries. We take pride in the fact that our Party sparked the movement for Canadian independence which is now being taken up by others.

Coincident with the struggle for Canadian independence, the Communist Party advanced the demand for the right to self-determination of the French-Canadian nation, relating this struggle for the national rights of the French-Canadian people to the struggle for economic and social equality. It fought and fights against the concept, peddled by Prime Minister Trudeau, of a single Canadian nation — as it fought and fights against nationalist, separatist tendencies as being detrimental to the best interests of the French-Canadian people and to the common struggle of the working class in English and French Canada against monopoly and U.S. imperialism.

The single-nation concept denies the national rights of the French-Canadian people, while separatism divides the working-class and democratic forces in English and French Canada, undermining their joint struggle against monopoly and U.S. imperialism, and for socialism.

In line with its position, the Communist Party has put forward the demand for a new confederal pact based on the equal and voluntary partnership of the two peoples in a sovereign, democratic, binational state. This demand, too, has become the demand of others.

These issues have been related to the struggle of the people against monopoly. Our Party has both initiated and participated in broad movements of the people. At the same time it has consistently worked to deepen the class and social-ist consciousness of the working class in the course of these struggles, and to help the working class find the path to independent labor political action.

The past 50 years show that our Party has a record of achievement we can all be proud of. The Party has always been true to the working class and the cause of socialism, and has never betrayed the interests of the working class or the cause of socialism. At every stage of development the Party has shown the way forward, focussed on the main issues which need to be resolved, and advanced the slogans which have moved millions into action. One can see this in the various movements around us — in the struggle for Cana-dian independence, the struggle for equality and the right to self-determination of French Canada, the struggle for peace, the upsurge of people's action against monopoly, the movements in defence of democracy and for its extension, the growing struggle of the working class in defence of its rights.

All these movements indicate a growing process of radicalization and a move leftward. This is not an even process but it is an inevitable process. The recent NDP convention illustrates this with the emergence of the Waffle as a crystallized left wing within it, as does the developing left in various movements including the trade unions. We are on the eve of significant developments arising from the growing crisis of capitalist politics and from the growing upsurge of the people.

These movements further indicate that conditions are maturing for the eventual emergence of a democratic, anti-monopoly and anti-imperialist coalition in Canada, led by the working class and its Marxist-Leninist Party. We see this democratic coalition and a government based on it as the pathway to socialism in Canada.

The strength of the anti-monopoly front depends upon the unity of the working class. The struggle for the unity of the working class is therefore of cardinal importance and demands a consistent struggle against the splitting actions of the right-wing social democrats, the revisionists and pseudo-leftists.

The objective conditions in Canada are stimulating the trend to unity of action between Communists and socialists, between all forces of the left. Our Party will work perseveringly to bring about such unity.

The illusions that the economic theories of Keynes have replaced Marxism are being shattered by fast-moving events. Despite the efforts of state-monopoly capitalism to adapt itself to the competition with socialism, and despite its efforts at regulating the economy, it has been unable to achieve full employment, stable prices and rising standards. Indeed, what we see, and what the recent currency crisis has further underlined, is the growing instability of the capitalist system. Unemployment, inflation, poverty and currency crisis are embedded in the system and threaten the well-being of the working people. Reality is daily shattering the illusion that capitalism has changed, that it has become "people's capitalism" and is now something other than it is. Monopoly and its governments are in classical style trying to place the growing consequences of the contradictions of the system on the backs of the working people, the small farmers, the young generation. Now they are speaking of selective controls, of an incomes policy. But what they are concerned with is not that the working people achieve a decent income, but rather that their incomes be undermined or frozen while profits and dividends rise. The working class, moreover, is beginning to realize that as long as the instruments of economic and political power remain in the hands of monopoly no permanent gains can be expected in their conditions of life.

The illusion that Marcuse had replaced Marx, an illusion widely spread among student youth and intellectuals, has also been dispelled. This was the theoretical basis for the "New Left" — that the working class has become bourgeoisified, conservative, has lost its revolutionary zeal and its place in the historical process leading to revolutionary change. The period which has elapsed since Marcuse advanced these theories has shown how wrong and bankrupt he is. The working class continues to be the main force of the anti-monopoly, anti-imperialist front, the main force for the revolutionary transformation of society in the capitalist world, while internationally the socialist world system, the embodiment of working-class power, is the leading force in the struggle for peace, democracy, independence and socialism.

Petty-bourgeois radicalism, pseudo-revolutionism, these have no future. They may appear on the scene temporarily and acquire a certain popularity and support, but they are a disappearing force, not a growing force. The future belongs to the working class and its Marxist-Leninist Party. The question at issue here is not alone the size of a party, but whether its program, its policies, its aims are sound and correspond with the real course of social and economic development.

The real course of development was shown most markedly at the 24th Congress of the Communist Party of the Soviet Union.

The capitalist press had speculated that the world Communist movement was in crisis. But what were the facts?

Some 102 fraternal delegations participated in the Congress, coming from all continents and representing not only Communist and Workers' Parties, but national-democratic movements and parties as well as left-socialist parties.

What that representation made clear is that the process of unity within the international movement is gaining strength. What it made equally clear is that the great Soviet Union and the Communist Party of the Soviet Union have become the center of attraction, the rallying point of the anti-imperialist forces of the world.

The capitalist press speculated that the Soviet Union was in economic difficulties.

But the 24th Congress showed that the eighth five-year plan had in the main been successfully carried through and that the ninth five-year plan had a new thrust to it, which was only possible because of the further development and growth of the socialist economy. That new thrust was expressed in the fact that the main aim of the ninth five-year plan is to raise living and cultural standards, based on the further development and utilization of the scientific and technological revolution, cybernetics and rising productivity of labor.

The Soviet Union's aim was always to raise living standards, but in the historical conditions in which socialism was being built, certain priorities had to be emphasized. These priorities were industrialization, the building of heavy industry, collectivization. Now socialist economy has reached a stage where it is possible to spread these priorities and to focus on raising standards through rising incomes, through the extension of social security measures, through the further extension of housing, through stable prices, including the reduction of prices on many articles — all this without foregoing the necessity of developing heavy industry and strengthening the defence capacity of the country.

But in addition to this focus, the ninth five-year plan undertook a further vast development of the economy throughout the length and breadth of the Soviet Union with particular emphasis on economic development in the Far East, Kazakhstan, and the Northern European part of the USSR.

The discussion at the Congress made clear the determination of the delegates of the Party and of the Soviet people to fulfil that plan. One of the delegates to the Congress, comrade Lebedev, a fitter from the Putilov-Kirov plant, underscored this point when he stated that he and his workmates had decided to carry out the five-year plan in three and a half years.

Contrast the spirit, the enthusiasm of the Congress based on grandiose perspectives with the picture in our country of rising unemployment, rising prices, uncertainty about the future for working people and the poor farmers, lack of jobs for a growing section of young people.

Contrast the grand plans of economic development based on rational development and scientific planning arising from public ownership with the situation in our country, where for a fast buck Canada's energy resources may be sold to U.S. imperialism, where planning is for profit and not the good of the people, where Premier Bourassa can report — as if a big victory had been achieved — that vast power resources will be sold to the USA rather than being used to develop the economy in Quebec and thus ensure work for a growing labor force.

Contrast the use of the scientific and technological revolution in the Soviet Union, aimed at creating abundance and making life easier and better, with the scientific and technological revolution here.

The STR creates objective possibilities for achieving an abundance of material and spiritual benefits, for increasing the leisure time of working people, for improving the welfare of the poor sections of society, but capitalism is powerless to turn these possibilities into reality.

The first conclusion of the 24th Congress, therefore, was that it was a congress planning for plenty for the people, and laying the technical and material basis for a communist society.

But the Congress did more than that. Indeed, its internal policy of raising living standards was integrally tied to its foreign policy, aimed at maintaining peace and preventing world nuclear and rocket war.

Here, too, the capitalist press speculated about a hard line in foreign policy, about a return to neo-Stalinism. But what are the facts?

The report delivered by comrade Brezhnev advanced a six-point program of peace. This program called for putting an end, based on political settlements, to the hotbeds of war in Indochina and in the Middle East. It called for acceptance of the territorial changes in Europe arising from the Second World War, for a European Security Conference, for the recognition of the German Democratic Republic. It called for the gradual elimination of the Warsaw Treaty Organization and NATO. (In his recent speech, comrade Brezhnev spelled this out by proposing to reduce troop strength in Europe on a mutual, balanced basis.) It called for nuclear disarmament and the convening of a conference of the five countries, the USSR, USA, China, Great Britain and France, to go into this question. It called for a world disarmament conference. It called for international action against colonialism, racism and apartheid. It called for international co-operation to deal with environment control, disease, and space research.

Where is the hard line? The capitalist press were compelled to eat their words and to write instead of a "peace offensive". This is what it is, a call for peace. Socialism has again demonstrated that it stands for peace and peaceful co-existence; that the fight for peace is in fact a fight for the future of mankind. At the same time the 24th Congress made clear that it will continue to give all-out support to all peoples struggling against imperialism and for their national and social independence. The sober, realistic position advanced by the 24th Congress contrasts sharply with the policy of confrontation pursued by Nixon, and the splitting policy pursued by some Chinese leaders which leads to a weakening of the anti-imperialist front.

The 24th Congress is therefore of profound international

significance. It will strengthen the Soviet Union and its defence capacity. It will strengthen the socialist system of states. It will ever more effectively advance the struggle for peace against the manoeuvres of imperialism. It will become an ever greater point of attraction for the peoples of the world. By its efforts and the endeavors of its people, the Soviet Union will exert an intensive influence on world development, strengthen the international position of socialism and give a further impetus to the cause of socialism on a world scale.

In truth, this Congress can be called the Congress of Peace, Progress and Plenty.

This event, which takes place during the 50th Anniversary of our Party, is a great source of strength for us. It brings out in sharp distinction two lines, two policies: the line and policy of imperialism, and the line and policy of socialism.

On the one hand, one sees the growing crisis of capitalism, the sharpening of its internal contradictions as well as its inter-imperialist contradictions, its growing inability to satisfy the needs of the people. The old world of exploitation and oppression is disintegrating and perishing.

On the other hand, one sees that the power of socialism grows day by day as does its unity, despite temporary difficulties and setbacks. The revolutionary movement on a world scale is on the offensive against imperialism and reaction. Despite all its efforts, imperialism cannot reverse the course of history. Socialist ideas are spreading over all parts of the world. The international communist movement is growing stronger and broader in scope, the all-round potential of the world socialist system is growing day by day, and imperialism, the all-powerful dominant force of half a century ago, is now powerless to prevent the complete triumph of socialism in the world.

This, too, is the scoreboard of these past 50 years, and that has had an influence on the course of events in our country.

This is why we express confidence and pride in our Party. We not only look back to the past. We study the past to do better now and in the future, to deepen our knowledge of Marxism-Leninism, to strengthen the Communist Party and its unity and to make it an ever growing force in the political life of the country.

The past 50 years have been years of hard and stubborn struggle, of self-sacrificing effort. But they have been rewarding years. Our work, our efforts, have helped extend the working-class movement and given it greater consciousness and understanding. We pay tribute to the founders of our Party in Montreal, to all those members who, day in and day out, despite difficulties, have worked to spread our ideas, our press, our literature and to build our Party.

State-monopoly capitalism has been doing everything in its power to isolate us from the people, from the working class which is our source of strength. Anti-communism has become the chief weapon of reaction against our Party and all progressive and democratic forces, directed to splitting them. However, the forces of reaction will fail because history is not with them.

As the resolution of the 24th Congress of the CPSU underscored: "The attempts of capitalism to adapt itself to the new conditions do not lead to its stabilization as a social system. The general crisis of capitalism continues to deepen. State-monopoly development results in an aggravation of all the contradictions of capitalism, and in the rise of the anti-monopoly struggle. The leading force in this struggle is the working class which is increasingly becoming the center of attraction for all the working sections of the population."

We shall succeed because we are on the right road, the road of victory for the working class, for democracy, for independence and socialism. History has conclusively shown that there can be no victory over monopoly capitalism without a revolutionary party based on the science of Marxism-Leninism. We are that Party.

Happy Birthday on our 50th Anniversary.

*Address at the Parti Communiste du Québec
banquet in Montreal to celebrate
the 50th Anniversary of the CPC.
Communist Viewpoint,
September-October, 1971.*

XI

The deepening crisis — and
the role of the Communist Party

Looking back over these past 50 years we have reason to be proud of the contributions our Party has made to the organization and advance of the working class and its democratic allies in the cause of peace, democracy, independence and socialism. Our Party has always been at the service of the working class. At every stage of the struggle it sought ways in which to strengthen its understanding, its class and socialist consciousness, so that it could carry through its historic mission, the achievement of a socialist Canada. We take pride in the fact that many of the issues advanced first by the Communist Party have since been taken up and acted upon by other political and social forces.

During this half century our Party has held high the banner of Marxism-Leninism and proletarian internationalism. It combined patriotism, love of country and its people with fraternal bonds and international solidarity with the first socialist country — the USSR — and with the socialist community of states following the Second World War, with the workers of the world and with all peoples fighting for their emancipation from imperialist rule.

These past 50 years have been years of rich and varied experiences for our Party, the working class and democratic forces, experiences which are of incalculable value.

We will continue to serve the working class, confident that it and its allies, through their own experience and the role of the Communist Party which integrates Marxism-Leninism with the mass movements of the people, will take the road to socialism.

In paying tribute to the Communist Party we at the same time pay tribute to those who founded it, to those who under the most varied conditions of the struggle stood firm with the Party, never wavered in their faith in socialism, never allowed themselves to be taken in by new fads and the appearance of new phenomena, and never lost their class orientation or sought to revise the fundamentals of Marxism-Leninism. They are the salt of the earth and we salute them.

We pay tribute to members of our Party like Dr. Norman Bethune who went to Spain and later to China where he gave his life for the cause of peace and socialism. Over the last few years an effort has been made in some capitalist circles to take over Dr. Bethune and pay tribute to him as a Canadian patriot, while eliminating from the record that he was a member of the Communist Party of Canada. There are some who want to transform him into a Maoist. Neither the one nor the other will succeed. Dr. Bethune's patriotism and internationalism were as one and arose from the fact that he was a Communist, an active and proud member of the Communist Party of Canada.

The special importance of this Convention lies not only in the fact that it coincides with the 50th Anniversary of our Party, it lies also in the fact that it has the task of adopting the Party Program and the Policy Statement, both of which have been actively discussed within the Party for three months or more. (The Party Program has been discussed for about six months.) These two documents need to be considered in the context of the significant changes taking place in the world arena and in Canada.

While they are two distinct documents, the Policy Statement in fact flows from the Draft Program. The Draft Program outlines the strategic aims, the forces involved in the struggle to achieve a socialist Canada, and the various stages leading to it. It situates the distinct stage of the anti-monopoly coalition and government based on it while emphasizing its relationship to the struggle for socialism. It

167

deals with the forms of struggle leading to the winning of political power by the working class and its allies.

We believe the redrafted Program is a significant contribution to the working-class and democratic movements. It will help give a perspective, a sense of direction to the growing struggles of the people against monopoly and U.S. imperialism, relating them to the struggle for socialism. It will assist the Party in the struggle against alien ideas, in the struggle for building alliances, the united front of the working class and a democratic coalition — the building blocks and pathway to socialism.

While the Program outlines the strategy of advance to socialism the Policy Statement focusses on the tactical line of the Party for the next immediate period of time and the specific tasks the Party is called upon to undertake.

GROWING CRISIS OF IMPERIALISM

There emerge specific moments in history which could be called crucial, when the balance tips more and more in favor of the peoples. We are in such a particular moment in history. This is characterized by a considerable weakening of the positions of imperialism, particularly of U.S. imperialism which has been the mainstay of world monopoly rule, by the further deepening of the general crisis of capitalism, and by a continuation and deepening of the revolutionary upsurge throughout the world.

The world capitalist economy is undergoing a period of serious difficulties. In many capitalist countries there is a slump in production, a decline in the rate of growth and continued inflation. The monetary and trade systems set up in the post-war period by the imperialist powers are showing signs of complete collapse. The steps taken by the Nixon administration to deal with the monetary and currency crisis and save the U.S. dollar at the expense of its allies have led to a sharpening of inter-imperialist contradictions and conflicts and to stepped-up attacks on the working people. The growth of unemployment, rising prices, a drop in real wages for workers, monopoly attacks on trade union rights, above all the right to bargain collectively and to strike — all of this leads to the growing economic and political instability of capitalism, to the further sharpening in all capitalist countries of the class struggle and a growing trend to working-class unity against the monopoly offensive.

The deepening of the general crisis of capitalism is also to be seen in the mounting anti-imperialist movement in the Asian and African countries and in Latin America. The newly born national states are extending the struggle for their economic and political independence against imperialist attempts to prevent their progressive development. Latin America is experiencing a massive upsurge of the liberation struggle as developments in Cuba, in Chile and Peru show, and as events in Uruguay may show. The national-liberation movement is more and more taking on a deeper social content and in a number of countries has advanced to, or is growing over into, a struggle to achieve a socialist society.

While imperialism is undergoing a profound economic, political and ideological crisis, the most acute of the post-war period, the world socialist system and the Soviet Union in the first place continue to progress in all fields. In contrast to a relative weakening and disintegration of world imperialism and of U.S. monopoly capitalism, the socialist world is growing in strength and authority. The socialist countries are not affected by economic crises, by unemployment, by rising prices and by currency crises. The temporary difficulties these countries have gone through have been the consequence of rapid growth and development, and not of the stagnation and decline characteristic of the capitalist countries.

Realization of these contrasts is more and more entering the consciousness of working people in the capitalist countries. The Soviet Union is using its growing strength and authority, and that of the world socialist system, to advance the struggle for peace and curb the aggressor. This can be seen in the peace offensive undertaken by the Soviet Union since the 24th Congress of the CPSU, a peace offensive that is already bearing important fruit. The evidence of this is to be seen in the Egypt-Soviet Treaty, the India-Soviet Treaty, in the Four-Power Agreement on West Berlin which, once the details are agreed to by the GDR and West Berlin, should finalize the West German-Soviet Treaty and the West German-Polish Treaty, and in turn create more favorable conditions for the convening of a European Security Conference.

These treaties, alongside the visits of Mr. Brezhnev to France, Mr. Podgorny to Hanoi, Mr. Kosygin to Canada and the agreements arrived at, strengthen the trend to peaceful co-existence of countries with different social systems, to international detente, to European security, to the tearing down of the edifices of cold war built up by imperialism, and to the promotion of world peace.

The statement by Prime Minister Trudeau that Canada will establish diplomatic relations with the German Democratic Republic before too long is to be welcomed as a significant contribution in that direction. The expression of a more realistic foreign policy found reflection in the joint communique signed by him and Premier Kosygin, covering agreements on approaches to political settlements in Vietnam, the Middle East, on European Security and a European Security Conference, on nuclear disarmament based on equality of security.

These indicate that new winds are blowing, that favorable conditions exist for compelling imperialism to retreat, that the imperialist drive to aggression can be curbed provided there is the maximum unity and co-ordination of efforts of all the anti-imperialist forces of the world.

The struggle for peace remains a priority task, a central problem in the struggle between socialism and imperialism, U.S. imperialism in the first place. Imperialism has not given up its efforts to reverse the course of history despite defeats and the weakening of its positions; it still wields considerable strength. However, it is coming up against the opposition of the peoples of the world and the changing relationship of forces. The historical initiative remains firmly in the hands of the revolutionary forces — the world socialist system, the international working class and the national-liberation movement.

Since our last Convention there has been a strengthening

and consolidation of the unity of action of the international communist movement. Temporary difficulties and differences are being overcome. A number of Communist and Workers' Parties which at first were critical of the action taken by the Warsaw Pact countries in relation to Czechoslovakia have since re-evaluated their positions and today recognize the correctness of the action taken. The growing cohesion in the international communist movement finds its echo in the growing trend to unity of action of the anti-imperialist forces of the world and in the trend toward unity of action between two of the three international trade union centers, the WFTU and the ICFTU.

The changing relationship of forces on a world scale in favor of peace, democracy and socialism, the military defeats suffered by U.S. imperialism in Vietnam and in other parts of the world, have compelled the Nixon administration to shift its tactics. This does not reflect a new progressive trend in U.S. policies, but rather the development of new tactics to carry out old aims.

One of these has been the decision to normalize relations with the People's Republic of China. This decision and the entry of the PRC into the United Nations constitute an historic defeat for U.S. imperialism and a victory for the socialist countries, the international working-class movement and the national-liberation movement, for all those who fought to defend the gains of the Chinese revolution and for normalization of relations between the People's Republic of China and all capitalist countries. Ever since the establishment of the PRC our Party has fought consistently for such normalization of relations.

The shift in tactics of the Nixon administration corresponds with a shift in tactics of the Chinese leaders — while maintaining their main aims. This shift also arises from failures in domestic and in foreign policy which brought about a serious crisis in China.

The Chinese leaders could not but note the historic offensive by the revolutionary forces of the world against the positions of imperialism, the growing upsurge of struggle of the peoples for peace and security. It is this which has compelled the Maoists to make a shift in their policies.

Previously, these leaders attacked the advocacy of peaceful co-existence of countries with different social systems as a "betrayal" of the revolution and as constituting "collusion" with imperialism. Now the Chinese leaders declare their support for the "five principles of peaceful co-existence" as the basis of relations between the PRC and the USA.

Previously, the Chinese leaders argued that world nuclear war was inevitable. Now they speak with the voice of a dove.

One could say that this is all to the good, that the Chinese leaders have moved away from a previously harmful and extremely dangerous line.

The facts, however, do not suggest this at all.

On all the main questions of peace, the unity of the anti-imperialist forces, the unity of action of the international communist movement, the Chinese leaders maintain their own special ideological-political platform, one that is anti-Leninist in its essence.

The Chinese leadership opposes collective security, both in Europe and in Asia. It is opposed to the treaties of the USSR and Poland with the Federal Republic of Germany. It throws roadblocks in the way of concrete steps leading to agreement on questions of disarmament and the prohibition of nuclear weapons. It has made anti-Sovietism and the struggle against other socialist countries and Marxist-Leninist parties an integral part of the policy and program of the Communist Party of China. The only difference here is that it pursues a policy of differentiation, aimed at dividing the socialist community of states.

As part of this approach and with the aim of dividing the anti-imperialist forces, the Chinese leaders have come forward with the thesis of "struggle against the two superpowers". This anti-Leninist thesis has become the watchword under which the Chinese leaders pursue their anti-Soviet course. This so-called "theoretical" proposition is aimed at covering up the non-class position of these leaders, of trying to negate the fundamental difference between the socialist Soviet Union — the mainstay of peace, independence and

172

socialism throughout the world, and that of U.S. imperialism — the most rapacious imperialist state and world gendarme, the upholder and defender of the system of exploitation and oppression, of death and destruction, as in Indochina.

The anti-Sovietism of the Chinese leaders is on a par with their discredited theory of the "world village freeing the world city". Both substitute hegemonistic petty-bourgeois nationalist positions for a clear working-class position. Both are calculated efforts to reject the main contradiction of our time — the international class struggle between the two world social systems, socialism and capitalism — and thus evade the real struggle against imperialism. This course is being conducted under the smoke screen of an alleged danger from the north, as the "theoretical" basis for working out a deal with U.S. imperialism at the expense of the anti-imperialist forces of the world.

All of this makes clear that the Maoist platform, despite tactical shifts, remains unchanged. It is anti-Marxist and anti-Leninist. No amount of demagoguery can cover this up.

Our consistent struggle against Maoism and for the principles of Marxism-Leninism and proletarian internationalism is a necessary part of the struggle for unity of action of all anti-imperialist forces, and for the unity and cohesion of the international communist movement.

Such unity is a vital necessity. While U.S. imperialism has suffered severe military defeat in Vietnam, it has not drawn the lessons of this military defeat by withdrawing from Indochina. On the contrary, while withdrawing some troops from Indochina, the Nixon administration has still left in that area 145,000 troops, including a large air force and navy. While talking peace, the Nixon administration, under cover of normalization of relations with the PRC and utilizing differences between the PRC and the USSR, has in fact stalled the Paris talks, stepped up the air war against the Democratic Republic of Vietnam, and continues to give unqualified support to U.S. puppet troops in South Vietnam for another assault through Laos and Cambodia against the Democratic Republic of Vietnam. At the same time, it has installed a military dictatorship in Thailand.

All this makes it clear that U.S. imperialism has no intention of withdrawing from Indochina and Southeast Asia.

Vietnam continues to be at the center of the global struggle against imperialism, particularly U.S. imperialism. Our Party must continue to do all in its power to unite the majority of the Canadian people in support of the demand that U.S. imperialism get out of Indochina totally and unconditionally and that the peoples have the right to determine their own affairs without outside interference. Our Party fully supports the seven-point Program of the Provisional Revolutionary Government of South Vietnam and will continue to give every assistance to the peoples of Vietnam, Laos and Cambodia in their struggle against U.S. aggression. The efforts of U.S. imperialism to prolong its aggression in Vietnam will not prevent its ultimate defeat.

Focussing on Vietnam is not to suggest there are no other serious tension points in the world. The critical situation in the Middle East, the outbreak of a military conflict on the borders between India and Pakistan, the struggle of the peoples of Bangladesh and Northern Ireland for their democratic and national rights, the necessity of a European Security Conference and the recognition in international law and by Canada of the GDR, nuclear disarmament — these are all questions requiring the close attention of the Party and of the peace movement in our country.

In light of the complicated and critical international situation our Party has a twofold task: first, to do everything in its power to strengthen unity of action of the anti-imperialist forces based on the unity and cohesion of the international communist movement; and, second, work to widen the peace movement in our country, helping the trade union movement become a vital and active force for peace and for an independent foreign policy, and to make Canada's voice heard as a foremost champion of peaceful co-existence of countries with differing social systems.

ECONOMIC SITUATION

The economic situation in Canada shows no signs of improvement. It continues in a state of near stagnation despite the Pollyanna-like statements of Finance Minister Benson and the various economic measures taken by the government. Industrial production has declined. What is particularly noticeable is the relative overproduction in the manufacturing industry, and with it, the consequent curtailment of production and the rise in unemployment. The situation has been further aggravated by the government's anti-inflation policies and by the devaluation of the Canadian dollar, arising from U.S. imperialist pressure which led to the closing down of many plants, particularly in Ontario, embracing over 16,000 workers. The situation has been further affected by the economic crisis in the USA which has flowed over into Canada and to other parts of the capitalist world.

The sharp rise in unemployment is due to many factors, ranging from technological change to speed-up, relative overproduction and closing down of plants — although at bottom it arises from the way capitalism works. In any case, in examining the immediate causes of unemployment technological change and speed-up should be seen as primary factors. The resulting prospect of this is that those workers who have lost or will lose their jobs will likely become *permanently unemployed,* added to by young people and school graduates who, notwithstanding diplomas of one kind or another, now find the doors to useful employment closed to them.

Workers have become "redundant", while a growing body of students and young people have become "superfluous" — an unwanted generation. These are the consequences of a so-called "free enterprise system" that denies young and old the right to a job.

Economic insecurity and unemployment, these have become a primary threat to the working people of our country.

The workers are not opposed to automation. What they demand are its fruits, in the form of reduced hours of work with no reduction in take-home pay and a redistribution of the national income which could begin to cope with poverty. Instead, the fruits of automation are going to corporate wealth which is amassing huge profits by intensified exploitation through technological changes, facilitated by government free grants to corporations. In the meantime the workers are being blamed for inflation stemming from the U.S. war in Indochina and from the Trudeau government's so-called anti-inflation policy. Moreover, they are now confronted with the threat of having some form of wage freeze or incomes policy foisted on them when the real need is an expansion of purchasing power of the working people, curbs on monopoly power, the adoption of the 32-hour work week with no reduction in take-home pay, and reduced prices and rents.

Confronted with the necessity of answering why unemployment has been climbing despite various government measures, the government has advanced the rather strange argument that the "participation rate" has risen. By this it suggests that too many people are seeking work. This is turning the problem upside down. The truth is that unemployment is rising because the economy is stagnating. Under capitalism, technological change and speed-up, modernization, rationalization and mergers do not create new jobs, they create unemployment. New jobs are created when new plants are built, existing plants expanded, new industries developed, hours of work reduced without reduced take-home pay and policies pursued directed to expanding the purchasing power of the working people.

All these measures require additional workers, technicians, engineers, scientists, white-collar workers, young workers. All these open the door to employment for graduating students.

The various measures taken by the government have not been based on this concept. Serving the interests of monopoly, government policy has been directed to making funds available to it, whether for regional development programs, technological change or research development — all paid for by taxpayers. This "trickle-down" theory, that if monopoly gets a big share of the pie it will give some of the crumbs to the working people, has proven to be completely bankrupt. The main beneficiary of this policy has been monopoly while its victims have been the working people. In point of fact, what this policy has accomplished is to provide substantial funds to U.S. corporations to further fasten their control over Canada. These funds could and should have been used for all-Canadian industrial development under public ownership.

When it comes to the unemployed, the "trickle-down" policy has gone together with a policy of "tokenism". The public works program is too little and too late to have any substantial effect this winter. The war on poverty remains on paper and will continue so to remain until government action is taken to achieve full employment and rising purchasing power for the working people through a minimum wage of $3.00 an hour, democratic tax reform, and the adoption of a guaranteed annual income of $3,000 for single people and $5,000 for married people. The argument that there is no money for a guaranteed annual income is false. If money can be found today to produce obsolete ships and planes, it can be found to battle poverty.

Our Party was on sound ground in raising the demand for one million new jobs and relating this demand to the need for new all-Canadian policies, for job security and the 32-hour work week with no reduction in take-home pay. Our Party has coupled this demand with the slogan *Put Canada Back to Work — Jobs or an Adequate Income for All Canadians as a Right!*

These demands, which won wide support in the labor movement, need to be directed ever more vigorously to all levels of government today, tomorrow and in the federal election campaign when it gets under way.

Rising unemployment, inflation, the effects of technological change on jobs, the pressure by monopoly for selective wage controls or an incomes policy — all these are compelling the workers to take more militant action, strengthen their unity and solidarity. This recently found expression in the united front achieved by the Quebec Federation of Labor, the CNTU and the Teachers' Union in support of the workers locked out by *La Presse* who were battling for job security and for a say over technological change. The powerful movement of solidarity in support of these demands merged at the same time with the right to demonstrate, which Mayor Drapeau had taken away. Police brutality in breaking up that demonstration did not deter the workers from holding an equally large mass meeting of protest a few days later.

These two actions show that significant processes are afoot in Quebec. The working class is beginning to emerge as the main force, not only in the economic but in the political struggle as well. Indeed, the class, democratic and national questions are merging more and more in Quebec.

In B.C., too, we have been witness to a rather major event, the historic half-hour general strike initiated by the B.C. Federation of Labor against U.S. imperialism's Amchitka nuclear test. This is the first general strike in B.C.'s post-war history and interestingly enough it was not called on a straight economic issue but around the slogan of survival. One can assume that, having taken such action once, this will not be the last time such a high form of struggle will be taken in B.C. or in other parts of the country, both to defend and to advance the interests of the working people. What is important to note in this action and in the demonstration by all the delegates to the Ontario Federation of Labor Convention in front of the U.S. Consulate, as well as the initiatives taken by other trade union bodies, is that the trade union movement is not only adopting resolutions on issues of peace but is becoming actively involved in the struggle for peace.

What these actions and the varied strike movements show is the increased and strengthened role of the working class. The weight of the working class in political life has grown. This finds its expression also in the increasing tendency to break away from support of the old-line parties, evidenced in various elections and in a growing trend to labor-farmer political action, particularly in Manitoba and in Saskatchewan.

All these developments taken together point not only to a continued radicalization but to a growth of class-consciousness among workers.

Not least, these developments expose the falsity of the claim that the working class has become reconciled to capitalism. Far from being reconciled, the reality is that the law of the class struggle is asserting itself. The working class is increasingly beginning to move onto the center of the stage in the struggle against state-monopoly policies. By its militant struggles it is helping to widen the movement for social change.

This in turn imposes on the Communist Party the task of bringing the ideas of scientific socialism into the working-class movement, thereby helping to increase the role and weight of the working class in the political life of the country as the center, the heart, the leading force in bringing together a democratic coalition in Canada.

CURRENCY CRISIS AND CANADIAN INDEPENDENCE

The present U.S. economic crisis which has overflowed to Canada has some distinctive features.

It takes place in conditions of a U.S. war of aggression in Indochina and continued militarization of the economy. It shows that war and militarization are not effective anti-crisis measures. At one stage war and militarization tended to promote and expand economic activity. But eventually this process turned into its opposite by distorting the economy, by curtailing markets and reducing demand for consumer goods, due to a heavy tax burden and a rising cost of living. This is the situation today.

A second distinctive feature of the present economic crisis is that it is not acting as a dampener on prices or inflation. Indeed, prices keep going up despite efforts by the government to curb inflation through the creation of unemployment. The fact is that inflation and unemployment have become built-in features of the capitalist system.

Concerned about its system, with the social consequences of continued inflation, rising prices and rising unemployment and with the drive for profits, state-monopoly capitalism is striving to resolve this dilemma by regulating labor and integrating it into its mechanism through selective wage controls or an incomes policy. These measures, taken in the USA by the Nixon administration as part of its attack on the workers and their unions, have so far not been brought into Canada.

This arises from the opposition of the organized labor movement to such controls and guidelines combined with the fact that Canadian monopoly and the government have not as yet agreed upon their necessity.

However, at some point this situation is likely to change. Indeed, this may well be the subject of behind-the-scenes discussions between government and monopoly at the present time. The workers will have to fight hard and unitedly, both on the economic and political fronts, against wage guidelines, selective controls, wage freeze or incomes policy. The essence of these measures, no matter how labelled, is to maintain wage inequalities and poverty, prevent workers from getting a larger share of the wealth they produce, undermine collective bargaining and the right to strike, while giving *carte blanche* to monopoly to rationalize industry and step up the exploitation of the workers through speed-up and technological change.

Not least, the present economic crisis is intertwined with a monetary and financial crisis, embracing the capitalist world. President Nixon's new economic policies, unilaterally imposed on the allies and trading partners of the U.S., underscore the fact that important or dominant sections of U.S. monopoly are veering to a policy of protectionism as a means of strengthening the sick U.S. dollar. These policies have the aim of overcoming the crisis at the expense of the U.S. working class, and by economic war on the allies and trading partners of U.S. imperialism. Inevitably they will affect the working class of all capitalist countries.

The cumulative effect of all this could lead to a capitalist world economic slump.

In any case, the monetary and financial crisis feeds back on itself. It aggravates the economic crisis and spreads it to other countries. Moreover, because U.S. imperialism continues its aggressive aims and military expenditures, it stimulates inflation both in the U.S. and in all capitalist countries, including Canada, and this, too, hinders the prospects of any immediate overcoming of the crisis.

The Nixon new economic policies are not a temporary phase of U.S. policy, a short-term affair to be quickly changed. The reality is much different. The dollar crisis marks the end of an era of unquestioned U.S. domination and leadership of the so-called "free world". The stability which imperialism thought it had established in the post-war era based on the dominant position of U.S. imperialism and of the U.S. dollar has proven illusory. The dollar crisis which has grown into a crisis of the monetary system of the capitalist world mirrors the growing crisis of U.S. imperialism and the changing relationship of forces within the imperialist camp, arising from the emergence of new trading blocs and countries that challenge not only the supremacy of the U.S. dollar but U.S. supremacy in general.

Under different circumstances such a challenge would find its outcome in war between the imperialist powers. However, the existence of a powerful world socialist system of states standing on guard for peace, and the fear that war would end their system impels U.S. imperialism as well as its competitors to find other ways of resolving their sharpening differences.

Meeting follows meeting in their feverish efforts to work out a new basis of stability, of exchange rates and trading rules. However, despite the efforts of the International Monetary Fund, these are not likely to stabilize the U.S. dollar or other currencies nor, for that matter, the monetary crisis of the capitalist world. On the contrary, differences on how to resolve this crisis will likely become sharper and inter-imperialist contradictions will become more acute. What they point up is the further deepening of the general crisis of capitalism.

The economic situation is worsened for Canada because of Nixon's new economic policies. Indeed, these policies have a particularly dangerous impact on Canada which is more vulnerable to U.S. policies than other capitalist countries.

The special relationship established between Canada and the USA has been rudely shattered by the unilateral actions of the Nixon administration. U.S. imperialism has made no bones about the fact that the "special relationship" it wants from Canada is a pound of flesh — a further revaluation of the Canadian dollar, an adjustment of trade policy as it affects safeguards in the Canada-U.S. Automotive Pact and in defence expenditures, and a continental energy policy.

This is quite a sizeable package, pressed for with the argument that what is good for U.S. imperialism is good for Canada. One can understand this crude blackmail being peddled by U.S. imperialism. But what can one say of those monopoly interests, their political spokesmen and their press in Canada who peddle the same sort of rubbish or who try to cover up for U.S. imperialism and act as its fifth column in our country?

What is good for Canada in a further revaluation of the Canadian dollar, which would raise the cost of Canadian exports and open the door for a massive increase in imports? In both cases further revaluation would create additional unemployment, slow down and undermine the industrial development of the country.

What is good for Canada in an adjustment of trade policy such as the U.S. administration wants with respect to the Automotive Pact and "defence sharing"? This too would promote unemployment, create an international balance of payments deficit and lead to a further tightening of the noose of U.S. control over the Canadian economy.

What is good for Canada in a continental energy policy that would hand over to U.S. monopoly energy resources including water — the very basis upon which to build, develop and expand industrial development in Canada?

What is good for Canada in the arbitrary closing down of U.S. branch plants and their transfer to the USA, something that could follow upon the adoption of the Domestic International Sales Corporation?

These plants have been paid for by the workers and by the Canadian people many times over from surplus profits extracted from the workers, by the prices charged to Canadian consumers and by depreciation and tax allowances granted by governments. These plants must stay in Canada under public ownership and be operated in the public interest.

Implicit in all these proposals is that Canada become a

hewer of wood and drawer of water, gas and oil for the U.S. — its raw material source of supply. This is denied by spokesmen for the U.S. government and by U.S. imperialism. Their denials hold no water, because the implementation of these policies would lead in one direction only — a decline in job opportunities, a decline in living standards, a loss of Canadian independence and sovereignty. The main decisions affecting Canada and her people would be made in the USA. The decline in job opportunities would be taking place at a time when according to government estimates 2,600,000 new jobs will need to created from now until 1980.

All these measures which would cause harm to the Canadian people, combined with the Amchitka nuclear test, have given further impetus to the demand for Canadian independence, for new trade policies and for an independent foreign policy. The demand for new policies is merging more and more with the demand for a greater measure of autonomy for the trade union movement, a battle our Party has waged these past 50 years.

The debates in the camp of monopoly on what to do with respect to the 10 per cent surcharge and Nixon's new economic policies generally are rather revealing. They show that monopoly is not united on what course of action to take to get out of the crisis.

One grouping, oriented to a large extent although not solely on resources industry, advocates fuller integration into the USA in the form of a common market or other arrangement and opposes any steps that would place curbs in the way of increased U.S. takeovers in Canada. It is interesting to note that those who advocate such policies veer to the right in Canadian politics, favor some kind of wage freeze, are critical of the visit of Premier Kosygin to Canada and of the agreements arrived at between Canada and the USSR which strengthen understanding, peace, trade and Canadian independence. These are the political forces that want to perpetuate the cold war, not eliminate it.

These political forces cut across the old-line political parties and include Social Credit and Action Canada.

The other grouping, which likewise cuts across old-line

party lines but is oriented on manufacturing to a large extent, is not opposed to some elements of integration with the USA in specific industries. However, their basic orientation is toward a greater measure of industrialization in Canada, an effort to assert a more independent position in foreign affairs, the seeking of new outlets and markets for Canadian manufacturing as well as the export of capital. It is interesting to note that those who veer in this direction are moving timidly in the direction of an independent foreign policy and a lessening to some degree of U.S. domination in Canada, as can be seen in the vague proposals for a screening mechanism with respect to foreign takeovers, and in efforts to establish and extend relationships with the socialist countries on the basis of mutual advantage.

This grouping reflects the views of a growing body of the Canadian people who are beginning to see that the path to real Canadian independence lies in friendship and closer political and economic relations with the socialist countries, and in the first place with our northern neighbor — for over 50 years the foremost defender of the independence and self-determination of nations — the socialist Soviet Union.

This grouping seeks new markets in the socialist countries, the only stable and growing markets in today's world. The advantages of trade with these countries are self-evident. The socialist countries are not plagued by economic crises or currency crises. Their currency is not tied to the U.S. dollar. Thus, even were the dollar and the entire monetary system of capitalism to collapse, it would not affect the stability of the rouble and the financial stability of the Soviet Union.

Trade with the Soviet Union and with the socialist countries, if based on long-term agreements and on mutual advantage, would therefore introduce a measure of stability into the situation and help overcome some of the negative effects of U.S. economic aggression against Canada.

The recent visit of Premier Kosygin to Canada, following Prime Minister Trudeau's visit to the Soviet Union, and the agreements arrived at have opened the door to the strengthening of trade, scientific, technological and cultural exchanges between our two countries. These agreements will help strengthen Canada's independence and make it a more vital force for peace. Those who attack the visit and the agreements echo U.S. imperialism and reaction in Canada. They undermine the true interests of our country. These agreements are in the interests of Canada, of the working people of our country, and should be actively defended and, above all, implemented.

It is useful to note the differences in the camp of monopoly and to utilize them in the interests of the struggle for genuine Canadian independence, peace, democracy and the well-being of the Canadian people.

However, it would be downright dangerous for the working class, or our Party, to pursue a policy that leads to tailing the bourgeoisie or a section of it. Canadian monopoly capital is not going to *lead* the struggle for Canadian independence, although individual capitalists and even groups will support that struggle. Their aim is the perpetuation of monopoly, a better deal for the Canadian capitalist class and the maintenance of the exploitative system of state-monopoly capitalism.

Indeed, monopoly interests in Canada have undertaken a widespread offensive against the proposed Canada Labor Code, particularly against those sections which would give workers a voice over the effects of technological change on the work force, against the proposed Competitions Act which could to some degree slow down mergers and influence prices, and against the proposed reform of taxation which, while totally inadequate, tips the hat somewhat in the direction of the low-income groups.

Monopoly is determined to prevent adoption of any legislation which could, to some degree, limit its right to exploit labor and hinder it from making profits at the expense of the Canadian people. The only restrictions it is prepared to consider and work for are those aimed at shackling labor and the working people of our country.

Clearly these aims do not coincide with those of the working class whose task it is to lead the struggle for genuine Canadian independence to the end. To free Canada from the present onerous domination of U.S. imperialism requires the political defeat of monopoly capital in Canada. The immediate crucial task is to win working-class support for that aim, linking up the struggle for genuine Canadian independence with the demand for a fully autonomous, united trade union movement based on class struggle policies.

Our Party, which has pioneered on the question of Canadian independence, must find the ways to get much more fully into the debate on the path Canada should take around the issue of fuller integration or genuine Canadian independence. This is really the central issue of Canadian politics today and will likely be the central issue of the federal election to be held next year. We should set ourselves the political aim of emcompassing the defeat of those championing fuller integration with the USA, and work to unite all the patriotic, democratic and progressive forces that can be united around a program directed to winning genuine Canadian independence from U.S. imperialism and liberation from the rule of Canadian monopoly capital.

The elements of such a program should include the following:

1. A long-term and balanced all-Canadian industrial development program, utilizing Canada's resources under public ownership for its implementation. Regional development programs to be merged with this overall program and developed under Crown corporations.

The main thrust of such a program should be the strengthening of Canadian independence, the achievement of full employment and rising standards. It should include public action on urbanization, housing, transportation, environmental control, parklands.

2. A restructuring of Canada's trade policies to make possible the extension of trade with the socialist and newly-liberated countries on a mutually advantageous basis making long-term, low-interest credits available where necessary.

3. An active policy of peaceful co-existence. Withdrawal of U.S. military bases from Canada and an end to flights by U.S. military planes over Canadian territory.

4. Economic and social policies directed to achieve full employment, rising standards, an adequate income, decent

health, housing and education as a right for all Canadians. Equal rights for women. A say on all questions affecting the lives of the people.

5. The adoption of a new Canadian Constitution based on the equal voluntary partnership of the French-Canadian and English-speaking peoples and on their right to self-determination.

6. A Bill of Rights which guarantees the rights of labor with respect to collective bargaining, the right to strike, to picket, to organize. No wage freeze or incomes policy.

ELECTORAL POLICY

Our Party should take such a program into the labor and democratic movement and undertake public mass campaigning for it on a level demanded by the situation. This should be seen as an essential part of the preparatory work for a federal election and the naming of Party candidates wherever it is decided to run.

Here it may be useful to draw your attention to the amendment proposed by the Central Executive Committee in connection with our electoral policy. The essential part of the amendment states as follows:

"The struggle over which path to take — the path leading to Canada becoming a hewer of wood and drawer of water, gas and oil, or one leading to industrialization based on Canadian control and public ownership — merges directly with the fight against monopoly policies and for jobs, adequate incomes and peace, and the movement for the right to national self-determination and for equality in French Canada.

"The issue of Canadian independence will be at the heart of the federal election and will shape political alignments. It is within this context that a very fluid and new political situation is developing. An effort is being made to knock together a reactionary right coalition of Conservatives, right-wing Liberals, Social Credit and Action Canada, aimed at pushing politics further to the right. The Communist Party needs to determine its aims and electoral tactic in the election campaign within the framework of these developments.

"Its aims should be to unite all the patriotic, truly national and democratic forces for the election of a large progressive bloc, including Communists, to Parliament.

"In pursuit of this aim the *main fire* must be directed against those monopoly interests which would more fully integrate Canada with U.S. imperialism through a common market or other forms which could undermine the political independence and sovereignty of the country, against those forces which stand in the way of implementing a policy of peaceful co-existence of differing social systems and of co-operation between Canada and the USSR; against all those who would try to push Canada further to the right and attempt to rekindle the flames of the cold war. At the same time the Communist Party must continue its vigorous criticism of the Trudeau government and its state-monopoly policies.

"The great issues to be fought out now, during the election campaign and following it — issues which our Party has pioneered and fought for in the broad labor and democratic movement — demand that the Party lift its sights and run a maximum number of candidates. This will enable the Party to boldly advance its program, place it before the whole country, stimulate the labor and democratic movements, help forge a democratic alternative to the policies of monopoly and relate it to the socialist perspective.

"The running of a large number of Party candidates is an ingredient essential to the achievement of unity of action of the labor and democratic forces. The Communist Party will advance the fight for unity of action, consistently and to the end, and struggle to achieve unity and the election of a large bloc of progressives including Communists to Parliament. The more effective the Party's campaign, the greater the likelihood of the above stated objectives being achieved. It is in this spirit that the Communist Party appeals for unity and co-operation of the labor and democratic movements. The developing situation opens up great opportunities and challenges which must be grasped with boldness and imagination."

From this it should be clear that the forthcoming federal election will be an extremely important one. Our Party can adopt a pedestrian approach to it and perhaps decide to run a minimal number of candidates, hopefully leaving it to others to raise some of the crucial issues. Or we can, if we will it, do what must be done — advance our specific contribution to the solution of the crisis, to the path Canada must take to get out of the crisis, and work to unite the labor and democratic movements for those alternatives which can take Canada along the path of genuine Canadian independence and toward a socialist Canada. The winning of the working class for these policies is crucial if it is to head the struggle for Canadian independence.

It is with full awareness of our responsibilities that the CEC proposes we run the maximum number of candidates we possibly can in the coming election. We know it will require a great effort but we believe the Party is capable of it and will respond to the challenge.

How does this correspond with the way the Draft Policy Statement puts the question of electoral policy?

The Draft proposes that "the Communist Party will nominate candidates in the coming federal election where an *effective campaign* can be waged around its program within the framework of the Party's electoral aims."

The amendment to the above by the·CEC, which appeared in the November 5th issue of *Convention 71,* after outlining the arguments for it proposes "that the Party lift its sights and run *a maximum number* of candidates."

Does the difference lie in running an *effective* as against a *maximum* number of candidates?

No, because we want to run an *effective campaign with a maximum number of candidates.*

The difference lies first in the crucial issues before the country and in the fact that the Party must make a major effort to advance its solution; and secondly, in the tendency that an effective campaign could be understood to mean that what we are undertaking is not a *maximum* effort but a *minimum* one, with the least number of candidates.

In line with the above the CEC asks the delegates to consider the proposed amendment on electoral policy, and urges the Convention to adopt it as Party policy.

In devoting considerable attention to the coming federal election one should not conclude that the municipal field is unimportant. On the contrary, the municipal arena has become an increasingly important center of struggle against monopoly, against the developers who are an essential part of monopoly and who, in many cases, have the municipal governments in their pockets and stand in the way of policies vital for genuine municipal progress. Our Party has some important achievements to record in various cities and towns where as a result of its work Communists have been elected and re-elected, despite the efforts of monopoly and the right wing in the labor and democratic movements to defeat them. This points up the need for the Party to develop its work more boldly and tenaciously in the municipal arena, to establish strong footholds wherever Party organizations exist and thereby create the groundwork for extending our political base on a provincial and federal scale. We need to see this relationship and begin a more concentrated and co-ordinated attack for its solution.

We should combine independent political work in the municipal field with a correct unity and coalition policy directed to defeat the spokesmen of monopoly and the developers in the municipalities.

This two-sided approach — the strengthening of the independent political work of the Party and the struggle for the united front — must become the very essence of the work of the Party. United front movements on specific issues, be they the fight for peace, independence, the national rights of the French-Canadian people, democratic rights, jobs and wages, a new deal for farmers, equality for women, Canadianization of culture, tax reform, educational reform, defence of the young generation, indeed, all issues of vital concern to working people, are not only important in themselves, but out of the struggles around these issues will arise the democratic

190

coalition our Party works for. The independent political work of the Party, unity and struggle are thus an essential part of the tactical line for building left and democratic unity, the achievement of a democratic coalition and a government based on it.

Keynote address, 21st — 50th Anniversary — Convention,
Communist Party of Canada.
November 27-29, 1971.

Abridged.

XII

A new direction for Canada — the coming federal election

As this report was being written President Nixon was en route to the Soviet Union; the West German Parliament ratified the treaties between West Germany, the Soviet Union, and Poland on the inviolability of frontiers arising from the Second World War; and the U.S. government continued bombing Hanoi, Haiphong and other cities and towns of the Democratic Republic of Vietnam. The scale of mass destruction surpasses the air destruction of the Second World War. The U.S. has escalated the war by blockading and mining all the principal ports of the Democratic Republic of Vietnam.

These contradictory developments reflect the contradictions in the international situation — the processes of detente on the one hand and international tension on the other — which go on simultaneously in today's world.

The ratification of the treaties between West Germany, the USSR, and Poland is an outstanding event, an important victory for the policy of peaceful co-existence waged by the Soviet Union and other socialist countries, opening up prospects for turning Europe into a continent of peace. Now that the treaties have been ratified, favorable conditions have been created for signing the four-power agreement on Berlin, for convening a European Security Conference (a course Canada supports), and to finally recognize the German Democratic Republic in international law, a step the Canadian government ought to take without any further delay.

Events in Europe take one turn favorable to peace and peaceful co-existence while, with the Middle East situation remaining critical, events in Indochina take yet a different turn.

Having failed, and failed miserably, in pursuit of its policy of Vietnamization, the Nixon administration has undertaken military escalation of its aggression against the Democratic Republic of Vietnam and the people of South Vietnam, coupling this with a highly provocative blockade of the ports of the Democratic Republic of Vietnam. This act of desperation and of brinkmanship is directed against the DRV with the aim of forcing it to its knees in abject surrender to U.S. imperialism. The blockade and mining of the rivers and ports are not directed to achieving a political settlement, which could easily be reached based on the seven-point program of the National Liberation Front and the Provisional Revolutionary Government. They are directed to seeking a military solution of the Indochinese question.

The blockade, the mining of the ports, and air attacks on the railway lines adjacent to China, are no less directed against the Soviet Union, China and all other socialist countries. By this military escalation the Nixon administration aims to use the "big stick", the policy of strength and of force to compel the socialist countries to stop sending assistance to the DRV, to acquiesce in the destruction of a socialist state and the defeat of the national-liberation movement.

This policy will not succeed. From the strictly military point of view the mining is of little value. The defenders of the DRV are fully equipped with the armaments they need, and they will continue to get replenishments, while the NLF gets its arms additionally from the puppet troops who "supply" it with modern U.S. arms and tanks.

President Nixon may hope through his show of strength to get some face-saving concessions from the Soviet Union, may hope that the Soviet Union would barter away a socialist country in exchange for some deal with U.S. imperialism. Only Nixon and Kissinger could continue such an approach and believe in its possibility. No one else in the world would. *The Soviet Union has made it unmistakably clear that there can be no barter of socialism, as it has made equally clear that it will defend socialism wherever it exists.*

For the Soviet Union there is no contradiction between the struggle for peace and peaceful co-existence, the pursuit of a realistic and flexible policy which helps to strengthen peace, and its active support of the national-liberation struggle and the struggle against imperialism. In this sense the Nixon visit to the USSR and the discussions and agreements arrived at cannot but help the cause of international detente and national liberation and be an important contribution to the cause of universal peace and disarmament which the Soviet Union has consistently fought for.

In the last few weeks the peoples of the world have seen two governments and two systems in action. On the one hand, they have seen the desperate actions of the imperialist Nixon administration, resulting from its defeats, talking peace while waging war, prepared to play with the peace of the world, using blackmail and worse in order to maintain its positions in Southeast Asia. On the other hand, they have seen the calm, sober and principled position of the socialist Soviet Union, directed to restrain the aggressor while continuing its assistance to the DRV and NLF. The world breathes easier today because the Soviet Union did not fall into the trap laid by the Nixon administration, did not reply to confrontation by a policy of confrontation and its possible consequence — nuclear war. The world breathes easier because of the historic peace offensive launched by the Soviet Union. Its consistent struggle for peace and peaceful co-existence, which exerts a determining influence on international politics, is breaking down the cold-war strategy of imperialism and compelling it, more and more, to accept the principles of peaceful co-existence. This is seen in the Moscow summit and the agreements arrived at.

This is not to deny that the blockade, the mining of the ports, the air attacks, are a threat to the DRV and to world peace. *The need here is to pull the claws of the aggressor without enlarging the conflict.* There is no doubt the Soviet Union is well aware of the old adage — "If you can't pass through the gate, go around it. If you can't get around it, go over it. And if you can't go over it, go under it." The main thing is that the material gets to the DRV and the NLF who are in the front line in the struggle for peace.

In this connection there are reports of discussions between the USSR and People's China, on the Soviet Union's initiative, with respect to the passage of such material through Chinese territory into the DRV. Assuming they are correct, they can only be welcomed by the forces of peace, democracy and socialism throughout the world. *Such co-operation in support of a common ally is absolutely essential, and it would be unforgivable if this co-operation were not forthcoming.* No ideological differences can be allowed to stand in the way, or be used as a pretext against such a common effort. The latest military escalation by U.S. imperialism points up again the overriding necessity for unity of action of all anti-imperialist forces in the world. The Chinese leadership cannot stand aside at this critical stage of the struggle. It must eliminate anti-Sovietism from its arsenal and take its place in the struggle for such unity to compel U.S. imperialism to change course and accept the right of the Vietnamese people to determine their own destiny free of outside control.

The actions of the U.S. government arise from a misjudgement and miscalculation of the actual relationship of forces in Vietnam and in the world today. No amount of military pressure and no threats will force the Vietnamese people to capitulate. The only way to solve the Vietnamese problem, the Indochinese problem, is by negotiations. This holds with equal force regarding the Middle East crisis which can only be solved through a political settlement based on the UN Security Council resolution of 1967.

As our recent Party Statement said: "End the blockade, end the bombing, return to the negotiating table, get out of Vietnam." This corresponds with the seven-point program of the NLF and the Provisional Revolutionary Government which we support. It corresponds with the need of maintaining peace on a world scale. This, not the whitewashing of U.S. imperialist aggression, ought to be the position of the Trudeau government.

The new dangers to world peace arising from this act of

195

desperation of U.S. imperialism emphasize anew the necessity of building a powerful peace movement in our country, in which the organized trade union movement must play a central role. The revitalization of the peace movement is an important step in this direction. The Canadian Labor Congress convention was compelled to reflect the urgency of the fight for peace in the positions it took on foreign policy. However, it must be said that the right wing in the CLC reflected the Nixon line, not a line leading to a just settlement, when it called for a settlement of the Vietnam question through the UN. This was not an act of solidarity with the struggles of the people of Vietnam. It was an act of solidarity with the position of Nixon. It is to be hoped that the trade union movement of our country will come forward in genuine solidarity by unequivocally supporting the seven-point program of the Provisional Revolutionary Government and National Liberation Front and by joining the campaign for an end to the blockade, an end to the bombing, a return to negotiations and the withdrawal of U.S. troops and bases from Indochina. This should be linked to a combined effort to compel the Trudeau government to separate itself from the U.S. military escalation.

The struggle for peace and peaceful co-existence takes place within the framework of growing difficulties for imperialism, expressed particularly in the declining role and prestige of the U.S.; a marked sharpening of inter-imperialist contradictions, and a growing confrontation between capital and labor. The crisis in U.S. policy and in U.S. hegemony is an essential feature of the deepening of the general crisis of imperialism. The period of the overall domination of the imperialist camp by U.S. imperialism is passing and is being replaced by the emergence of three main centers of imperialist rivalry — the U.S., Western Europe, and Japan. The unresolved monetary crisis reflects this change which arises from the law of uneven economic development under capitalism. This very unevenness of development prevents long-term stability in the capitalist world and sharpens inter-imperialist rivalry.

The causes which brought on the dollar crisis are still here and will result in a further depreciation of the U.S. dollar, a slowing down of economic growth and a further splurge of inflation in the capitalist world. The impressive gains of socialism stand out in sharp contrast to the process of decay and disintegration in the imperialist camp.

The growing crisis of imperialism leads the most reactionary circles to seek solutions by a drive against democracy at home and by adventures abroad.

There are still forces bent on perpetuating the cold war and stimulating anti-Sovietism. These forces have not given up. They will try in every possible way to throw obstacles in the path of an all-European Conference on Security and Co-operation. This holds true with equal force in the Middle East where the Israeli annexationists, backed by U.S. imperialism, are determined to prevent a political settlement.

In both these critical areas there is an obvious need for a maximum effort by the democratic and peace forces of our country to help influence developments in a direction favorable toward detente.

In this situation, as the events in Vietnam illustrate, there is need for maximum vigilance, maximum escalation of the struggle for peace and the struggle for democracy, the ever-present urgency of building working-class and democratic unity so as to prevent imperialism from finding a way out of its internal contradictions.

Developments in Canada cannot be seen apart from the framework of the deepening of the general crisis of imperialism and the growing crisis of U.S. imperialism, which monopoly capitalism is trying to overcome at the expense of the working class and other peoples, including the Canadian people. This poses in all sharpness the necessity of revising economic and political relations with the U.S. and strengthening Canadian independence.

CANADIAN SCENE

Twenty-seven Communist candidates have already been nominated for the coming federal election and efforts are being continued to reach the target of 30 we set for ourselves. However, whether we reach this figure or not, the fact that the Communist Party has undertaken to nominate the maximum number of candidates it can, and has succeeded in doing so, is an important political victory.

By running the maximum number of candidates it should be possible for the Communist Party to make an impact on Canadian politics, stimulate the labor and progressive movements, focus attention on the central issues of the election, advance our alternative policies and strengthen the progressive forces inside and outside of Parliament.

The prospects of so doing are becoming increasingly favorable.

Dissatisfaction with the Trudeau government is growing, made public by a recent Gallup Poll which showed that support for the government has declined with no appreciable gains for either the Conservatives or the NDP.

The most revealing feature of the poll was the high percentage of uncommitted voters, 43 per cent to be exact. This trend, not the lack of an overriding issue or issues, was undoubtedly a decisive factor in Prime Minister Trudeau's decision to delay the election, and in the various measures taken by him to mend political fences and rebuild the political fortunes of the government, particularly in its relationship to big business and the U.S. government.

Big business had begun to look down its nose at the government because of its original bills on tax reform, on the Competition Act, on the Labor Code and technological change, all of which it felt were unfavorable to it. The U.S. government had taken a critical attitude to the Canadian government's independent stance with respect to the withdrawal of troops from NATO, its recognition of People's China, its efforts at establishing closer relationships with the USSR. The U.S. government was concerned over the possibility that the government, under pressure of the rising demand for Canadian independence, would curtail U.S. monopoly operations in Canada.

The Conservative Party tried to utilize these developments for its own political advantage and to become the preferred party of monopoly.

The government undertook a number of measures to correct this situation. It amended the tax reform bill in favor of big business. It withdrew the Competition Bill. It amended the Labor Code referring to technological change so as to emasculate those sections that might help the workers affected by such changes. It has taken a hard line on wage policy as it affects workers in the civil service, in Air Canada, and in the CBC, and with respect to the important issue of job security. The essence of its policy has been to regulate wages in the interests of monopoly and to refuse to guarantee job security.

Simultaneously with this it undertook a number of measures to strengthen the positions of monopoly at the expense of the Canadian people, the latest and most blatant being the budget. This budget gives cake and icing to the corporations, the U.S. corporations in the first place, in the form of a half-billion dollar giveaway program, while giving literally pennies, 72 cents per week, in increased pensions to pensioners and veterans. Moreover, this budget has a hooker to it. The Canadian people will be called upon to pay an additional three per cent personal income tax while corporation taxes are reduced.

The trickle-down theory which motivates this budget and is ostensibly aimed at promoting new employment, by providing the corporations with incentives to expand, will not produce new jobs. Indeed, modernization of plants, new machinery and equipment based on new technology may create unemployment rather than alleviate it. Furthermore, with manufacturing industry running at below 80 per cent of capacity, such incentives are not likely to be acted upon. The main thrust of the budget is to strengthen monopoly and guarantee high profits to the big corporations, Canadian and U.S. alike.

The government has been equally energetic in establishing a new atmosphere and a new image in its relationship with the U.S. government. From a position in which it seemed to be developing an independent posture with respect to foreign policy, it has moved back to a position of whitewashing U.S. foreign policy. Instead of condemning U.S. military escalation in Vietnam with all its dangerous consequences, it has minimized the escalation and, in the name of not "taking sides", become an echo of U.S. imperialist foreign policy. Indeed, it seems to have returned to a position in which Canada's foreign policies are increasingly being co-ordinated with those of the USA, presumably in return for a lessening of U.S. imperialist economic pressure on Canada.

The capitulation of the Trudeau government to U.S. imperialist pressures with respect to foreign policy, peace, and peaceful co-existence, finds its counterpart in the retreat of the government with respect to Canadian independence. After the preparation of voluminous reports on the issue of U.S. control, of U.S. investments in Canada and their impact on the Canadian economy, the government finally came up with the proposal of a screening mechanism which in fact is not intended to prevent foreign takeovers or strengthen Canadian control over the economy. All it will do is legitimize such takeovers. Moreover, foreign takeovers are the least of the problems having to do with growing U.S. domination of the Canadian economy. The proposed mechanism leaves unchanged both foreign domination over manufacturing industry and natural resources, and the increase of U.S. monopoly in Canada. By focussing on a screening device, by stating the screening mechanism is all it is prepared to undertake to curb the power of U.S. corporations and investment in Canada, the government has exposed the pretence that it would stand up to the U.S., proceed with the Canadianization of the economy and strengthen Canadian independence.

The retreat of the government on foreign policy, on Canadian control over the economy, emphasizes anew the fact, as the Communist Party Program and Policy Statement indicated, that one cannot depend upon monopoly or its governments in Canada to uphold Canadian independence, that such a struggle can only be effectively waged and won by a united working class and its allies and by a new government based on them.

The retreat also emphasizes that U.S. imperialism is determined in every way it can to prevent Canada and the

Canadian people from moving toward an independent position either in foreign policy or in economic development. Nothwithstanding the lovey-dovey statements of President Nixon and Prime Minister Trudeau during President Nixon's recent visit to Ottawa and the demogogic deception of the president about upholding Canadian independence, the "get tough with Canada" policy remains the guideline of U.S. imperialism. This is made evident in the recent steps taken by the U.S. government with respect to DISC, by the drive to adopt the Burke-Hartke Bill, by the countervailing tariffs with respect to Michelin Tires, and so on.

The *Financial Post* in a recent editorial sees these measures and the Turner budget as part of a developing trade war between the two countries. All these pressures go together with a continuing drive by the U.S. government to compel modifications and changes in the Auto Pact. What appears likely is that following the election in Canada, and assuming the Trudeau government is re-elected, the Auto Pact will be revised in favor of U.S. monopoly and at the expense of the jobs of Canadian auto workers.

Notwithstanding the position of the Trudeau government, the acceleration of the offensive by U.S. imperialism against Canada is sharpening the antagonism between U.S. imperialism and Canada and broadening the base of opposition to U.S. domination. Conditions are becoming more favorable for extending the movement for Canadian independence and for a fully autonomous trade-union movement.

For the Trudeau government the screening mechanism may be the end of the measures it will take to uphold Canadian independence. For the Canadian people, however, it can only be the beginning of an ever larger effort led by the working class: to press for public ownership and control of natural resources and industries based on them, as well as of energy; for all-Canadian development of secondary industries; for development of the North with due regard to the interests of the Northern people and the ecology; for the expansion of trade on a mutually satisfactory basis with the socialist countries, and for an independent foreign policy for Canada.

These questions need to be at the center of the election campaign.

The turnabout by Trudeau on all fronts is at the same time a calculated and cynical ploy. *The Trudeau government sees the Conservatives, not the NDP, as its main opponent in the coming election and is veering to the right, so as to take the ground away from the Conservatives who have been attacking the government on precisely these issues.*

We need the sharpest possible critique of the government and its polities. At the same time we should make clear, as we do in our electoral policy statement, that *the alternative we strive for in this election is not a Tory minority or a majority government or a coalition on the right, but the election of a large progressive bloc including Communists and NDPers who would constitute a genuine opposition to the policies of the government.*

WORKING-CLASS UPSURGE

What stands out today as a main feature of Canadian politics is the sharp labor-capital confrontation.

The monopoly offensive against the working class has been stepped up as can be seen in Quebec, B.C., and Metro Toronto strikes and in numerous other struggles. The monopoly offensive is aimed at weakening the power of the working class, at undermining trade union rights, the right to strike, the right to collective bargaining. It is a get-tough-with-labor policy with the workers getting less of the carrot and more of the whip.

While the immediate targets of the attack are the workers in the public service, as can be seen in Quebec, B.C., and Ontario, the attack will not stop there. Once legislation is adopted to prevent strikes in the public service, this would become the signal for imposing compulsory arbitration in negotiations everywhere. United working-class action is necessary to defeat this drive and prevent the implementation of such restrictive legislation.

Underlying this offensive is the government-inspired effort to regulate the trade unions, to set the terms of settlement and integrate the trade unions into the mechanism of state-monopoly capitalism. The aim is to make the trade unions pliable tools of government policy in the trade wars now developing, to undermine their militant and class character and transform them into tools of class collaboration with the active aid of the right wing in the trade union movement and in the NDP. This is the essence of Mr. David Lewis' remarks to the CLC convention about the need for a "modern" approach to collective bargaining.

The offensive against the working people takes place on the background of continued economic uncertainty despite a slight increase in production. This slight improvement in production has not resulted in any appreciable decline in unemployment which continues to hover at six per cent of the labor force, although hidden unemployment would push this figure up considerably. One reason for this is that manufacturing industry operates at below 80 per cent of capacity at the same time that there is a rapid growth in the young adult labor force. Nor has it given workers an increased share of increased production. Indeed, rising prices and continuing inflation which will accelerate in the coming period are continually eroding the purchasing power of working people. Moreover, faced with the prospects of trade wars, monopoly and its governments are undertaking modernization of industry including technological change at the expense of the working people under the slogan of increased productivity.

In response to this attack the workers are uniting their ranks and undertaking ever more militant forms of struggle in defence of their jobs, their living standards and trade union rights. *The battle for jobs and for job security has become a major feature of working-class action. Gainful employment, the right to work, has become a major issue for the working class and finds its reflection in the growing demand for the 32-hour work week with no reduction in take-home pay.* Despite the efforts of governments to check the working class and push it back, *despite the role of the right wing in the labor movement, the unity, solidarity and class consciousness of workers are growing. This is a significant feature of the situation today.*

A great and historic class battle is presently under way in Quebec. Starting as an economic struggle for a $100 dollar weekly minimum wage, substantial wage increases, and for job security, it has increasingly taken on the character of a major political struggle against the state and the parties of monopoly.

Our Party drew attention to the processes at work in Quebec at our 21st Convention when we stated: "Significant processes are afoot in Quebec. The working class is beginning to emerge as the main force not only in the economic but in the political struggle as well. Indeed, the class, democratic and national questions are merging more and more in Quebec."

This indeed is what is taking place in Quebec. It is of great historic significance that the workers virtually took control of cities and towns such as Sept-Iles and Thetford Mines, took over countless radio stations, that the workers in the Ste. Thérèse GM plant could tell a junior executive of that company who had been stopped by the picket line and who inquired under what authority it had been done, "by the authority of the workers of Quebec."

These developments evoked fear in the hearts of reaction and its press, which in effect called for a blood bath against the working people of Quebec. It evoked fear in the hearts of the right wing in the NDP and trade union movement also. How else can one characterize the statements of Messrs. MacDonald and Lewis that "chaos" exists in Quebec? How else can one characterize the claim that no conspiracy existed against the trade union movement on the part of government, the corporations and judiciary? How can one characterize such statements except as an attempt to whitewash monopoly and its governments, and as an expression of fear of the militancy of the working class?

It is of utmost importance to the future of our country and the cause of democratic progress and of socialism that the working class of English-speaking Canada identify itself fully and unreservedly with the just struggle of the working class

204

in French Canada, that the bonds of *class unity* be cemented to the utmost in support of the struggles of the working people of Quebec for parity in wages, improved social security, for national equality, for the right to self-determination of French Canada based on an equal voluntary partnership in a new confederal pact.

The measures of solidarity taken by the CLC convention, by provincial federations of labor and countless unions throughout the country and by the National Farmers' Union, point up the fact that the workers and farmers are becoming increasingly conscious of their responsibilities in the present critical situation.

Their own strength, their unity, the growing unity of blue- and white-collar workers, their solidarity — which neither government nor press could undermine — coupled with the solidarity of the working class throughout Canada, compelled the Bourassa government to agreed to the release of the three arrested leaders and to reopen negotiations with the Common Front. This constitutes an important victory for the working class in Canada.

The negotiations are taking place in conditions when a monopoly-inspired drive is afoot to divide and splinter the trade union movement in Quebec. The CNTU is the special target of this drive, of which one of the aims is to undermine the ability of the Common Front to win its just demands, and to undermine the Common Front itself.

This attack on the developing class unity of the organized labor movement needs to be resolutely defeated. It is the ever-strengthening unity of the Common Front and the growing solidarity of the working class of Canada which can lead to victory for the just demands of the workers, the repeal of Bill 19, and the unconditional release of all those arrested.

There are some rich lessons from this historic struggle of the working class in Quebec which our Party and all those concerned with democratic progress need to study.

The working class is learning about the role of the state: that far from being neutral, the state is an instrument of coercion by monopoly against the working class and the people; that the judiciary is an integral part of this instrument of coercion, no less than are the police and the armed forces.

It is no less important for the working people in French Canada who forged the Common Front to advance their vital interests in the public service; to learn that the Common Front needs to be extended into the political arena and find its expression in the building of a mass federated party of labor.

The lack of a viable political vehicle through which the working class can advance its economic, social and political aims — in conditions where there is increasing disgust with the parties of monopoly, and more particularly, with the Bourassa government — could lead to the Parti Québecois or Social Credit becoming beneficiaries of the turnaway from the old-line parties. The NDP, including its Waffle wing, is facilitating this process of support for the Parti Québecois, which is a petty-bourgeois neo-separatist party, in return for its support in the federal election. Such a line is not only an expression of sheer opportunism, it is dangerous for the working-class and democratic forces. *There is no future for the working class in French Canada in becoming the tail end of the Parti Québecois, as there is no future for the working class and the country in separatism. The future of the working class lies in strengthening its class unity in Quebec and on an all-Canadian scale against monopoly, and in uniting its allies on an all-Canadian scale around a democratic alliance for fundamental change.*

The way forward at this stage in Quebec lies through a mass federated party of labor, open to all segments of the working class — the NDP, the Parti Communiste du Québec, the trade unions, and other forces.

The upsurge which characterizes the situation in Quebec finds its own reflection in other parts of the country where the workers are showing equal determination to win justice and to defeat the wage-freeze and anti-labor policies of municipal, provincial and federal governments. This is particularly the case in British Columbia where the united action of the trade union movement, in alliance with the teachers and other groups, compelled the Bennett government to retreat. However, this has not deterred the government from continuing on a course of imposing compulsory arbitration on the trade unions.

The struggles of the recent period show that the white-collar workers in the public service, including teachers, are developing a high degree of militancy and solidarity, a firm determination to maintain their right to strike, to unite their efforts to win their demands. The monopoly offensive is stimulating the trend to unity and creating new opportunities for unity of action of the working class and all anti-monopoly forces.

Not least, the sharpening struggle gives us additional proof of the leading role played by the working class. All the various theories advanced in the past period of time about the loss of revolutionary spirit of the working class, about the elimination of class distinctions and therefore of the class struggle, have quickly evaporated. *The working class, as the events in Quebec have again emphasized, is the main driving force in the struggle against monopoly and for the rights of the working people.* This will be underscored time and time again in the coming period of sharpened class confrontation between labor and capital.

The general strike of public employees in Quebec, followed by a virtual general strike of blue- and white-collar workers in almost every industrial center in Quebec, makes it clear that irrespective of the outcome of the present struggle, the working class in French Canada will never be the same.

It is this that leads us to believe that it will increasingly draw the lesson that economic struggle alone cannot bring about a fundamental change in its position, that political action is required — not any kind of political action to replace one party of monopoly by another, but political action that aims at achieving fundamental change. What is needed in Quebec is a large influential revolutionary party of the working class based on the principles of Marxism-Leninism and proletarian internationalism. Such a principled party exists in the Parti Communiste du Québec. It is still small, but unless the working class builds it into a powerful force for revolutionary change there will be no fundamental change in the position of the working class. It is this challenge to which we need to apply ourselves with ever greater vigor, seeking in every way to strengthen our roots in the working class.

DRIVE FOR A SHIFT TO THE RIGHT

The Conservative Party is striving to take advantage of the growing disillusionment and disenchantment with the Trudeau government. It aims to shift politics more to the right, and to become a credible alternative for monopoly policies. Its programmatic positions reflect this as does the choice of its candidates. It is not accidental that the Conservatives are going out of their way to select candidates from the extreme nationalist and reactionary ethnic groups. The alliance they are building up is part of their objective of establishing an important electoral base for their reactionary program.

In the Social Credit Party this drive to the right finds its reflection not only in the program of that party but in the fact that the Edmund Burke Society has taken it over in Ontario as a political vehicle through which to push its reactionary, pro-fascist policies. At the same time in B.C., the Social Credit Bennett government is pursuing a policy aimed at strengthening the political fortunes of the Conservatives in the federal arena.

Action Canada has become a vehicle through which to rally right-wing Liberals. It has chosen wage and price controls and anti-communism as its main programmatic points through which to rally monopoly support and that of the petty-bourgeoisie in an attack on the trade union movement and the working class.

These developments are now added to by the introduction of the ultra-right John Birch Society into Canadian life, brought here by the CIA and by reactionary interests in Canada.

So far these political groups have not coalesced. Notwithstanding, they constitute a dangerous reactionary current in Canadian political life. These parties feed upon dissatisfaction with the policies of the Trudeau government, at the same time using demagogy, deception and proposals for reform to create a wider base for their more reactionary policies. While some of their aims may differ, all are united in support of a continentalist position, in support of U.S. imperialist policy, and of a hard line against the working class and trade union movement. They are united in restrictions on democratic rights. At this stage their aim is to build up sufficient public support to compel a shift to the right in the policies of whatever government is formed, or to help bring about a right-wing coalition.

This appears to be the electoral strategy of the Conservative Party.

The working-class and democratic forces would be wrong to underestimate this reactionary political current which is at the same time a reflection of an international trend in the capitalist world. The drive to reaction can be blocked by the united struggle of the workers and all democratic forces in defence of labor's rights. Indeed, the necessity of a democratic coalition to counter and defeat these aims becomes an increasingly pressing and urgent task. The big challenge before the working-class and democratic forces in the coming election is that of checking the drive to the right and strengthening the forces of democracy and progress.

It should be self-evident that there is no advantage for the working-class and democratic forces in jumping from the frying pan into the fire by ceasing to vote Liberal and voting Conservative instead. The present situation calls not for new slogans but for real change.

The opportunity for achieving this exists. It lies in the election of a large progressive bloc including NDPers and Communists to Parliament. It rests in the search for new policies and the turnaway from the old-line parties which are increasingly evident.

CRISIS IN NDP

And yet in this situation of opportunity and challenge the prospects for major advance are endangered by the policies of the right wing in the NDP who, in alliance with the right wing in the trade unions affiliated to the NDP, have precipitated a crisis within that party. While the crisis centers in Ontario, it is country-wide in scope. The immediate cause of this crisis is the decision to expel the Waffle from the NDP unless they dissolve their forms of organization. The deeper cause lies in the adaptation of the NDP to capitalist policies, and the inevitable emergence of a left wing in opposition to these policies of class collaboration. If the expulsion of the Waffle takes place it will seriously weaken the NDP and help the parties of monopoly which would hope to take advantage of the situation to their own benefit.

The decision to expel is not something new. In the 30's the right wing in the CCF undertook a similar operation against the left wing, under the slogan of cleaning out the Communists. It attacked and expelled all those who advocated unity for democratic progress, all those who favored co-operation with the Communist Party instead of co-operation with capitalism. The end result of that struggle was to strengthen capitalist ideas within the CCF.

Today the situation is being repeated. In alliance with the right wing in the trade unions affiliated to the NDP, the right-wing expulsion of the Waffle, if it proceeds, would shift the NDP to the right, to the political center, where the Liberals and Conservatives are to be found. *It would tend to blur whatever areas of distinctiveness the NDP has in the political spectrum.* This of course is part of the electoral strategy of the right wing, to give it an aura of respectability with which to appeal to the petty bourgeoisie and the middle class.

Evidence of this orientation and of making state-monopoly capitalism work for monopoly is to be seen in the declaration of Mr. Lewis that he would support a Prices Review Board and, if that didn't work, wage and price controls. Evidence is to be found in his declaration to the Canadian Labor Congress convention that labor needed a "modern approach" to collective bargaining — that it should stop being unreasonable in its demands and accept what monopoly is prepared to give, no more, no less, a proposition even Mr. MacDonald, CLC president, couldn't stomach. This approach is seen in the position of Mr. Barry Mather who called on the workers to forego wage increases in the name of some mythical national interest and, in effect, agree to intensified exploitation of the working class by monopoly.

All these non-class concepts are expressions of a policy of class collaboration reflected in the right-wing trade union leadership also.

The aim of the right wing is not directed to help the working class find a way out of the growing contradictions of capitalism at the expense of monopoly, but rather to help monopoly resolve its contradictions at the expense of the working class and its jobs, standards and trade union rights.

At the same time the proposed expulsion of the Waffle is a clear warning against those who advocate genuine autonomy and independence in the trade unions, as it is a warning against those who in the NDP advocate socialism as a basic solution to the fundamental problems confronting the country and the Canadian people.

While right-wing policy is responsible for the crisis within the NDP, the position often taken by the Waffle has made the struggle against the right wing more difficult. The Waffle too are in crisis, reflecting the crisis of "new left" policies. The rhetoric of the Waffle, their pseudo-radical posturing and "new left" theorizing have not been calculated to win support for their policies, often repelling the very forces that condemn right-wing policy. *Above all, by spreading the false assumption that the basic problems of the Canadian people could be solved through and within the NDP, that the NDP is the vehicle through which to achieve the socialist transformation of our country,* the Waffle have misled those who aspire to genuine socialism, and at the same time have stood in the way of uniting the forces of the socialist left for common aims.

Certainly there is more than enough international experience, as well as performance in Canada, to disprove such an assumption. The NDP was and remains a social-democratic party operating within the framework of capitalism. Its aims are not scientific socialism but the seeking of reforms within capitalism. It is not formed to challenge the class structure of capitalism.

If this situation is to change, *if the NDP is to become part of a democratic coalition opening the door to genuine Canadian inde-*

pendence and to socialism, right-wing policy in the NDP and in the trade-union movement needs to be defeated. To accomplish this objective requires unity of the left for genuinely socialist policies. It does not lie, as is suggested in some quarters, in a breaking of the alliance with the CLC.

We believe the expulsion of the Waffle will be helpful only to the parties of monopoly. Their expulsion, however, will not prevent the re-emergence of a left in the NDP. This is as inevitable as day follows night.

Certainly the Communist Party should do everything in its power so that the expulsions, if they take place, will not lead to a withdrawal of Wafflers from the struggle for Canadian independence and for socialism. Rather it should result in their more active involvement in the many-sided struggle, including joining the Communist Party for all those who want genuinely socialist policies based on the principles of Marxism-Leninism. Irrespective of what takes place in the NDP, the Party should undertake an open, friendly dialogue with Wafflers. Experience shows this is both possible and fruitful. This dialogue needs to be devoid of sectarian hang-overs which would get in the way of co-operation for common aims.

In any event, the crisis within the NDP underscores again and again that if changes in the relationship of forces are to take place in the broad political arena, and in the democratic movement in the first place, the working class must be the driving force for such changes.

This puts to the forefront the development of our policy of industrial concentration the aim of which must be, over the next period of time, to have the unions become *carriers of left policies.* The fight for such policies and for a leadership to implement them will take time. Obviously this is not a short-range task, but is an absolutely necessary task, closely bound up with the building of the Party in industry without which there will be no genuine left. Without this it will not be possible to put an end to the alliance of the right-wing leaders of the trade union movement with the right-wing leadership of the NDP, win the majority of unions for social-ist policies and thereby bring about a change of relationships within the labor and democratic movements.

The prospects of achieving such changes are not as far away as some would think. The CLC convention mirrored the struggle between two policies, right-wing and left-wing. The growing pressure of the workers was seen in the various policies adopted — on economic policy, solidarity with the working class of Quebec, the issue of peace and foreign policy, the question of bringing unions into the CLC, the organization of the unorganized, particularly the white-collar workers, and not least in the very significant vote given Mr. Bell running for president and Mr. Stewart running for the executive.

What the votes signify is that the cold war is on the wane in the trade-union movement; that the working class is faced with the reality of a hot war by monopoly on its standards, its jobs and rights; and that it sees the need for policies and for people to lead it in struggle. The votes are a criticism of class-collaborationist policies which are exposing themselves more and more as completely bankrupt and aimed to prop up capitalism at the expense of the Canadian people.

At this new stage of the struggle the organization of the unorganized, particularly in the white-collar field, has become a vital necessity to enable the working class to play an ever more effective role in the economic and political arena. Our Party should do everything in its power to make that drive successful, in the same way as we helped in the bringing of the industrial unions into Canada.

The results of the CLC convention show that we are on sound ground in striving to strengthen the unity of the trade union movement on the bases of autonomy and independence, that we are on sound ground in striving to bring about left unity in union after union, and in working to actively involve the trade union movement in the struggle for peace, for Canadian independence, and in the social and economic issues facing the people. The results show no less clearly that one can't fight monopoly with monopoly arguments and positions.

Congratulations are due to all left wingers at the CLC convention, like Bill Stewart of Vancouver, to all those who advanced sound working-class policies. *The convention showed that our Party is not an isolated force. It is a growing force based on the correctness of its policies which the working class is increasingly recognizing as valid and necessary for its advance.* Precisely because this is so we need to seek out ways and means by which Communists in the trade unions can come forward as public spokesmen for Party policy, combining this with consistent defence of the interests of the working class and exposure of right-wing policies.

MAIN THRUST OF COMMUNIST ELECTION STRATEGY

Generally speaking, the Party welcomed the decision to run a maximum number of candidates as can be seen in the number already nominated. However, the discussions, particularly around the election platform, brought forward various conceptions of how to develop our position which could tend to weaken the impact of our electoral policy.

One conception was that the Party focus its campaign around the slogan "Trudeau must go". A slogan of this kind would in our view only serve the interests of another wing of monopoly capital, one which is even more reactionary than that supporting the Trudeau government. For the working class and democracy, it is not a matter of indifference whether a more or less reactionary government is in power. *But above all, such a slogan places in a secondary and minor position that which is the essential thrust of our electoral tactic — the election of a large progressive bloc including NDPers and Communists to Parliament.* This thrust merges with the continuing battle of the Party for working-class and democratic unity against monopoly capitalism. It would at this time be the best outcome of the election, particularly when the situation is not yet ripe to raise the issue of forming a government, *and when, arising from the possibility of a minority government being elected, such a large progressive bloc could conceivably hold the balance of power.*

The question of the action slogan is therefore of considerable importance and bears directly on our electoral policy, on how and against whom we develop the main fire, including the absolute necessity of sharp criticism of the

Trudeau government as an instrument of monopoly policies.

Another view holds that we should spell out who are the progressive forces in the "large progressive bloc". In our view it would be premature to do so. Developments have not yet reached a stage, as in some other capitalist countries, where one could speak of a distinct left grouping within this or that capitalist party. Undoubtedly as the struggle develops and sharpens, such a situation may emerge but it does not exist now, and to orientate on it would be wrong and dangerous.

The essential element of our electoral tactic is thus the election of NDPers and Communists. *One should note that we do not call for the election of the NDP as such, but of NDPers. We believe the change is important in that it gives the Party more flexibility and at the same time enables it to pursue a policy of differentiation toward the NDP, sharpening its criticism of right-wing policy in the democratic and labor movement while simultaneously pursuing a policy of struggle for united action.*

In addition to the above views there are still some voices in the Party, feeble it is true, which suggest the Party only run a small number of candidates or none at all, and throw all its energy into the battle to elect the NDP. *Experience, however, has already shown us that such an electoral policy is self-defeating in that it tends toward liquidationism in the Party, opens the door to unqualified and uncritical support of social democracy and social democratism, rather than a policy of conditional and critical support. This distorts the united front. There will be no united front electorally without a strong Communist Party, including Communist representation in Parliament, federally, provincially and municipally.*

Moreover, our electoral policy is not related only to a particular election. It is an integral part of the struggle to bring into being a democratic coalition of which the Communist Party is a part. *The running of Communist candidates, irrespective of the vote at a particular time, is therefore a decisive component of our overall strategy and needs to fit into it as a hand fits a glove.* At the same time our running is bound to stimulate the left and progressive forces in the NDP, the trade union and farm movements, among youth and women, and thereby become an important part of the battle for unity of the left.

In this regard one must say that while all the objective conditions are maturing for the realization of a democratic coalition, what is still lacking and hampering its development is the subjective factor, that is, the weaknesses among the democratic forces and the resistance of the right wing in the labor and democratic movement to the formation of a united front which includes the Communist Party.

The major factor in changing this situation and in bringing about a democratic alliance is the all-sided strengthening of the Communist Party. At the expense of repeating, it must be said again and again that there will be no united front without a strong and effective Communist Party which fights for it. There will be no change of relationship in the working-class movement without a strong Communist Party rooted among the industrial workers. There can be no democratic alliance without a strong Communist Party including Communist representation in Parliament.

It is necessary to place the question this way to correctly situate the electoral policy of the Party and its relationship to the coming election, as well as to the overall struggle for democratic reforms and fundamental change. *It is particularly necessary to do so in order to place in the sharpest way the decisive task of Party, YCL and press building as an integral part of the election campaign.* Indeed, we should view the results of our campaign not only in the number of votes obtained, although we must fight for every vote and the expansion of the political influence of our Party, but also in the extent to which we build our Party, the YCL and press in every constituency in which we run.

In short, electoral work is mass work and should be seen as such, in the same way that mass work assists the electoral work of the Party. The work of Communists in the trade union movement, among farmers, women, working youth and students, in the various mass movements, including the peace movement — these are the necessary ingredients of a sound electoral policy. We have some positive experiences in Party and YCL building. This is true in Ontario, in Alberta, in B.C. and elsewhere. We need to collate these experiences which show the Party can be built.

In view of the vital necessity of Party, YCL and press building, perhaps we should consider launching at this Central Committee meeting, for a period of a year, a consistent, many-sided fight to build the Party, YCL and press, including the organized sale of the Party Program, and focussing on the ideological, organizational and political strengthening of the Party. The need to do so is self-evident. At the heart of it is the need to make our Party the effective vanguard of the working class. The turbulent events throughout the country, the leftward move in the CLC, the crisis within the NDP and within the "new left", the election campaign itself, the changing international situation — all these constitute the ingredients, the nutrients around which and with which to undertake such an effort. If it is agreed to by the CC meeting, the CEC should be instructed to work out the details of such a campaign in close consultation with Provincial Committees and the Party membership, linking this up with a consistent struggle against anti-communism, anti-Sovietism, revisionism, leftism, all those roadblocks used by monopoly to place obstacles in the way of Party growth.

The date of the election is still a matter of speculation, even though we now know it will not take place this summer. However, whether it takes place this October or next year, our Party should use whatever time is available for election campaigning. There is a view that we should wait until the election is actually called before getting into the campaign. In our view this would be short-sighted and wrong. While it would be premature to distribute our electoral platform or to establish election headquarters, unless this or that constituency can afford to do so, it is not too early to start campaigning now and in a way that would lead to an ever greater effort as we get closer to an actual election. This requires that the Party relate all its activities to the election and integrate them in a proper fashion. Grass-roots work in every constituency is election campaigning.

What is required is that ways and means be found to have our Party candidates identified with issues, be they local, provincial, or federal, although all of them should be linked to the federal campaign. A case in point is the action undertaken by the Party in Alberta around the demand for an increase in oil royalties.

We propose that from now until an election is called, the Party undertake a countrywide campaign, with due regard for flexibility and change if the situation requires it, around the following slogans and issues:

Put Canada back to work, process our natural resources and energy based on public ownership — build an all-Canadian publicly-owned Mackenzie gas and oil pipeline — develop secondary manufacturing industry based on planned all-Canadian economic development — jobs or an adequate income for all Canadians as a right!

As you see, we do not advance a single slogan but a series which ties in the questions of jobs, independence, incomes for working people. It would be useful for the comrades to indicate their opinions on the above in the course of the discussion. While we have not worked out the concrete details, what would be involved would be an action by the CC, supported by the Party throughout the country, around which to develop campaigning preliminary to the actual election. This could take on the form of a folder, stickers, posters.

This leads me to a third proposition, the need to work out a strategy to break through the mass media. So far the national media have closed us off as if our Party were not running an appreciable number of candidates. We have to find ways and means of changing this situation, while doing everything possible to break through the local mass media as well, although here we have had more success. The CEC should be instructed to devote considerable time and attention to this problem which is decisive to our ability to make an impact on Canadian politics and the overall outcome of the election.

While focussing on preparations for the federal election we should not forget that a provincial election is likely soon in B.C., and that municipal elections are also on the agenda in some of the large cities this fall and winter. All these require our close attention.

I come to the end of my remarks. We have set ourselves

large but not impossible tasks. If we can combine our work in the electoral arena with the necessary mass work — in the fight for peace, Canadian independence, the vital needs of the working class, the youth, women and farmers, and in the battle to build the Party, YCL and press — we can begin to make an appreciable impact on Canadian politics. This is the challenge before us.

Report to the Central Committee,
Communist Party of Canada.
May 27-28, 1972.

Abridged.

XIII

The federal election — what next?

For most Canadians including the pollsters, politicians and the mass media, the results of the October 1972 federal election were totally unexpected. The general expectation was that the Trudeau government would be returned with a smaller majority. The Communist Party was among the few who foresaw the prospect and possibility of minority government, although not the seesaw minority government we have today.

Minority government is of course not new in Canadian politics. But it has become particularly pronounced in the postwar period. Seven general elections over the past 15 years produced five minority and two majority governments. This is Canada's fifth postwar minority government.

This recurring and significant development of the postwar period reflects the crisis of capitalist politics in our country, the turnaway of growing sections of working people from the old-line parties. This expression of growing lack of confidence in these parties and their programs does not go in one direction. It takes one form via the NDP and another via Social Credit. One leads in a generally progressive direction, the other has reactionary overtones. But at bottom this trend is an expression of the inevitable breakdown of the parliamentary monopoly of the two-party system, of a process of fragmentation and polarization of Canadian politics which was evidenced particularly in the elections of NDP provincial governments in Manitoba, Saskatchewan and more recently in British Columbia.

The results of the election bear out the analysis of the 21st

Convention of our Party last November, 1971, which declared:

"What is qualitatively new is that a polarization of class forces cutting across party lines, as well as a fragmentation within the traditional bourgeois parties, is taking place in Canadian political life. This process of developing shifts and changes creates a fluidity in Canadian politics which suggests that the return of a majority government may be short-lived *and that the next federal election may conceivably return a minority government.*"

Clearly our Party hit it on the button.

We are back at minority government, a state of affairs that alarms big business but has certain possibilities for the working-class and democratic movement.

WHY THE LIBERAL SETBACK?

Before dealing with some aspects of strategy and tactics for the next round it would be useful to analyze those factors which brought about the unexpected setback for the Trudeau government, transforming it from a majority into a minority government.

The political experts with their Maginot-line complex, those who always fight the last war's battles, are still trying to fathom the basic reasons for the setback. Some hold the opinion that it was an anti-Trudeau backlash based on a condemnation of his personal traits, his arrogance and general behavior. Others say it was due to an anti-French backlash. Still others claim it was an expression of dissatisfaction with unemployment and inflation.

In our view, no single factor determined the outcome of the election. Indeed, if one basic factor dominated above all others, it was the economic and social policy of the government and its management of the economy. The government was held responsible for rising unemployment, rising prices and rising taxes, for alleged fraud by recipients of unemployment insurance and for undermining the "work ethic". It was attacked by big business for advancing its original proposals with respect to tax reform, the Competitions Act and the Labor Bill, and by the labor and democratic movements for having capitulated to the pressures of big business on these issues.

Moreover, instead of advancing a bold and dynamic program leading to a strengthening of Canadian independence and full employment, both of which could have ensured its return with a comfortable majority, the Trudeau government strategy was to stand on its record while in fact retreating from any pretence of strengthening Canadian independence both in economic and foreign policy. This strategy was based on over-confidence, on the conception that the election was going to be a "shoo-in". Instead, it almost turned into a "shoo-out".

This strategy included the creation of a new image of Trudeau, a serious man concerned with affairs of state. Stanfiield, of all people, became the swinger and Trudeau become the serious philosopher holding a dialogue with the Canadian people. As it turned out, the dialogue became a monologue. Clearly, the new image in which Trudeau was cast did not bring the desired results.

There is an effort by the Anglophone press to deny that a chauvinist, anti-French backlash had anything to do with the outcome of the election, that the *only reason* for the setback suffered by the Trudeau government was its economic and social policy. *However, one cannot separate its economic and social policy from its approach to Quebec.* The Regional Development Program was geared in large measure, although not only, to Quebec, as were other aspects of economic policy.

One should not forget that in 1968 there were strong separatist tendencies in Quebec. The Trudeau government which was elected around the slogan of "One Canada, One Nation", strove to mitigate the sharpness of the then existing situation by economic measures directed to overcome some of the worst features of economic inequality, including regional inequality in Quebec. This found expression in the Regional Development Program. Together with this the government increased French-Canadian representation and "power" in government and in various fields. At the same time it introduced bilingualism in government offices, in the study of the French language outside of Quebec where 10 per cent of the population were French and desirous of preserving their language. All of this was directed to imply that French-Canadians had an equal voice in Canada.

By these measures the government strove to undercut separatist tendencies in Quebec and at the same time do away with the reality of the existence of two nations in Canada.

However, the government's preoccupation with Quebec, the role of French-Canadians in Canada and with bilingualism, was not balanced with sufficient attention to other parts of Canada, particularly the West. Diversification of industry using natural resources for this purpose, as an integral part of an all-Canadian program of industrial development, was ignored. Instead these resources were sold to U.S. monopolies for a fast buck. This led to the alienation of the Trudeau government in the prairie provinces and in British Columbia.

There is no question but that a skilful effort was undertaken to build up a backlash against the government on its position with respect to Quebec, to "French Power", and to bilingualism.

The efforts of the Anglophone press to minimize the backlash or deny its existence cannot cover up the dangerous crisis of English-French relations which the election results have brought about.

At the same time it would be wrong to accept the viewpoint of those in Quebec, including the Francophone press, who say the anti-French backlash was the *only reason* for the Liberal government setback.

Incorrect policies, the backlash around economic and social policy and "French Power", as well as a poorly devised election strategy, all these were the ingredients determining the outcome of the election. As was pointed out in the Communist Party election platform, "Growing dissatisfaction and disillusionment with the policies and performance of the Trudeau government are being seized upon by the most reactionary circles to turn politics to the right." It further declared that "the Conservative Party is becoming the main center of attraction for the right in Canadian politics."

Events bear this out. The Conservative Party became a significant beneficiary of the chauvinist anti-French and anti-Quebec backlash which it helped to stir up, even though Mr. Stanfield disclaims any responsibility for it.

It undertook a skilful exploitation of anti-French and anti-Quebec feeling based on resentment of French power, bilingualism and the Regional Development Program.

The Conservative Party combined this with the exploitation of a backlash on welfare, the unemployed, the so-called fraud in unemployment insurance, the "work ethic", rising unemployment and rising prices. All these issues were calculated to appeal to the farmers, small business, the petty bourgeoisie and sections of the middle class, and to turn them against the working people. *In a cynical and irresponsible way the unemployed were made to appear responsible for unemployment, and the working class for rising prices and inflation.*

In the course of the campaign the Conservative Party attacked the right to strike, proposing limitations of that right for workers engaged in "essential" industries. But what industry is not essential? It coupled this attack on democratic rights with the proposal for wage and price controls.

The exploitation of the reactionary backlash paid off in increased votes and increased seats for the Conservative Party.

Another element giving objective assistance to this reactionary backlash was the line of the right-wing NDP and trade union leadership.

During the course of the entire election campaign the trade union leadership maintained virtual silence in face of the Conservative Party attacks on so-called fraud in unemployment insurance, even though it was clear that their aim was not the elimination of fraud but the emasculation of unemployment insurance benefits to ensure an ample supply of cheap labor. They maintained virtual silence when the right to strike was attacked and when proposals for wage and price controls were being advanced.

Instead of condemning the reactionary attack on labor's standards and rights Mr. Lewis, too, spoke in favor of limiting the right to strike in essential industries, for limitations on collective bargaining and in support of an incomes policy.

While seeming to criticize both the Liberal government and the Conservative Party as being Tweedle-Dum and Tweedle-Dee, *in practice the NDP right wing concentrated their main fire on the Trudeau government.* It consistently under-estimated the Conservative drive and the Conservative line, brushing them off as Mr. Lewis did in one of his election speeches as an "inept campaign". How inept can be seen from the election results that almost swept the Conservative Party into power.

Objectively this line helped the Conservative Party and opened the door to NDP setbacks in Saskatchewan and to no gains in Manitoba as well as in Alberta.

Not least, the trend to the right was objectively facilitated by the campaign of the Parti Québecois. The Parti Québecois campaign called upon the French-Canadian people to stay away from the polls, a campaign they later modified. While falling short of its total objective this campaign had a certain effect on the vote in Quebec, which was lower than that in Ontario, and negatively affected the vote of the NDP and of the Communist Party.

These are among some of the factors leading to the set-back suffered by the Trudeau government in the federal elections.

IMPLICATIONS OF THE ELECTION

How should one estimate the overall result of the election? Does it indicate a shift to the right?

While it marks a change in the relationship of political forces in Parliament, it would nevertheless be simplistic to draw this conclusion.

An examination of the votes and the seats won gives a picture of a contradictory process, *a tendency to the right as well as a tendency to the left.*

The tendency to the right is evidenced in the gains made by the Conservative Party which increased its vote by 796,062 from 1968 and its seats by 36. It is also to be seen in the gains of Social Credit which increased its vote by 353,306 over

1968, mainly in Quebec around a single campaign issue, the guaranteed annual income. This demand had a particular appeal to the lowest-income groups and the unemployed in the most poverty-stricken areas of Quebec but less so, as the total vote showed, in other parts of Canada. For the first time Social Credit was able to extend its base of support in and around Montreal.

The increased Quebec vote for Social Credit from 16.7 per cent to 24 per cent made it the second party in Quebec, replacing the Conservative Party which traditionally had held that position. Social Credit's main support came from Quebec in this election. Out of a total of 714,359 votes throughout the country, 615,476 came from Quebec and 98,883 from the rest of the country.

Concurrently with increased votes for the Conservatives and Social Credit, the NDP likewise achieved some gains in votes and in seats — increasing its seats from 25 to 31, and its vote from 1,378,260 or 17 per cent in 1968, to 1,695,978, an increase of 316,818 but still 17.8 per cent of the total vote. Complete results may show the NDP having reached close to two million votes.

As can be seen, the percentage remained almost the same although the absolute vote increased. To be noted also is the fact that the NDP increased its seats in the industrial centers of Ontario and B.C. — 11 seats in Ontario and 11 in B.C. This was a direct consequence of the militant struggles of the workers and the trade unions in these two provinces which thereby helped to widen the movement toward independent labor political action and for social change. In fact about 25 of the 31 seats came from the big cities and industrial centers, suggesting that the base of the NDP has shifted somewhat from the agrarian to the industrial areas.

The increase in votes for the NDP was uneven. In Quebec its vote declined from eight per cent to five per cent. This is a direct consequence of its ambiguous position on the right to national self-determination. No small cause for the decline in its popular vote was the refusal of the Parti Québecois to support the NDP.

What seems apparent is that the Conservative Party hold

in the three prairie provinces and particularly in the countryside has been maintained and to some extent strengthened in the recent election.

The shifts in the voting pattern require further study.

For example, the Liberal Party vote declined by 49,898 over 1968. But at the same time over 1.5 million more Canadians voted than in 1968. Where did these votes go? If one adds up the increased votes of the Conservatives, Social Credit and NDP, one might conclude that these voters divided their allegiance among these three parties.

Among these voters a goodly percentage may have been 18-year-olds or those who voted for the first time since 1968. Where did their vote go?

It would appear from the results of the vote that only a small percentage went to the Liberals, with a higher proportion going to the NDP and Conservative Party.

If this is so, it suggests that the voting pattern among the young people or first voters was in the main not different to the voting pattern of other age groups. *This is not surprising because youth is not a separate class.*

It is probable that a percentage of these young voters did not exercise their franchise at all in the belief that meaningful change within the present structure is impossible of achievement.

However, the election results give no ground for the belief that the young people are satisfied with the *status quo*. The high percentage of young people in the category of permanently unemployed, the negative consequences of the scientific and technological revolution resulting in layoffs, the nature of work in many industries with its monotonous and non-creative character, bear out the contention that they are seeking changes. From this *one may expect an upsurge of militant action, particularly among working youth* arising from their conditions of life.

The shift in voting patterns is also to be seen in the increased vote for the Conservative Party at the expense of Social Credit in B.C. and in Alberta. In B.C. it doubled its popular vote to over 300,000 or nearly 34 per cent of the total vote, mostly, it would appear, at the expense of Social

Credit. On the other hand, in Quebec Social Credit by and large increased its vote at the expense of the Wagner Conservatives. There the Conservatives went down from 21 per cent to 17 per cent of the popular vote compared with 1968, while Social Credit, as already pointed out, increased its vote from 16.8 to 24 per cent.

The result of the shift in voting patterns led to the election of just two Conservatives in Quebec, only one of whom is French-Canadian.

An important outcome of this election therefore is the fact that the Conservative Party has been virtually excluded from French Canada, appearing in the eyes of the French-Canadian people as the party of the Anglophones, the party of the backlash against the French-Canadian people.

A significant outcome of this election is the improved showing of the NDP. This has made the NDP an important political factor in Canadian politics, one which neither the Liberals nor the Conservatives can afford to ignore. Previously each of these parties saw the NDP as an unpleasant nuisance to be used against the other political party. *Now they see the NDP as a threat to both their parties, particularly since the election of three NDP provincial governments.*

Following the election there has been a systematic effort by the mass media to minimize the results of the NDP vote. Indeed, one columnist wrote recently that "the NDP did not suffer a rout, it simply failed to make gains." True enough, the NDP with all the enormous free publicity given it, and Mr. Lewis and the "corporate welfare bum" theme, did not achieve a massive breakthrough. *It did, however, become an important political factor by virtue of its holding the balance of power in Parliament.*

We are correct, therefore, in avoiding a one-sided estimate of the overall results of the election. The election results did not express a general shift to the right. *At the same time the electoral gains of the Conservative Party and of Social Credit create favorable grounds for more conservative and reactionary policies. The Conservative Party will obviously try to influence and exert pressures on the government for the adoption of measures inimical to the best interests of the working people.* By the same token and by virtue of the NDP balance-of-power position in Parliament, the working-class and democratic movements can through their mass actions exert pressures in a left direction.

In a certain sense the struggle between right and left policies, which found expression in the course of the election campaign and its inconclusive results, will now be continued in Parliament as well as outside it. How well it is fought out by the working-class and democratic forces will have an important effect on the results of the next election.

Not least, the election indicates a process of polarization corresponding with a growing crisis of capitalist parties and capitalist policies. These reflect the inability of state-monopoly capitalism and its parties to cope with the requirements of the modern world, with the rising expectations and real needs of the people. This compels larger numbers of people to strive for change.

The impulse for change federally is not yet wide and deep, as can be seen in the fact that 82 per cent of Canadian voters continue to vote for the parties of monopoly and for Social Credit (a reactionary petty-bourgeois party at the service of state-monopoly capitalism, although one should differentiate between the leaders of that party and its supporters). Illusions about the old-line parties are still widespread, based on the mistaken notion that a change-over from Tory to Liberal or vice versa represents a real change. This is not to deny that tactical and other differences between them may be made use of to good advantage by the working-class and democratic movements. The illusions about these parties have a certain material basis, arising from a policy of concessions they are compelled to undertake so as to hold the working people within the confines of the old-line parties.

The process of breakaway from these parties is not a simple one. This is to be seen in the following figures showing the combined percentages of the Liberal and Tory vote in postwar elections: 1945 — 68 per cent; 1949 — 78 per cent; 1953 — 80 per cent; 1957 — 80 per cent; 1958 — 87.2 per cent; 1962 — 75 per cent.

These figures indicate the immensity of the task and the challenge before us and all those genuinely concerned to help the working class break away from the old-line parties and find the path to independent labor and labor-farmer political action.

This task, and the deepening of the political and class-consciousness of the working class to help it become a class for itself, remain central and permanent tasks for the Communist Party of Canada.

THE COMMUNIST PARTY'S CAMPAIGN

The whole course of the election and its outcome bear out the correctness of the electoral policy of the Party as set forth at our 21st Convention and elaborated in the election platform.

The Party accomplished by and large what it set out to do in the election.

It brought our policies to millions of Canadians through our platform, TV, radio, press advertisements, public meetings and all-candidates meetings.

There is no doubt that the voice of the Communist Party came through loud and clear in this campaign. Our platform, which was well received, brought forward a clearly defined democratic alternative to the policies of state-monopoly capitalism. The bourgeois press could not ignore our Party's position. We were able to break through the blackout of the mass media and establish the fact that the Communist Party is a viable political force in the country. It is not too much to say, therefore, that the Party's stature grew in the course of this campaign and that it came out of the campaign with its authority enhanced.

The Party's campaign and electoral line were factors in the overall outcome. As our election platform declared: "As against those who want to shift politics to the right, the Communist Party works to shift politics to the left. It believes the best result would be the defeat of the right and the election of a large progressive bloc to Parliament in which Communists and NDPers would play a major part." To a certain degree, this objective was achieved. There is no doubt that the Communist Party's campaign and electoral line helped in making NDP gains possible. The Communist Party can take pride in the fact that its campaign was an important factor in *blunting* the right-wing offensive. The progressive forces in the ethnic group field and their press played an important role in the struggle against the reactionary offensive. Had there been unity of action between the NDP and the Communist Party, the reactionary offensive could have been set back.

The Party's battle for working-class and democratic unity in this election, alongside the advancement of its own program and candidates, will have long-term value. It is not accidental that very few, if any, voices were raised among workers that we were "splitting" the vote. This is important from the standpoint of the continuing struggle for working-class and democratic unity, a struggle we need to wage in the course of strengthening the independent work of the Party.

The results of the campaign show what the Party can do with a sound working-class policy once it sets its mind to it.

All of us are mindful, of course, that the vote for our candidates was small as yet. But this was not the main feature of the campaign. Its main feature was the total impact of our effort on political developments. What stands out in this campaign was the receptive and more friendly attitude displayed to our campaign everywhere. This was particularly the case with young people. It suggests that cold-war attitudes are breaking down, that more interest is being displayed in our program and policies. While this is so, we were at the same time confronted with the widespread points of view that "your Party hasn't got a chance of being elected this time", and "I don't want to waste my vote", coupled with continuing prejudices and misunderstandings about our Party which find expression in anti-communism and anti-Sovietism.

These were important factors in the low vote we received. These votes, however, do not correspond with the impact of the Party's policies on the election outcome.

It indicates the scope of the problem and the task facing the Communist Party to help raise the level of political consciousness of the working class. *As the vote showed, worker militancy in negotiations with monopoly does not yet express itself in a mass breakaway from the old-line parties, and radicalization among working people, young and old, does not yet express itself in votes for our Party.* This is a process — the changeover to class and political consciousness will be accelerated in so far as the Communist Party and its members are able to win their spurs as vanguard fighters, a task to which we must give constant attention, combined with a systematic struggle against anti-communism and anti-Sovietism.

There is reason to believe our vote would have been higher had it not been for the intervention of the Maoists and their misuse of the honorable name of our Party. This was done to create confusion among voters. The Maoists in Canada, who mirror the anti-Marxist and anti-Leninist position of Maoism, constituted a disruptive force in the election, purposely put forward at this time to deflect and confuse people who are beginning to move leftward.

The Communist Party has the responsibility of exposing the Maoists' program and its pseudo-revolutionary positions which are in essence anti-labor, anti-socialist, anti-Soviet and counter-revolutionary. These positions substitute wishes for reality, by-pass intermediate stages in the transition from capitalism to socialism, substitute abstract generalities for concrete analysis of a concrete situation, which Lenin called the essence of Marxism. Such pseudo-revolutionary phrases if followed would lead to reckless actions and to alienation of the working class. The Maoists' pseudo-revolutionary phrasemongering serves the interests of reaction and must be thoroughly exposed in the working-class and democratic movements and in the popular movements of the people.

In exposing the pseudo-revolutionary position of the Maoists we do so from the standpoint of a revolutionary party, the Party of Marxism-Leninism which relates every stage of the struggle to the aim of achieving a socialist Canada.

The Party was on solid ground in undertaking a systematic criticism of the right-wing NDP in the course of the election.

Mr. Lewis, by and large, reduced the fight against monopoly to one of overcoming loopholes in taxation. It was, of course, useful to expose these loopholes. It was not in the interests of the working class, however, to whitewash the corporations and thereby undermine the possibility of waging an effective and united struggle against monopoly, directed to curbing its power.

This same line was attempted at the recently held Ontario Federation of Labor convention where a statement on unemployment, taxation and the corporation rip-off declared that "our fight is not with the corporations". Fortunately, due to the intervention of the left and of the Communists, it was deleted.

The workers from bitter experience know that their fight is with the corporations against whom they are compelled to struggle daily. What they are beginning to learn more and more is that the struggle is not just with one corporation but with state-monopoly capitalism, which embodies the state power of the corporations.

The line of the right wing is not accidental. It flows from their pursuit of a policy of class collaboration, a policy designed to help state-monopoly capitalism resolve its contradictions at the expense of the working people. The substance of their position is to administer capitalism more efficiently, to come to the rescue of the ruling class when capitalism is in difficulties, instead of organizing the mass action of the people to solve those difficulties through the ending of capitalism and the building of socialism. It is precisely such a policy of accommodation that opens the door to the reactionary backlash to which President Archer of the OFL recently drew attention. The policy of class collaboration must be replaced by a working-class policy of unity based on policies of class struggle. Otherwise the working people will be made to bear the burden of state-monopoly capitalist economic and social policies.

At this critical period the NDP has two choices: it can take the anti-monopoly road, uniting with all genuine forces of the left including the Communist Party to push politics to the left, or it can capitulate to the pressures of monopoly and contribute to the forces striving to push politics to the right. Unfortunately, as was seen in the Vancouver municipal elections and elsewhere, it still rejects the united front, it rejects the left within the NDP, as was to be seen in the attack on the Waffle. In so acting, the right wing in the NDP and in the trade union movement may believe they have dealt a death blow to the left in the NDP. This is an erroneous point of view. The left goes beyond the Waffle although it includes it. In any case socialist ideas cannot be wiped out. They will grow and develop in the NDP and in the working class. Experience shows that right-wing policy must be defeated, without which an effective, consistent and united struggle against monopoly cannot be waged.

While the main thrust of criticism must necessarily be directed against right-wing policy, one cannot overlook the left-sectarian position of the Waffle, now named the Movement for an Independent Socialist Canada (MISC), in the course of the election. Instead of pursuing a course of co-operation directed to the election of a large progressive bloc, MISC decided instead on a "non-campaign". In effect they sat out the election, covering up their desertion of the struggle by meaningless leftist phrases.

The only ones benefitting from this "strategem" were the old-line parties.

From all appearances the Waffle continue to waffle. Some opt for staying in the NDP and fighting for their point of view as individuals. Others opt for forming another political party. What they continue to avoid is the necessity of co-operation with the Communist Party for common aims.

This thrashing around on the part of the Wafflers arises from their lack of a clear perspective of the road ahead, of the strategy of advance to a socialist Canada, of the necessity for left unity around which to build a democratic coalition, with the working class as the leading force, as the necessary transition to an independent socialist Canada.

In conditions when monopoly capitalism and its henchmen are doing everything in their power to encourage opportunist trends and tendencies among working people, ideological work by the Communist Party is of major importance. Indeed, it must be at the center of its activities and focus on *combining* criticism of right-wing policy, of reformism, Maoism, Trotskyism, and revisionism with a systematic struggle for the united front of the working-class and democratic forces. Such duality of approach should never be overlooked.

The Communist Party should, in this connection, seek out opportunities for a dialogue with NDPers, with the left in the NDP, as well as with members of MISC, and above all with the left in the trade unions and in farm and democratic movements, directed to creating conditions for a common struggle against monopoly. This should be combined with the popularization of our socialist policies and with systematic efforts to help the left get rid of the poison of anti-communism and anti-Sovietism.

THE NEXT STAGE

How long the Liberal minority government will exist is anyone's guess. There is no doubt that the Conservative group in Parliament will work for its early collapse so that the Tory party can become the government. Its aim may include making some concessions to win the support of the NDP. More particularly, it may use these concessions to extend its base of support throughout the country with the hope of becoming the majority government in the next election. The Conservatives believe they have two things going for them: a tide of support for their policies, and the backing of important sections of big business.

The Liberal minority government undoubtedly has plans of its own which may include making some concessions to the NDP as well as to the Conservatives, playing for time until it considers the situation more favorable for calling an election.

This is obviously a period of intensive manoeuvres, of sharp tensions, particularly between the Liberal and Conservative parties.

It is also a period when the working-class and democratic movement might be able to extract some concessions from a minority government.

The relationship of forces in Parliament with a Liberal minority government and with the NDP holding the balance of power gives certain openings to the working-class and democratic movement which it should try to make use of. In line with this possibility and in order to prevent a snap election that may prove disadvantageous to the labor and democratic movement, a policy of "conditional and critical support" should be given the government provided it enacts legislation in the interests of the people. Such "conditional and critical support" necessarily includes condemnation of the government if it gives way to reactionary pressures.

There is no doubt that the reactionary forces in Canada will try to make use of the inconclusive results of the election to prevent the adoption of progressive legislation. These reactionary forces, using the Conservative Party as their vehicle, are reponsible for the backlash against the working people, the unemployed, the poor, the national and demo-cratic rights of the French-Canadian people.

Their aim is to place the burden of the crisis on the backs of the working people, while pressing for policies to guaran-tee maximum profits for monopoly.

Their aim is to push the Liberal minority government further to the right and win adoption of legislation directed at watering down the Unemployment Insurance Act, thereby assuring an ample supply of cheap labor for monopoly.

Their aim is to win legislation directed at imposing a wage freeze on the working people, the limitation of labor's right to strike and its replacement by compulsory arbitration.

Their aims include the forcing of an early election through which they hope to achieve a Conservative majority or a right-wing coalition government to implement such a reactionary program.

Democratic opinion must be alert to these manoeuvres and work to defeat them, combining this with an all-out effort to win legislation in the interests of the working people.

The Communist Party believes such a legislative program should include: a policy of full employment, the right to a job or an adequate income for every Canadian, the processing of our natural resources in Canada based on public ownership and the building of secondary industry, a crash program of public works, guaranteed- prices and markets for farm products, a guaranteed annual income, a low-rental, low-cost housing program, reduction of hours of work to 32 with no reduction in take-home pay, increased pensions and voluntary retirement at 60, reduced taxes for all those earning up to $10,000, effective measures to curb price gougers and profiteers in the food industry, in land, housing and rents.

The democratic and labor movement should not leave it to the NDP group in Parliament to press for such legislation. To rely on the NDP group to fight for such a program without the mass action of the working class, the farm movement and democratic forces would not bring the desired results. Gains will not be achieved by parliamentary manoeuvres but only through united mass action. Parliamentary action should merge with non-parliamentary action, each buttressing the other to compel the government and Parliament to act on these demands. The trade unions and farm organizations should be at the center of such action. Such pressures are all the more important in view of monopoly's call for a squeeze on the working people.

The battle needs to be waged in such a way as to strengthen the progressive forces inside and outside of Parliament. There is nothing that the Liberals and Conservatives (and monopoly for whom they speak) would like more than to set back the trend to independent labor-farmer political action, weaken the NDP and create the conditions for majority government and a turn to the right.

The decision of the NDP to support legislation which is worthwhile but not to support a coalition with the Liberals is sound. A Liberal-NDP coalition would be a setback for independent labor-farmer political action, while a Liberal-Conservative coalition would be dangerous to democracy and to the working class.

The battle for legislation to protect the interests of the working people must take this into account and go side by side with flexible tactics and active preparations for an early election.

PREPARE FOR THE ELECTION NOW

It seems fairly obvious that an election is likely within the year, *that is, at any time. We need to be prepared for it now, combining public mass campaigning with the nomination of Party candidates.* Our aim should be to double the number of candidates we run. The minimum should be 50. We need 50 to register and appear on the ballot as the Communist Party. But more than that. The experience of the recent election shows that the more candidates we have in the field, the more effective is the Party's campaign. *We must oppose any tendency to retreat or limit our participation,* based on the argument that our forces are too weak, that we should concentrate on a few constituencies only, and so on. If we follow such a course we shall be unable to influence the development of events in the coming crucial election in an increasingly progressive direction, or to compel debate on the basic issues before the country and people. Fifty or more candidates means 50 or more public spokesmen for the Communist Party, means promoting young and promising cadres for the Communist Party, the working-class and democratic movement, means strengthening the public debate on the main problems facing Canada.

Can the Communist Party run a large number of candidates? Basically it is not a financial question, although finances obviously play a role here. By and large it is an ideological question, based on an understanding of the role of the Communist Party, its struggle for the realization of a democratic coalition of which it is part.

Like the previous one, the present electoral tactic of the Communist Party is not designed only for a specific election. It is bound up with an overall and longer-term objective, the ending of the rule of the parties of monopoly by a new people's majority based on a democratic coalition and the formation of an anti-monopoly government as the transition to socialism in Canada.

As the Communist Party has had occasion to say before, there won't be a democratic coalition without a strong Communist Party which advocates and works for it, and without Communist representation in Parliament. There will be no democratic coalition without decisive left influence in the trade union movement, the farm movement and people's organizations, including youth and women. The fight today in the parliamentary arena combined with our work in the non-parliamentary field is part and parcel of forging such a democratic coalition.

The nomination of a large number of Communist Party candidates is therefore not in conflict with the aim of helping to build such a coalition, or with the struggle for working-class and democratic unity.

Indeed, the starting point for the development of such a democratic coalition is to win ever-wider support for it in the working-class and democratic movement. The Communist Party's participation in the election and the nomination of a large number of candidates is an integral part of the fight to bring it into being.

The Communist Party will strive to have as candidates more workers from the shops, more women, more farmers, in addition to younger people. In the last election eight of the candidates came from the shops. The Communist Party will aim to double that in the next round, combining this with a systematic struggle for legalization of the Communist Party in the trade unions by the elimination of anti-communist clauses in union constitutions. The Central Committee will be pleased to know that the Ontario Committee is thinking of nominating 25 candidates in Ontario and that the Communist Party in Quebec has its sights on 10 candidates. With this kind of spirit we should be able to reach our objectives.

What should our objective be in the coming election as part of the struggle to bring a democratic coalition into being?

In the last election we called for the defeat of the right and the election of a large progressive bloc including Communists and NDPers.

In the coming election we should bear in mind that both the Liberals and the Conservatives will be attacking the NDP as well as each other. They must seriously weaken the NDP and take away support from each other as well as from Social Credit, if either of the old-line parties hopes to form a majority government.

If either party succeeds in that objective and, more particularly, if

239

the Conservative Party forms a majority government or a coalition perhaps with Social Credit, there could be a more definite shift to the right and more open attacks on the working class and working people generally.

It is fairly clear what a Conservative government would do — impose bans on strikes in essential industries, introduce some form of wage and price controls, and weaken the unemployment insurance benefits.

A Liberal majority may veer in the same direction.

As matters stand now there is no realistic prospect of a democratic alternative to either old-line party with sufficient strength to form the next government.

The best alternative in the circumstances would be the return of a larger progressive group to Parliament fighting for truly alternative policies to those of the parties of monopoly and dedicated to the struggle for full employment and for genuine Canadian independence. The larger the group elected the less likely the election of an old-line majority government and a shift to the right.

Bearing the above in mind the Communist Party believes the following slogans embody the general line it should pursue in the forthcoming election: For a new direction — New policies for Canada — Defeat the drive to the right — Elect a large progressive group to Parliament, vote Communist!

THE THREE MAJOR CONFRONTATIONS

The election settled nothing. The main issues were not even debated. The mass media and the establishment saw to that by sweeping these issues under the rug. Only the Communist Party advanced the central issues confronting the country and the people, but its voice was not strong enough to change the character and content of the election campaign. However, these issues remain and are pushing themselves to the fore. At this time they find reflection in three major confrontations: the confrontation between the working class and democracy on the one hand and monopoly on the other; the confrontation between French and English

240

Canada; the confrontation between Canada and U.S. imperialism.

THE WORKING PEOPLE VERSUS MONOPOLY

The economic situation is far from satisfactory and can best be described as economic instability. Recovery has given way to stagnation and rising unemployment as well as to rising prices. Unemployment and inflation, these twin evils of capitalism, constitute the Achilles heel of capitalist governments.

The latest report of the Economic Council of Canada is compelled to admit that it is impossible to maintain full employment, rising standards and stable prices — that the aims set in 1964 are not realizable.

It is compelled to state that the original declared aim of reducing unemployment to three per cent has gone by the board; that even lowering present unemployment to four and a half per cent by 1975 cannot be achieved. Government policy is directed to keeping unemployment at the level of about five per cent and calling this full employment.

This means, as our Party has warned, that working people, men and women alike, including a portion of the young generation, will be faced with the prospects of permanent unemployment. Since 1965 unemployment among working women and young people between the ages of 14 to 24 has more than doubled. Unemployment among university graduates has increased.

Unemployment and inflation have now been built into the system of state-monopoly capitalism and mirror its growing instability. The basic roots of inflation lie in monopoly control of the economy, in militarization of the economy and U.S. aggression in Vietnam. Inflation can only be dealt with by far-reaching measures of radical reform. To successfully tackle inflation requires democratic controls and structural changes in the economy. These of necessity include controls over prices, over capital inflow, investments, trade — both import and export; restrictions on monopoly growth, struc-

241

tural changes aimed at developing the state sector of the economy, and nationalization of key industries.

This is not what either the Liberals or the Conservatives propose.

The pretence that either the Conservative or Liberal Party can solve unemployment and inflation is pure poppycock.

Neither tax reductions by themselves nor incentives to big or not-so-big companies will eliminate unemployment. The Liberal government has given ample incentives to big business. But unemployment continues to rise. The trickle-down theory, which gives handouts and gravy to monopoly and crumbs to the people whether it is pursued by a Liberal or Conservative government, will not, as experience has amply shown, achieve full employment, rising standards and stable prices. These incentives are being used to modernize existing plants, stimulate rationalization in industry and achieve mergers. They do not create new jobs, they create unemployment. Thus, with all the incentives given it, Canadian manufacturing industry continues to operate at 17 per cent less than capacity.

What incentives do is guarantee profits for the corporations, enabling them in turn to buy new technology to increase production and decrease jobs.

In point of fact what government incentive policy has accomplished is to grant substantial funds to U.S. corporations with which to fasten further their control over Canada, funds which could and should have been used for all-Canadian industrial development under public ownership.

Neither will the Conservative Party panacea for inflation — wage and price controls — eliminate inflation. What it will do is undermine purchasing power in conditions when technological development is leading to increasing productivity and loss of jobs. Such action would narrow the home market and accelerate tendencies to recession.

The orthodox monetary and fiscal policies pursued by both the Liberal and Conservative Parties with regard to unemployment and inflation have failed and any continuation of similar policies will likewise fail. This underscores the fact that the mechanism of state-monopoly capitalism is in crisis. Monopoly is seeking a way out of its dilemma through an incomes policy, that is, wage and price controls.

All the signs point to the readiness of monopoly to impose such controls and thereby undermine the collective bargaining rights of the trade unions, their right to strike, their democratic right to decide on settlements.

Wage and price controls if enacted would seek to freeze inequality. With over 25 per cent of all Canadians living below the poverty line, with wealth by and large concentrated in the hands of a few, wage and price controls would perpetuate inequality, legalize poverty and reduce the workers' share of the wealth they produce.

Moreover, with the technological revolution developing apace, productivity is rising and ensuring higher and higher profits for monopoly. In these circumstances monopoly could afford to maintain the pretence of a freeze on costs and prices, confident that profits will rise in line with productivity increases. Thus the monopolies would be, as in fact they are, the main beneficiaries of change through rationalization of industry, automation and technological advance, as the workers are its main victims.

The workers should be on their guard against a wage freeze covered up by the sweet-sounding term of incomes policy. They should be equally alert to proposals for selective wage controls. Wage controls, no matter by what name, mean freezing present economic relationships, when in fact the overriding need is to change these relationships and introduce economic planning based on public ownership, through which to ensure steady growth and development and a rising standard of life.

One of the reasons behind the monopoly-inspired campaign for wage controls is next year's negotiations which will involve large numbers of workers in key industries in a sharp confrontation with monopoly.

The aim here is to undertake psychological war against the workers, directed to impose cheap settlements on them. As against this monopoly attack directed to increase profits at the expense of living standards, the aim of the trade union movement, of all workers, should be to get the largest possible increases they can, combining this with the struggle for job security and improved benefits. Rising living costs and increased productivity make that absolutely essential. Indeed, increased purchasing power is essential to expand the home market.

Increased purchasing power combined with stable prices and stable markets is no less essential for the farmers. The increased sale of wheat on the world market, particularly to the USSR and to China, cannot mask the fact that the share of the gross national product going to the farmers is steadily declining. Next year it is expected to decline by 4.4 per cent. This deterioration in living standards takes place at the same time as the family farmer is being pushed off the land at an increasingly rapid pace. Less than seven per cent of the population live on farms today compared with 12 per cent 10 years ago.

The defence of the family farm, adequate incomes, stable markets — these aims will not be achieved by reliance on the old-line parties of monopoly which gouge the farmer; they will be achieved through co-operation of worker and farmer against their common enemy, monopoly. Labor-farmer co-operation in the fight for new policies is the way forward.

Furthermore, instead of allowing reaction to emasculate unemployment insurance benefits, the working-class and trade union movement should press for further improvements in the Act. Benefits should be increased to 80 per cent of earnings, payable from the first day and to continue for the entire period of unemployment. The two-week waiting period should be abolished. Vacation pay and severance or termination allowances should not be classed as earnings.

In conditions when the working class has become the main target of monopoly's attack, with the offensive on working-class standards, jobs and rights mounting; with inflation, unemployment, rising prices and taxes placing a heavy burden on the working people, the Communist Party has the responsibility of working for unity of action around common aims on all fronts: the trade union front, the working-class front, the democratic front, the front of labor-farmer co-operation — while further developing its strategy and tactics to enable the working people to beat back the monopoly offensive.

The development of strategy and tactics should include the impact of new immigration on the composition of the working class, on the development of its political and class consciousness and the necessity of winning those new sections of the working class for the anti-monopoly struggle. It should include the impact of methods used by governments acting in collusion with monopoly directed to nullify the right to strike in essential industries, as well as the need for refining forms of struggle in these industries that would prevent companies from breaking strikes. Not least, it should include an effective strategy to cope with the multi-national corporations based on the achievement of international solidarity and unity.

The struggle against capitalist exploitation and reactionary policies is assuming a wider and more militant form.

The rejection of wage controls by the Ontario and B.C. Federations of Labor conventions, and by the Canadian Labor Congress, shows that the working class is prepared to fight against being made the scapegoat for state-monopoly economic and social policies. The workers instinctively feel the need for unity and solidarity. This found expression in the demand by these federation conventions for the inclusion of militantly led unions in the CLC, pressure the CLC could not withstand. The inclusion of unions like UE and the Fishermen in the CLC represents a defeat for the cold war, for right-wing policy. By the same token it represents a victory for the forces of unity.

These developments show that the working class is in a mood to fight back, that it has the strength to fight back and move forward provided it is united around sound policies.

FOR CANADIAN CONTROL
THROUGH PUBLIC OWNERSHIP

The monopoly offensive on the jobs, standards and democratic rights of working people takes place on the background of a growing trade war. The recurring currency crises are an expression of it. The aggravation of the currency crisis, the latest example of which is the British pound, is undermining the entire currency system of capitalism. Basically this expresses growing lack of confidence in the U.S. dollar and reflects the weakening of the economic and political positions of the USA in the capitalist world.

What is increasingly clear is that the international monetary system has broken down and that the General Agreement on Trade and Tariffs is being undermined, a further evidence of the sharpening of inter-imperialist contradictions.

The problem is further aggravated for Canada by the process of integration in Western Europe through Britain's entry into the European Common Market. This fact, alongside the trend toward protectionism in the USA, is bound to seriously affect the Canadian economy and the jobs of thousands of Canadians.

The trade war and intensified competition between capitalist states is being turned into a war against the working class. The Canadian working class is already feeling the effects of sharpened competition with the USA and Japan in the form of rising unemployment.

Now that the Nixon administration has been returned in the USA, pressure will mount on Canada to give way to the demands of U.S. imperialism. The U.S. government has made no bones about the fact that *it wants to change the terms of trade with Canada to its advantage at the expense of the Canadian economy and the jobs of Canadians.*

What it is striving to do is export its crisis to Canada and make the Canadian people pay for it. What it is pressing for particularly is a change in the auto pact and a "partnership" in Canadian energy.

Canada's future, the strengthening of its independence, does not lie in becoming part of an economic bloc or in integration with the USA. Nor does it lie in continuing the role of supplier and reserve of raw materials for the USA. It lies in a new national policy which could transform Canada into a great independent industrial state, pursuing an independent foreign policy.

In this situation in which the confrontation between Canada and the USA will sharpen, central to the struggle to strengthen Canadian independence and to the struggle for jobs and rising standards is the battle for new national policies, for balanced independent all-round industrial development, including northern development, for Canadian control through public ownership starting with natural resources and energy, the processing of natural resources and the building of secondary industry, effective measures to prevent further takeovers and closing down of plants, the extension of exchanges of trade, science, technology and culture with the socialist countries on a mutually satisfactory basis.

New national policies have particular meaning for the western provinces whose natural resources have been sold for a mere pittance at the expense of industrial development. Such a continentalist policy, a policy of integration, would have disastrous results for the working people of Western Canada, standing in the way of all-sided and balanced industrial development. Such a policy would not only lead to the loss of irreplaceable natural resources necessary for Canada's development, it is already leading to a loss of human resources in some of the western provinces and a further undermining of Canada's independence.

The future of the people of Western Canada, as for Canada as a whole, lies in diversification of industry, the building of secondary industry by processing natural resources in Canada on the basis of public ownership. Industry should be built close to the source of Canada's natural resources.

Canada needs a 10-year plan of balanced industrial development, utilizing its great natural resources under public ownership for its implementation. The 10-year plan should include a fully integrated and comprehensive program of northern development with due regard to safeguarding the ecology and the interests of the northern peoples.

The starting point in such a development program of the North should be the interests of the Canadian people and the strengthening of Canadian independence.

This means that the concept of Canada as a corridor through which the riches of the North, particularly gas and oil, can be shipped to the USA needs to be scrapped. Canada is not a second Panama Canal. The gas and oil of the North should be used for Canadian development, a source of energy to satisfy the needs of the Canadian people and for development of industry. Surpluses only should be sold to foreign countries.

The concept of tokensim should also be rejected. Tokenism would find expression in nominal Canadian ownership of the pipeline while the resources are owned by U.S. corporations.

Not only the pipeline or pipelines, but the resources of the North, starting with gas and oil, need to be publicly owned also. Only in this way is there the assurance that the wealth of the North will accrue to the benefit of Canada and the Canadian people.

If funds are needed for development of the North they should take the form of state loans to be repaid in gas or oil at prevailing world prices.

Only by such new national policies will it be possible to adequately cope with the crisis of development in Canada and reverse the government's present policy of handing over publicly-owned enterprises to private monopolies.

Such new national policies require a change of direction — the curbing and eventual abolition of the power of the monopolies over the life of the country.

The Communist Party must continue to stand out as a foremost champion of genuine Canadian independence, of Canadian control of the economy through public ownership. More and more Canadians will be impelled to move in that direction and to give support to those who fight for it. The working class must be at the center of that fight as it should be at the center of the fight for peace, for nationalization of key industries and for new trade policies. In this way it will challenge the capitalist class for leadership of the nation.

The demand for Canadian control and ownership should be linked to the demand to put Canada back to work. Moreover, as our Party has emphasized before, the battle for genuine Canadian independence and for a fully autonomous, united trade-union movement based on class-struggle policies needs to go together with the struggle for a democratic coalition led by the working class, for a new majority and a new government.

As the Communist Party program, the *Road to Socialism in Canada* states: "The fight for autonomy lays the basis for the achievement of an independent and sovereign trade-union movement. This will decisively strengthen the political struggle of the working class for genuine Canadian independence, against monopoly rule."

NATIONAL SELF-DETERMINATION AND EQUALITY

The struggle for genuine Canadian independence is organically linked with the right to national self-determination and equality for the French-Canadian nation.

Only on the basis of national equality do conditions exist for realizing a truly democratic solution of the problem of the co-existence of the two nations in one federal state, and only in this way will the necessary conditions be created to unite French- and English-Canadians for the independence of Canada from domination by U.S. imperialism. Multi-culturalism and bilingualism, the "solution" offered by the Trudeau government, is no substitute for the demand of French-Canadians for full national equality and recognition of the right to determine their own national life.

The Communist Party warns against the dangers of chauvinism and racism, as well as narrow nationalism, which the results of the election may accentuate. Such dangers exist and it would be folly to close one's eyes to them. These divisive and harmful developments can best be countered by strengthening the fight for the right to national self-determination and equality for the French-Canadian nation, the adoption of a new Canadian Constitution based on the equal voluntary partnership of the French-Canadian and English-speaking peoples in an independent, democratic bi-national state, and by democratic measures of structural reform that could begin to come to grips with national and economic inequality in Quebec.

It is precisely such a democratic solution that creates the necessary preconditions for strengthening the unity of the working people and for enabling the working class to realize its historic mission of achieving socialism.

The touchstone of solidarity in English Canada is the attitude of the working-class movement to the French-Canadian struggle for national equality; and in French Canada, it is solidarity with all democratic forces in English-speaking Canada.

It is this sound internationalist approach, the only sure guide for the working-class and democratic movements, that can unite all genuinely national and democratic forces in active struggle against monopoly and for the realization of a democratic coalition.

The rich lessons of the Soviet Union in solving the national question, an historic event that is at the center of the 50th anniversary of the formation of the USSR, should be popularized as widely as possible.

History has confirmed that the national question can only be solved in a fundamental way through the victory of socialism and the building of a socialist society.

History has confirmed that socialism does away with national antagonisms and replaces them by a new community of peoples based on the principle of the right to self-determination, including separation, which establishes the conditions for equality and creates conditions for voluntary fraternal unity.

History has also shown that only socialism can eliminate the roots of national oppression and national inequality by eliminating their source, capitalist exploitation. By establishing new economic relations the necessary conditions are created for overcoming economic and cultural backwardness and lifting up the lowest regions to the level of the highest.

These lessons have validity for Canada. We can see how, despite the measures taken by state-monopoly capitalism, despite regional development programs, poverty and inequality continue as before.

We can see that even limited democratic measures such as bilingualism are resisted and nullified in practice, and how the anti-French backlash is used to maintain inequality.

We can also see that the French-Canadian bourgeoisie — no less than their class brothers and competitors, U.S. and Canadian monopoly alike — dispense class justice with a heavy hand, as in the case of the three trade union leaders in Quebec; impose anti-labor legislation to compel strikers to return to work, and enact legislation giving the state the authority to search without warrant and to seize documents.

On the occasion of the 50th anniversary of the formation of the USSR we salute the Soviet peoples and wish them every success. The example of the Soviet Union in solving the national question serves as a model for peoples of other lands. The Soviet peoples have built a society which has shown the world how to end exploitation of man by man as well as national oppression, and now, on the basis of a developed socialist system, are laying the material and technical basis of a communist society.

On this occasion, too, we call for strengthening the bonds of good-neighborly relations, trade, cultural and scientific exchanges between Canada and the Soviet Union, a policy which helps to strengthen Canadian independence and international security.

THE FIGHT FOR PEACE

Preoccupation with domestic affairs should not lead us to overlook developments internationally, developments with which Canada's future and that of the Canadian people are so closely bound up, such as the necessity of strengthening the fight for peace. *In this connection the struggle to compel the U.S. government to sign the agreement with the Democratic Republic of Vietnam must be at the top of the list.* The unsigned agreement represents an acknowledgment by U.S. imperialism that its aim of military victory is unattainable and that it has no other choice than to end its shameful aggression through a political agreement. However, imperialism does not give up easily.

From all appearances the Nixon administration has

undertaken a strategem to continue the war with other people's hands. It continues to arm the puppet regime of South Vietnam which now has the third largest air force in the world. It continues to attack the DRV by air, destroying everything in sight. The only conclusion one can come to is that U.S. imperialism has not given up its aim of imposing a military settlement on the DRV and on the people of Vietnam. Moreover, even if the draft agreement is signed, settlement of the internal affairs of South Vietnam will not be automatically guaranteed. U.S. imperialist arming of its puppet troops is directed to ensuring continuation of the war, and its direct as well as indirect presence in Indochina and in Southeast Asia.

However, U.S. imperialism cannot succeed in imposing a military settlement on the people of Vietnam, particularly if the solidarity movement of the peoples of the world reaches a higher level, backed by the socialist countries and above all by the Soviet Union which continues to give unsparingly to the heroic people of Vietnam.

Our Party will continue to give all-out support to the people of Vietnam, for the victory of their just cause. It will continue to work for the withdrawal of Israeli troops from all occupied Arab territories, for the observance of the lawful rights of the Arab people of Palestine, for a political settlement based on the UN Security Council Resolution of 1967.

Developments in Vietnam and in the Middle East take place on the background of a changing world, of an international setting which opens up prospects for a further relaxation of international tensions and the elimination of the cold war. The latest example of this process is the conclusion of a treaty between the GDR and West Germany, the significance of which cannot be overestimated. Its significance lies in the fact that this treaty and others already agreed to, such as the treaties between the USSR and West Germany, confirm the results of the Second World War and postwar developments and open up prospects of turning Europe from a continent of conflicts into a continent of security and co-operation.

This also confirms the fact that the battle waged by the

socialist countries, the GDR, the Communist and Workers' Parties including the Communist Party of Canada, has borne fruit. It is now necessary, with greater vigor, to press for Canada's recognition of the GDR and for Canadian support of a collective security system in Europe. It is all the more important to do so because the reactionary forces in West Germany, despite the recent election outcome which demonstrated the desire of the majority of West Germans for detente, as well as the cold warriors of Western Europe, in the USA and in Canada, have not given up their aim of maintaining international tensions. In this they are helped by the Maoists.

It is a matter of record that the government of China and the Communist Party of China are among the few who have come out in opposition to the treaties and the trend toward easing international tensions, as well as to the proposed European Security Conference. This disgraceful position is on a par with its opposition to the convening of a World Disarmament Conference, its refusal to recognize Bangladesh, and its persistent anti-Sovietism which leads Maoism more and more to act as the left bower of imperialism.

The Chinese leaders oppose collective security both in Europe and in Asia. They throw roadblocks in the way of concrete steps leading to agreement on questions of disarmament and the prohibition of nuclear weapons. They have made anti-Sovietism and the struggle against Marxist-Leninist parties and other socialist countries an integral part of the policy and program of the Communist Party of China.

As part of this approach and with the aim of dividing the anti-imperialist forces, the Chinese leaders have come forward with the thesis of a struggle against the "two super-powers", or its variation, the struggle against "one of the two super-powers". This anti-Leninist thesis has become the watchword under which the Chinese leaders pursue their anti-Soviet course. As a so-called "theoretical" proposition, it is aimed at covering up the non-class position of these leaders, and trying to negate the fundamental difference between the socialist Soviet Union — the mainstay of peace, independence and socialism throughout the world — and

U.S. imperialism, the most rapacious imperialist state, the world gendarme, upholder and defender of the system of exploitation and oppression, of death and destruction, as in Indochina.

The anti-Sovietism of the Chinese leaders is on a par with their discredited theory of the "world village freeing the world city". Both substitute hegemonistic petty-bourgeois nationalist positions for a working-class position. Both are calculated efforts to reject the main contradiction of our time — the international class struggle between the two systems, socialist and capitalism — and thus evade the real struggle against imperialism. All this is being conducted under the smokescreen of an alleged "danger from the north", the "theoretical" basis for working out a deal with U.S. imperialism at the expense of the unity of the anti-imperialist forces of the world.

All of this should make clear that the Maoist platform, despite tactical shifts, remains unchanged. It is anti-Marxist and anti-Leninist. No amount of demagogy can cover this up.

A consistent struggle against Maoism, and for the principles of Marxism-Leninism and proletarian internationalism is a necessary part of the struggle for unity of action of all anti-imperialist forces, for the unity and cohesion of the international communist movement, and in making the struggle against imperialism more effective.

New perspectives are undoubtedly opening up for relaxation of tensions in Europe and this in turn could have a salutary effect all over the world. These developments reflect the changing balance of forces in favor of socialism and peace, due above all to the successes of the world socialist system. The growing economic, political and military strength of the socialist community, and of the USSR, is the decisive factor strengthening peace and international security.

What is evident is that the co-ordinated efforts of the socialist countries and all forces opposed to imperialism have compelled the forces of imperialism and of war to retreat. This does not mean that imperialism has been completely muzzled. Imperialism, notwithstanding the agreements it is compelled to accede to, remains an aggressive, predatory system — compelled to adapt itself to the new conditions. However, it has not changed its nature or its essence. Its policies are fundamentally hostile to the interests of the working people and need to be combatted day in and day out. Its aggressive forces continue resisting any easing of tensions. Imperialism continues the war in Indochina, prevents a settlement in the Middle East and stimulates armed conflict in that part of the world. It has its hand in the recent events in Chile whose aim was the overthrow of the Allende government.

Vigilance and unity of effort, as we have stressed more than once, remain a must. The Communist Party will work perseveringly for unity of action of all anti-imperialist forces. It will work perseveringly to strengthen the peace movement. Any letdown of the peace movement and of peace action can only help the aggressors.

The initiative and leadership displayed by the Communist Party on all fronts, the united action it is able to forge around them, will create more favorable conditions for bringing into being a broad democratic alliance directed against reaction, against U.S. imperialism and Canadian monopoly. The heart and the main force for such an alliance is the working class. It is its unity, for which the Communist Party works, that will rally around it other democratic forces.

The starting point for bringing such a democratic coalition into being is the various mass movements that presently exist and will continue to develop. Our Party and Party members need to be actively involved in all such movements and work to unite them into one powerful anti-monopoly stream.

The Communist Party is the prime factor in the struggle to bring all those who are victims of monopoly policy, all working-class and democratic forces, together in a broad alliance capable of replacing the power of monopoly by a new majority, a new government. The strength of the Party is the decisive factor in the success of this struggle.

Everything dealt with above finally focusses on one central task, that of building the Communist Party, the YCL and the working-class press.

Experience shows that Communist Party building is possible in the course of public activity. In fact it is the best time to build the Communist Party. That should be our approach now. What is proposed is a year-round campaign of Communist Party, YCL and press building and that 1973 be the year to carry this out.

The need for building the Communist Party is self-evident. The period we are entering is not likely to be one of relative calm or stability, but rather one of sharpened struggle over which path Canada should take to get out of the crisis. This struggle will merge with ever-growing working-class action against the policies of monopoly, for the economic and social needs of the working people, the rights of the French-Canadian people, the movements for peace and democratic rights and for Canadian independence.

In this period of growing upsurge and demand for change much depends upon the work and leadership of the Communist Party.

The Canadian working people need a much stronger Communist Party — rooted in industry, in the countryside, among working youth and students, women and intellectuals, and among the new immigration of working people. It is this strength that will enable the Communist Party to play an ever more effective role in the political arena, in the struggle for left unity, for a breakthrough in the parliamentary arena, and in the continuing struggle to bring about a democratic coalition as the transition to socialism in Canada.

The campaign for Communist Party, YCL and press building should not be conceived of in a humdrum way. It should be approached in the same way the election was tackled.

Our aim should be to consolidate and extend the ideological and organizational base of the Communist Party in each constituency where we ran, as well as where we did not.

Our aim should be to build the Communist Party in new areas. It should include systematic efforts to extend the Communist Party's ideological and organizational influence among the large mass of postwar immigrants, the majority of whom are working people.

Let us agree to go all-out in the battle to build the Communist Party, YCL and the press and make 1973 a banner year for the Communist Party — the year of growth and expansion of the party of the working class, the party upholding the true national interest, the party of socialism in Canada.

A strong Communist Party is the best guarantee of the unity of the workers and the people, the strengthening of the workers' political and class consciousness, the defeat of alien and hostile ideas in the working-class and democratic movement, and in the struggle for Canadian independence, social progress, democracy and socialism.

In the rapidly changing world where the forces of peace, democracy and socialism are gaining ground, we appeal to Canadians who seek to be part of this great world change to join the ranks of the Communist Party and together build a happy, peaceful and socialist future.

Pamphlet,
January, 1973.

XIV

Unite against monopoly — a Communist plan of action

Our Policy Resolution states: "We are entering a more turbulent period of history, a period of great challenge and rapid change."

The evidence is all around us.

The forces of peace and socialism, in the first place the Soviet Union and the socialist countries, have achieved major successes in the struggle for peaceful co-existence.

At our 21st Convention a major preoccupation of our Party was centered on helping to bring an end to the cold war. At this Convention we can register the fact that the cold war has begun to give way to detente. This is of great historical significance.

Indicative of the profound changes shaping the international scene are: the accords to end the Vietnam war, although peace is yet to be achieved; the implementation of decisions on a ceasefire in the Middle East and prospects of a peaceful settlement in that area; the relaxation of tensions in Europe arising from a number of bilateral and multilateral agreements and treaties, all of which recognize the outcome of the Second World War and the territorial questions related to it; recognition of the GDR in international law; the strengthening position of Cuba; the accomplishments of the second stage of the Conference on Security and Co-operation in Europe; the first moves toward restriction of the arms drive; agreement on averting nuclear war between the USSR and the USA; and an ever wider development of economic, scientific, and cultural co-operation between countries.

What has made these changes possible is the growing strength of socialism and the influence socialist achievements have on the peoples of the world. It is the continuing shift of the world balance of forces in favor of peace and socialism which has created favorable conditions for detente. It is this which has led to a consolidation of the victories achieved by socialism after the Second World War, and at the same time opened up new prospects for democratic advance in the capitalist world.

DETENTE MUST BE MADE IRREVERSIBLE

Detente has sharpened inter-imperialist contradictions. It has sharpened contradictions among monopoly groups in each capitalist country between those who favor and those who oppose detente. It is stimulating a process of differentiation in social democracy and creating more favorable conditions for unity of action of the working-class and democratic movements.

Thus, detente is not only a matter of state relations, of bringing about an improvement in the international situation. It has a direct bearing on the further development of the working-class and democratic movement in the capitalist world, including Canada.

Detente is not an automatic process. It had to be fought for every inch of the way by the Soviet Union, other socialist countries and all peace-loving forces throughout the world. Today, too, it has to be fought for in face of an imperialist counter-offensive to extract concessions from the socialist countries with the objective of opening them up to capitalist ideas.

Notwithstanding detente, preparations for war continue and intensify, arms expenditures grow, as evidenced in Canada also. New and ever more destructive weapons of war are being perfected.

Nuclear disarmament has slowed down. U.S. imperialism stands in the way of implementation of the peace treaties with respect to Vietnam and Indochina. It stands in the way of a peace settlement in the Middle East based on Resolution

242 and other pertinent UN resolutions, all of which call for a return to the 1967 borders and recognition of the rights of the Palestinian Arab people.

What one sees is an alliance of the U.S. military-industrial complex, the Pentagon, NATO forces, West German revenge seekers, reactionary Zionist forces, the ultra-right, the ultra-left, George Meany and company, and Maoism whose aim is the undermining of detente, a return to the cold war, the arms race and a policy of confrontation.

This unholy alliance opposes peaceful co-existence and the need for detente and mutually beneficial relations with the socialist countries. Alongside direct attacks on peaceful co-existence, other voices are raised which call upon the Soviet Union to open its frontiers to the spreading of capitalist ideas, to cease criticism of capitalism, to give up the ideological struggle. In this they are joined by right-wing social democrats.

The opponents of detente have undertaken an unscrupulous and co-ordinated campaign for "liberalization" of the socialist system, that is, the elimination of the real gains of socialism. This was the purpose of the recent campaign around Solzhenitsyn, a campaign to undermine detente, attack the Soviet Union and socialism as well as the progressive forces in the capitalist world.

These gentlemen and their press, so concerned about the "rights of man", connive in taking away the individual and collective rights of man and of peoples. Capitalism will never be able to give to the people rights that those in the socialist countries presently enjoy.

Maoism has joined the opponents of detente. The Maoists describe the treaties and agreements arrived at as "mere scraps of paper". They attack the policies of the socialist countries directed to achieve peaceful co-existence of different social systems. They spread the false claim of "superpower collusion", of the "renunciation" by the Soviet Union of revolutionary principles. In line with its adventurist aims, the Peking leadership opposes the banning of nuclear, chemical and bacteriological warfare and the restriction of strategic armaments. Maoism stands opposed to peaceful co-existence, claiming that this policy hinders the struggle for social progress, democracy and socialism. In reality however the conditions of peaceful co-existence facilitate the revolutionary struggle as events throughout the capitalist world and the underdeveloped countries underscore.

The ultra-left try to imply that peaceful co-existence means acceptance of the permanence of capitalism. This, however, is completely false. Peaceful co-existence does not mean class peace. It applies to interstate relations between capitalist and socialist countries, not to class relations within capitalist society, the class struggle on an international scale, or relations between the peoples of the colonial and dependent countries and the imperialist states oppressing them.

The policy of peaceful co-existence, by weakening the aggressive circles of monopoly capitalism, advances the best interests of the working class, the struggle for democratization, for social and political rights, for socialism. It creates more favorable conditions for the peoples oppressed by imperialism, in their struggle for national and social liberation.

What has become evident is that objectively Maoism has lined up with the reactionary forces of imperialism against socialism. Thus to fight for peace demands consistent and continuing struggle against imperialism as well as Maoism.

Detente and confrontation, these two contradictory processes that reflect the world reality, show that peaceful co-existence as the only real alternative to nuclear war does not mean the elimination of contradictions and differences. It reflects the clash of interests of different social forces and opposite social systems and ideologies.

Recent events emphasize anew that the road to peace is not an easy one. Reactionary imperialist circles are trying and will continue to try to prevent the implementation of the principles of peaceful co-existence and detente. They will seek to revert to cold war and military confrontations, the creation of divisions within the socialist community of states and in the international communist movement. This is why vigilance is essential. One must have no illusions about imperialism.

Clearly the struggle for a just and democratic peace is far

261

from over. It is today the issue of issues that mankind must resolve to prevent a third world war. The central question of the fight for peace is to make detente an irreversible process. The security of the Canadian people lies in detente and a world at peace.

As the Policy Resolution states: "The fight to maintain and extend detente and make it irreversible, and ensure that the principles of peaceful co-existence become a norm of relations between states with different social systems, is now at the center of the struggle for world peace. Political detente must lead to military detente and cover the entire world."

CANADA NEEDS A FOREIGN POLICY FOR PEACE

This is a task in which all democratic and peace-loving forces in Canada must engage. Canada's voice must be raised loud and clear for an end to U.S. interference in Indochina; for the full implementation of the Paris Peace Treaties; a political settlement in the Middle East based on the UN Security Council resolutions; the successful completion of the European Conference on Security and Co-operation; for nuclear disarmament based on equality of security. What is decisive is that the people be brought into action for the cause of peace.

The U.S. nuclear alert during the Middle East crisis brought the world to the brink of nuclear disaster, and showed how dangerous it is for Canada to be tied to NATO and NORAD, It showed how urgent is the need for an independent foreign policy for Canada. On this, the 25th anniversary of NATO, renewed efforts should be undertaken to have Canada withdraw from this U.S. military bloc and from NORAD, both of which undermine its sovereignty and its ability to pursue policies based on the real, all-Canadian interests of the country.

We welcome the initiative of the Canadian Peace Congress in formulating a Peace Charter for Canada. We believe this can play an important role in rallying wide sections of the Canadian people in support of measures to assure a just and democratic peace, in support of the peoples striving for their freedom and independence.

The Communist Party pledges support to the Canadian Peace Congress and the various campaigns it undertakes.

The Communist Party considers it of particular importance that everything humanly possible be done to extend the movement of solidarity with the democratic forces in Chile. This should include the demand on the Canadian government that it break off diplomatic relations with the military junta, call for the release of all political prisoners including Senator Luis Corvalan, general secretary of the Communist Party of Chile, that Canada open its doors to all political refugees from that country.

Democratic opinion cannot but note the rapidity with which the doors of Canada were opened to allow entry into our country of thousands upon thousands of Hungarians in 1956 and Czechoslovakians in 1968, following upon unsuccessful attempts to restore capitalism in those countries. Large numbers of fascist elements from other countries have been admitted to Canada. Compare these examples with the resistance displayed to the entry of Chilean patriots whose sole "crime" was support of a constitutionally elected government.

In this time of great trial for the Chilean people, we want to state from this platform: All Canadian democrats are with you in your great democratic struggle which one day will be crowned with victory over fascism!

Our task in the field of international solidarity demands also that we help widen the movement of solidarity with democratic Spain. We must assist in the creation of a strong solidarity movement against apartheid, racism and colonialism in Southern Africa, and in support of the liberation movements in Guinea-Bissau, Angola and Mozambique. We must do the same with respect to all-out support of Greek democracy. At the same time there is need to support in every way the heroic struggle of the DRV and the Provisional Revolutionary Government of South Vietnam to implement the Paris Peace Treaties, despite the sabotage of the Thieu administration and the U.S. government. That same support must be given the Cambodian people. In all of this we must not overlook the role of Canadian imperialism, particularly in Latin America, we must expose it.

There is a great reserve of anti-imperialist sentiment in Canada, particularly among the young people. This must be tapped and united into organized support of the anti-imperialist struggles of the peoples against U.S. imperialism, racism, anti-semitism and genocide.

The struggle for detente and in support of the anti-imperialist forces everywhere is an essential part of the movement to achieve a just and democratic peace in the world.

A NEW PHASE IN THE GENERAL CRISIS OF CAPITALISM

Detente, while it has led to an improvement in international relations, has not altered the laws of capitalism.

The general crisis of capitalism has deepened. Indeed, we have entered a new phase of the general crisis.

This is to be seen in the inflationary price spiral affecting all capitalist countries. It is to be seen in the monetary and financial crisis, the collapse of the postwar structure created by U.S. imperialism and the inability of the imperialist states so far to work out a new structure. It is to be seen in the energy crisis affecting all capitalist countries in varying degrees and accentuating the inflationary price spiral. The deepening of the general crisis is also to be seen in the sharpening of inter-imperialist contradictions which have become more acute, particularly between the USA, West Germany and Japan; in the crisis of relations between the underdeveloped countries and imperialism; and in the crisis of foreign policy arising from the bankruptcy of "brinkmanship, roll back of communism, containment" and armed suppression of socialism.

Bourgeois democracy is in growing crisis as evidenced in Chile, Uruguay and the USA (Watergate).

This crisis of bourgeois democracy shows again that whenever and wherever the positions of capitalism are threatened, the most reactionary section of the capitalist class quickly forgets its allegiance to "democracy" and the "free world", and does not stop at any violence to hold on to its positions.

The new phase of the crisis finds reflection in increasing political instability in the capitalist world, in a growing crisis of the capitalist parties.

How true this is could be seen in the first week of March. During that week there was a crisis in Great Britain arising from the Tory attack on the working class and its electoral defeat. During that same week there was a crisis in Italy with the government resigning. Similar resignations took place in France and in Israel. In West Germany the social democrats suffered defeat in state elections, while in the USA the political crisis continues to deepen around the growing demand for impeachment of President Nixon.

From this, Mr. Reston of the *New York Times* concludes that these governments do not have the confidence of their people and that "political instability is the rule of the day". He then went on to say, "The political decline of the West is no longer a subject for theoretical debate, but an ominous reality, particularly when the leader of the West, the USA, has so much trouble at home."

Since these remarks were made the fascist regime was overthrown in Portugal after more than 40 years of rule. As a consequence, a new chapter opened up in the struggle of the Portuguese people for democratic reform and fundamental change, and in the struggle of the peoples of Guinea-Bissau, Angola and Mozambique for national liberation.

Since then the presidential elections took place in France, resulting in François Mitterand receiving almost 50 per cent of the vote for President of France. This is striking evidence that the Socialist, Communist and Left-Radical co-operation around a common program has opened up real prospects of France taking a new road of advanced democracy, away from the rule of the reactionary right. A similar process is underway in Italy as the recently held referendum on divorce showed.

These events show how correct is the statement that detente and peaceful co-existence, rather than hindering, create the best conditions for advancing and strengthening the working-class and democratic forces.

They show how sound was the proposition of the 1969 Conference of Communist and Workers' Parties that imperialism has lost its historic initiative and is unable to determine the course of history. As it stated: "The main direction of mankind's development is determined by the world socialist system, the international working class, all revolutionary forces."

The new phase of the general crisis of capitalism is reflected in a growing crisis of the regulatory mechanism of state-monopoly capitalism. The thought that state-monopoly capitalism would bring prolonged and lasting political stability has been proven wrong. Present-day capitalism is in a state of profound and ever increasing crisis. It is showing itself unable to advance an effective program or programs to cope with the economic, social and cultural needs of our time.

GROWING INSTABILITY IN THE CAPITALIST WORLD ECONOMY

The energy crisis, the monetary and financial crisis, the inflationary price spiral, and an economic downturn are all taking place at the same time and affecting all capitalist countries.

In point of fact this is the first time in the postwar period that there has taken place a synchronization of the cycle in the advanced capitalist countries, an event which is increasingly commented on in the capitalist media. Previously when the economy was down in one part of the capitalist world, it was up in another. The economic cycle never met or synchronized.

This time it is different, suggesting the possibility of severe economic dislocations. The general secretary of the Organization of Economic Co-operation and Development, Mr. Emile van Lennep, felt impelled to say in a speech in Toronto recently that there was "an increasingly synchronized world business cycle, itself showing a worrying tendency towards excessively severe peaks and troughs." These remarks were further underscored by the Credit Suisse (Canada) Ltd., which stated in a market letter that the world faced "staggering global problems" that include chaotic conditions in currency markets, competitive devaluations, a move toward protectionist trade policies, and over extended liquidity which could lead to a 'domino-like series of bankruptcies'." It then went on to say: "For the first time in history, an economic boom has been worldwide, with all major countries simultaneously running at top speed. In consequence, 1974 presents for the first time the challenge of a synchronized worldwide slow-down in economic activity." This prospect raises "the spectre of spiralling recessionary forces, indeed of depression."

These notes of uncertainty and of pessimism are not misplaced. They point up the fact that relative stability is coming closer to an end in the capitalist world.

This is also to be seen in a shift in the anti-imperialist struggle, expressed in the sharpening antagonism between imperialism and the underdeveloped countries. Imperialism is out to strengthen its domination over these countries through new forms of neo-colonialism. In this they come into conflict with countries striving to restrict and eliminate neo-colonialism and develop their economies, free of outside control. This struggle is focussed on oil and natural resources, the raw materials of which imperialism is increasingly short.

Previously the underdeveloped countries had been compelled to sell their resources at below value to the benefit of imperialism which in turn sold them manufactured goods and other commodities at the highest possible price. Now, arising from changes in the balance of power, from nationalization, and from the support given them by socialism, the underdeveloped countries are striving to redress the balance. Oil and natural resources have become important weapons in their political struggle, helping to shift the balance in favor of the countries possessing these resources. This constitutes a major shift in the struggle of the third world countries to achieve economic liberation from imperialism.

The struggle over the price of energy essentially reflects the battle for national sovereignty over one's own resources and for economic and political independence.

It should be noted that the capitalist world is not only faced with an energy crisis. It is increasingly faced with the prospects of a crisis of raw materials. The USA imports 53 per cent of its consumption of zinc, 56 per cent of tungsten, 83 per cent of tin, 80 per cent of nickel.

The struggle of the underdeveloped countries for national sovereignty, for economic and political independence, for real control and the development of their own resources as they see fit, is thus an important factor in the battle against imperialism. It should be given all our support.

Alongside the growing anti-imperialist struggle, inter-imperialist contradictions are becoming more acute. The sharp exchange between President Nixon and Mr. Kissinger on the one hand and the European Economic Community on the other reflects the sharpening struggle for markets and raw materials in the imperialist camp. This is to be seen in the energy crisis, in questions of trade, in the U.S. nuclear alert and its consequences last fall. Behind the façade of "western unity," a bitter struggle is on between U.S. imperialism, the EEC and Japanese monopoly.

In the EEC itself contradictions have become more acute, threatening the very existence of that trade bloc.

What is evident is that the effort to reform the NATO alliance, on its 25th anniversary, around an Atlantic Charter is foundering on the rocks of sharpening inter-imperialist contradictions. The attempt by U.S. imperialism to restore the postwar structure and maintain its leading position in the imperialist system is meeting increasing resistance. A military alliance is as strong as its economic base. The economic base of NATO is being undermined by sharpened industrial and commercial competition and by inter-imperialist contradictions which become more acute. These in turn help shift the balance of world forces increasingly in favor of peace, democracy and socialism.

While the imperialist world is confronted with increasing instability, there is growth and stability in the socialist world. The Soviet Union and other socialist countries continue to achieve new successes in the fields of economic, scientific and cultural development and in foreign policy. The socialist world is not faced with economic crisis, energy crisis, inflation. There are no land speculators there. Nor is there inequality of women, or national inequality. The sense of insecurity that pervades working people in the capitalist world does not exist in the socialist countries.

The contrast between socialism and capitalism is to be seen in economic and social policy. While workers' real wages decline in the capitalist world, they continue a steady upward pace in the socialist world. Real income will go up 5 per cent this year in the Soviet Union. Average wages will rise by 3.5 per cent while collective farmers' earnings will rise by 6.1 per cent. According to the UN Economic Report on Europe, prices tend to decline in all socialist countries. In the Soviet Union for example price reductions of 1.2 per cent have already taken place in a number of commodities. Moreover, free medical treatment, holidays, grants and scholarships have added nearly an extra third to wages. Real income per head of population during 1971-73 rose by 13½ per cent.

Stability in prices and steady pay increases — this is the reality in the socialist countries. The example of the socialist countries shows that the price of commodities can be fixed, controlled and stabilized, without any harm to the economy.

These developments, made possible by socialist planning and public ownership, point up the fact that inflation is not worldwide, just capitalist-wide.

Profound political decline of the West, that is, of capitalism. Growth and development of socialism. These two realities reflect the changing balance of forces in the world. This is increasingly penetrating the minds of the working people. Mounting discontent with capitalism — mounting confidence in socialism. These have become constant factors in the world we live in.

In this period of growing crisis of capitalism we need not only to popularize the achievements of socialism. We need to defend it and show that only socialism can extricate the people from crisis.

Canada is not immune from the instability and crisis phenomena evidenced in the capitalist world. Inflation, like unemployment, has become a permanent feature of state-monopoly capitalism, and is seriously undermining the living standards of the working people.

The Canadian people were sold the idea that a new world had been created, a crisisless, affluent world and that a new capitalism had replaced the old capitalism.

The facts have turned out differently.

The spokesmen of state-monopoly capitalism spread the illusion that it would provide full employment. Instead, unemployment is up and may go to seven per cent this year. It has had a particularly serious effect on young people who have been among its main victims. Now unemployment is spreading into the auto industry. This is part of a restructuring of the industry in the USA which is presently underway, a restructuring that could threaten the auto industry in Canada. The consequences of this will be growing *permanent* unemployment among auto workers, and in turn among the workers in industries related to the auto industry.

The discussion in capitalist circles is not how to lower or eliminate unemployment but how to convince the Canadian people that five to six per cent unemployment is equivalent to full employment. This goes together with an attack on the Unemployment Insurance Act, led by sections of big business and pushed by the Tories. The aim is to weaken the Act and compel working people to accept low-paying jobs. Proposals are being advanced to rewrite the Act with this in mind. What monopoly wants is a reserve army of unemployed that can be used to depress wages and living standards.

The spokesmen of state-monopoly capitalism spread the illusion that it would achieve stable prices. Instead, inflation developed at a rate of 10 per cent last year. This year sugar rose by 60 per cent, fresh vegetables by 7.4 per cent, pork and poultry by 22 per cent, beef by 22 per cent. Transportation costs rose by 7.7 per cent and housing costs by 7 per cent.

What the Canadian people are faced with is wholesale robbery on a scale never seen before and with governments apparently helpless to stop it.

The claim that rising prices are due to shortages is so much balderdash. There are no real shortages of goods produced in Canada. There are artificial shortages created by monopoly which then uses the situation it created to jack up prices as if the sky were the limit.

One has only to look at the profit sheets of the corporations to see how true this is.

Falconbridge Nickel in 1973 increased profits by 770 per cent over 1972. International Nickel increased profits by 107 per cent. Abitibi Paper Company increased profits by 260 per cent, Gulf Oil by 58 per cent and Exxon increased profits in the last three months of 1973 by 59 per cent.

The *Globe and Mail* showed recently that fourth quarter profits in the industrial mining sector increased by 3,196 per cent, while base metals showed a lesser profit of 566 per cent, and paper and forest industries, 344 per cent. In the last few days we have reports on the profits of the food processing industry, and the pattern is the same.

Thus, rather than stable prices, the Canadian people are confronted with rising prices and a profit orgy.

The spokesmen of state-monopoly capitalism spread the illusion that it would achieve rising living standards. The reality is different. Rather than rising, there has been a deterioration in living standards for working people. Inflation and rising prices have cut real wages by over five per cent. The real purchasing power of the average worker is back to where it was in 1970 because real gains, whatever they were in 1972-73, were wiped out by rapidly rising prices. And this does not include increased productivity and speed-up. If these are taken into consideration the situation is much worse.

The *Financial Post* admits:

"The Canadian corporations have managed to keep productivity ahead of wage increases ..." Between 1967 and 1972, "average hourly earnings (in constant 1961 dollars) went up by 26.6 per cent." (*Financial Post*, Feb. 23, 1974.)

In light of the huge profits of monopoly and its wholesale robbery of the people, the cry that wages are responsible for inflation and rising prices has been temporarily shelved. What cannot be hidden any longer is that increased profits come out of the increased exploitation of the workers. This increased exploitation of the workers takes on many forms. One way in which this is being pushed is by the 10-hour day and four-day week, through which the rights and standards of blue- and white-collar workers are being undermined.

Instead of keeping ahead of inflation, the working people are increasingly being submerged by it. Particularly hard hit are the unorganized workers, the working poor, the poor who do not work, pensioners and those on small and fixed incomes.

Through inflation monopoly has further redistributed the national income in its favor, at the expense of the living standards of the working people. Indeed, this is a primary purpose of inflation.

Working people should note that while they often need to strike to win wage increases, and while governments are used to impose settlements on them "in the national interest", as was the case with the railway workers, there is no "national interest" when it comes to the corporations raising prices. Here the government appears helpless. What is obvious is that capitalist laws are made to protect the corporations and to keep the working people in their place. This includes legislation denying the right to strike of railway workers, hospital employees, teachers and others.

The spokesmen of state-monopoly capitalism spread the illusion that it would eliminate poverty and inequality. Here too the reality is different. The fact is that there has been no real change in the redistribution of the national income since Confederation. In any case what is evident is that the poor are getting poorer, that there are more of them, and that the rich are getting richer. The concentration and centralization of capital and production have grown by leaps and bounds in the postwar period, added to by the multi-national corporations. This has strengthened the economic and political power and domination of monopoly and of the multi-national corporations in all spheres. The working men and women who produce the wealth of the country get less and less of that wealth while the corporations become bigger and stronger and profits soar. Poverty has increased while regional disparity and inequality continue as before.

The spokesmen of state-monopoly capitalism spread the illusion that it would achieve stable growth. However, instead of an expanding economy, the prospects are of a decline in the growth rate this year. Last year the growth rate was seven per cent. This year it may decline to four per cent. It requires no stretch of the imagination to see that, alongside a growing labor force, this will bring about a considerable increase in unemployment.

This situation will be further aggravated by the energy crisis which affects both prices and jobs; by economic recession in the USA, Japan and Western Europe; and by the sharpening struggle for markets.

What is clear from the above is that the working class and all working people are being made to bear the main burden of the growing contradictions and developing crisis of the regulatory mechanism of state-monopoly capitalism.

State-monopoly capitalism is showing that it cannot satisfy the real needs of the working people. Whatever the changes that have taken place, capitalism remains as before — an exploitative crisis-ridden system that breeds unemployment and perpetuates poverty and inequality.

INFLATION — PERMANENT FEATURE OF CAPITALISM

Today the most serious and urgent problem is the struggle against inflation and its effects. Inflation, now a permanent feature of capitalism, bears heavily on the living conditions of working people. The wholesale robbery of the working people, the deterioration of living standards, layoffs and unemployment are bringing about widespread dissatisfaction and discontent, creating conditions for an upsurge of the class struggle and the struggle of the people against monopoly.

The Conservatives are trying to capitalize on this situation by creating the impression that wage and price controls and an incomes policy will solve inflation. At the same time they have joined the big business campaign for a curtailment of government spending, as if this would solve inflation. What they have in mind, and what big business has in mind, is that social service, welfare, and unemployment insurance expenditures be curtailed. What they also have in mind is opposition to the extension of social security to include a guaranteed annual income. While attacking government expenditures they continue clamoring for additional billions of public funds to be handed over to big business, as was the case with last year's half-billion-dollar gift to the corporations. The Tory solution to inflation is a freeze on wages, the maintenance of inequality and poverty while allowing profits to soar.

The Trudeau government has continued to hide behind the claim that inflation is "worldwide", although in reality it is only capitalist-wide, using this as a pretext to do very little about the effects of inflation. Under public pressure it has added a cost of living escalator to pensions, family allowances and veterans' payments. But when it comes to rising prices and profiteering by the corporations the Trudeau government, like the Conservatives, considers monopoly and the multi-national corporations to be "untouchables". It set up a Prices Review Board but then made sure it would have no power to deal with rising prices. The working people can see the results of this approach in the rise of prices of staples, including bread and milk. The government provided subsidies on some commodities but then did nothing to prevent the corporations from becoming the sole beneficiaries of these grants. Prime Minister Trudeau declares that inflation is caused by people "who want to take more out of society than they put into it". He couples this with a statement that wages are not responsible for inflation. But so far he has done nothing to curb those — whom he named as "the price gougers and profiteers" — who are responsible for it.

More recently, under public pressure, he came forward with proposed legislation on profiteering but like the Prices Review Board it had very few teeth in it.

Even so, the howls of rage emanating from monopoly and the mass media, as well as from the Tories, against the proposed legislation show that monopoly is determined to maintain at all costs its "sacred right" to superprofits, come what may.

Both the government and the Conservatives refuse to face up to what is central — that there can be no attack on inflation without curbing the profits and power of the monopolies and the speculators. This is so because monopoly controls the economy and is able to raise prices at will. Its uncontrolled domination of the market makes that possible. It is monopoly and the capitalist state, that is, state-monopoly capitalism, that is responsible for inflation. This is not to say that Canada does not feel the effects of inflation from the outside, particularly the effects of the U.S. military program. Indeed, it is the expenditure of vast sums of money for non-productive purposes by U.S. imperialism and the NATO alliance that has stimulated capitalist-wide inflation. As the evidence of the socialist countries proves, there is no need for inflation, rising prices and deteriorating standards.

BEAT BACK EFFECTS OF INFLATION

If inflation is to be dealt with at its roots the workers and working people generally must challenge the political power of monopoly, limit and curb its power, and undertake a profound democratic transformation of society. This must include nationalization of the key industries and the banking and credit system. Until this is done working people will continue to be the victims of inflation with all of its evil consequences.

This does not mean that there is nothing to do now to protect the workers and all working people from the effects of inflationary price rises. Mass united action, mass pressures of all kinds — centered on the demands *for a roll back of prices, for price controls on food, fuel, housing and rents, for curbs on the profiteers, for substantial wage increases* — can play an important role in protecting the working people to some degree from the effects of inflation. What is required now is the creation of a powerful and united movement, a coalition of forces embracing the trade union movement, the farm movement, consumer organizations, all democratic organizations, the NDP and the Communist Party whose aim is the defence of the living standards of the working people and the incomes of the petty bourgeoisie.

This latter aspect of the question must be given close attention. It is important to advance demands that could in part protect the middle strata of the population from the effects of inflation and win them as allies in the struggle against monopoly exploitation. Past experience has shown, at great cost to the working-class movement, how reaction uses the petty bourgeoisie or sections of it against the working class and democracy. It is therefore necessary to include in the overall demands such questions as protection of small savings, insurance policies and the like.

The fight back against the monopoly offensive must also include demands for a vast low-cost, low-rental housing program; for decisive measures against the land speculators; for making housing a public utility; for reduced taxes on working people and an excess tax on profits and the elimination of federal and provincial sales taxes.

Inflation, rising prices, higher productivity rates, speed-up and rising profits, all these have stimulated widespread anger among workers, coupled with a determination to defend their standards and improve on them. The struggle between labor and capital has grown in intensity. All signs point to an upsurge of working-class struggle. Indeed, as we can see, strikes have become a daily occurrence in most parts of the country. As we know, one of these strikes forced us to change the date of our Convention. The focus of the struggle is centered on winning substantial wage increases plus cost of living escalator clauses. In addition, the workers are demanding a say over technological change and production, over questions related to speed-up, pensions, denticare and pharmacare. In Quebec, this struggle has been dramatized by the Common Front, which embraces the QFL, CNTU and teachers, in the May Day demonstrations in Montreal and other centers in Quebec.

The struggle for substantial wage increases and cost of living escalator clauses as well as wage openers is of particular importance, because it is the way the working class is striving to protect itself from the effects of inflation. All democratic forces must support it in this effort, as they should support the demand for opening up long-term contracts to protect living standards.

However, action on the economic front must be buttressed by effective political action. Every working man and woman can see how gains won in negotiations are being nullified by inflationary price rises, the consequence of monopoly rule and policies. Inflation won't be defeated by economic action alone. It requires a combination of militant, united economic action and united political action against monopoly policies to do the job.

WORKING-CLASS UNITY ESSENTIAL

New sections of workers have entered the struggle, the latest example being the teachers in Ontario. They have been conducting a determined struggle against compulsory arbitration, for the right to strike, the maintenance of proper educational standards and increased salaries.

The scope of this struggle can be seen in the march of 60,000 teachers on the Ontario Legislature and other government agencies throughout that province. This struggle was preceded by the general strike of public and para-public workers in Quebec, and by militant actions in B.C. and elsewhere.

Monopoly interests are striving in every possible way to take away the right to strike from the workers in public service and impose compulsory arbitration on them as a substitute for collective bargaining. It is a measure of the changing situation that white-collar workers and workers in the public service industry are showing themselves to be as militant as the blue-collar workers in their determination to defend their vital interests.

The upsurge of struggle shows that the working-class movement is entering a qualitatively higher stage of its development. The workers are demonstrating time and again their determination to protect and advance their standards, their jobs and trade union rights. The struggle between a reformist and revolutionary policy in the working-class movement is developing, as is the trend to unity to beat back the monopoly offensive. This trend to unity finds expression in joint action in negotiations and against the effects of the inflationary price spiral, in various forms of action against anti-union legislation in different parts of Canada, in actions in defence of Chilean democracy, in the battle for peace and detente.

In the course of all these actions the task of Communists and of the Communist Party is to help make the working class conscious of itself as a class, able to unite around itself all anti-monopoly, democratic and anti-imperialist forces.

Of particular significance is the growing demand for autonomy and independence of the trade union movement and for the establishment of a relationship of fraternal equals between the Canadian and U.S. trade union movements. This was shown in the recent vote among paper workers who overwhelmingly opted for the establishment of an independent and united trade union in Canada, and for the establishment of relationships of fraternal equality with their counterparts in the USA. Their decision demonstrates that, given an opportunity, the workers will increasingly move in that direction. Not least, it points up the fact that workers are increasingly aware that in this period of multi-national corporations, the Canadian trade union movement cannot limit itself to relationships with the U.S. trade union movement only, but must work for international co-operation, unity and solidarity on a world scale.

This was reflected by the CLC convention where the majority of the delegates showed in no uncertain terms their determination to establish full autonomy for every U.S.-

based union in Canada, on the road to a fully independent, sovereign and united trade-union movement. The stand on this issue was made possible by a wide coalition of forces embracing provincial federations of labor, Canadian unions and substantial forces among the international unions. It was this coalition of forces that fought through and secured the specific rights of the QFL in Quebec. It is a tribute to the majority of delegates at the CLC convention that they understood and supported measures that in their own way mirror the national rights of the French-Canadian people. It is a tribute to the French-Canadian delegates from Quebec that, in fighting for these rights, they emphasized that these will lead to a further strengthening of the unity of the trade union movement on an all-Canadian scale. Indeed, these measures taken together should help to strengthen the unity of the trade union movement both in Quebec and throughout the country.

The Communist Party and Communists in the trade union movement who fight consistently for a truly independent, sovereign and united trade union movement greet these developments which result in greater autonomy for U.S.-based unions in Canada. However, they are only first steps that must lead in the direction of a fully independent, sovereign and united trade union movement — based on the class struggle and actively working for detente and the unity of the trade union movement on a world scale. This would constitute a significant victory for the working-class and democratic movements and the cause of genuine Canadian independence.

What is evident is that the working class is more and more becoming the center of the struggle against monopoly. Working-class struggles are having wider political repercussions. The organized labor movement is exerting a steadily growing influence on the life of Canadian society. In French Canada the working class is increasingly coming to the fore in the battle in defence of national rights and the economic and social demands of the working people. The increased support given the proposal for the formation of a mass party of labor in Quebec shows a growing trend by workers away from support of the parties of monopoly and for a party through which they can advance their aims on the political front. The working-class struggle is increasingly influencing and stimulating various peoples' movements to battle monopoly control. In supporting all democratic movements directed against monopoly we are called upon to pay particular attention and give unstinting support to the movement against rising prices, the farmers' demand for guaranteed markets and incomes, the rising struggle of women for democratic rights, the Bill of Youth Rights advanced by the Young Communist League, the demands of the Indian and Innuit peoples.

In this connection I would like to focus particular attention on two fields: one, work among women; the other, work among young people.

WOMEN'S RIGHTS

The year 1975 has been declared International Women's Year by the United Nations. This is a fitting tribute to the ever increasing role of women in all fields of endeavor and to their selfless and devoted struggle for peace, democracy and socialism. To these struggles has been added the struggle to overcome inequality for women in the capitalist world and to win their full democratic rights. In this connection, narrow feminist positions are giving way·more and more to participation in the working-class struggle and to the struggle for social change. There is growing recognition that the active participation of women is vital to the struggle for democratic progress. Our Party, the working-class and democratic movements should use the occasion of International Women's Year to go all-out in the battle to win full democratic rights for women, the promotion of women to all levels of leadership, the strengthening of the democratic women's movements, and not least, the strengthening of the Communist Party by the addition of many, many more women to its ranks.

I would like to use this occasion to express deep appreciation to our women comrades who, under all conditions and situations, have given their all to the work of the Party, the various activities of the Party and to the cause of socialism. Our Party will take second place to none in its indefatigable struggle in defence of the democratic rights of women, the cause of peace and that of socialism — without which the "woman question" will not be fully solved.

YOUTH AND THE CLASS STRUGGLE

This is the year of the 18th Convention of the Young Communist League, an event which also marks the 50th Anniversary of the YCL. It is an important event not only for the YCL but for the entire Party and the working-class movement. This is so because in the YCL we see our best helper, our strongest and firmest supporter, a source from which to replenish the cadre of the Party and the working-class movement. Above all, this is so because in the YCL we see the best defender of the interests of the young generation. Part of this generation, after going through a process of development and experience, has begun to move away from the false concept of "young versus old" instead of class versus class. It has begun to move away from false concepts that Marxism-Leninism is obsolete and has been replaced by Marcuse, by the technocrats, and by the Maoists with their "theories" of the "world village" replacing the "world city".

Implicit in all these theories was the false concept that the working class had ceased to perform its historic mission of gravedigger of capitalism, had become bourgeoisified, and that the Communist Party had become a spent force. Life, which is a hard taskmaster, is destroying these false concepts. This is not to say that all illusions have been destroyed. Capitalism tends to create illusions and feed on them. However, what is true is that interest in Marxism is growing. An increasing number of students are becoming aware that only close ties with the working class and with the Communist Party can help give young people a truly revolutionary perspective. The growing interest in Marxism finds expression in the growth of the Communist Party and the Young Communist League. But we cannot be satisfied with whatever progress has been made. The Convention of the Young Communist League and the preparations for it must be the occasion for strengthening it in every way among working and farm youth and among high school students. At the same time it should be the occasion for strengthening the Party in the universities where some promising advances have been achieved.

THE STRUGGLE FOR CANADIAN INDEPENDENCE

If inflation mirrors the many-sided offensive by monopoly on living standards, the energy crisis mirrors the many-sided offensive of U.S. imperialism on Canadian independence.

Pressure for a continental energy policy has been stepped up, this time under the high-sounding name of "synchronization" of effort. Presumably what is meant is that Canada "synchronize" its energy with that of the U.S. and make it available to U.S. imperialism. This effort merges with pressures for having the Mackenzie Valley pipeline under U.S. control, with the longer-term aim of fastening its control over the Athabasca Tar Sands, the North and the Arctic where the last great Canadian reserves of oil and gas are to be found. U.S. imperialism would like nothing better than to achieve complete U.S. ownership and control over these reserves. Nor does it stop there. U.S. imperialism wants to gain control over all other sources of energy in Canada — uranium, hydro power, coal, water as well as the mineral wealth of Canada.

This bears out what John Foster Dulles said many years ago: "There are two ways of conquering a foreign nation. One is to gain control of its people by force of arms," — the world has been witness to this effort of U.S. imperialism in Vietnam, and in Indochina — "the other is to gain control of its economy by financial means." The Canadian people are witness to this effort in our own country.

Pressure on Canada for a continental energy policy has gone together with other types of pressure, such as the U.S. Trading with the Enemy Act. U.S. imperialism uses this act for two purposes — to pursue its policy of economic blockade against Cuba and other socialist countries, and to undermine the sovereignty of Canada by deciding with whom Canada is to trade. This interference was made possible and continues to be made possible by virtue of U.S. ownership and control over decisive sectors of the Canadian economy and by the refusal of Canadian governments to defend the real national, i.e., all-Canadian, interest.

In the particular case of the MLW Worthington Company which had a sale of $18 million with Cuba for 25 locomotives, a stratagem was worked out which enabled the sale to go through. However, U.S. ownership and control over decisive sectors of the Canadian economy have not been changed as a result. Nor has the Foreign Investment Bill checked this process. Indeed, there has been an increase in foreign take-overs and ownership despite the Bill.

To avoid a repetition of the locomotive affair, legislation must be adopted that makes it mandatory for all foreign-owned companies to abide by Canadian law. Where this is not done these companies should be taken over and operated as Crown Corporations.

PUBLIC OWNERSHIP IS THE ANSWER

Dissatisfaction with the present situation has been widespread and has reached out to new sections of the Canadian people. This is seen in the fact that 73 per cent of the Canadian people, according to a recent Gallup poll, expect the government to step in and maintain Canadian control over the economy. This may explain the declarations of the government about processing raw materials in Canada and for stronger measures to deal with the U.S. Trading with the Enemy Act.

It indicates also that the dominant sections of the capitalist class in Canada are increasingly conscious of the fact that they are sitting on a "gold mine", in light of diminishing non-renewable resources in the capitalist world. They want to make sure maximum profits accrue to them instead of to U.S. imperialism.

For the working-class and democratic forces, however, the question is not whether these resources should be taken over by this or that imperialist power, or by Canadian monopoly. These resources should be publicly owned because only in this way can the Canadian people benefit through industrialization, balanced economic development, employment and rising standards. Without public ownership there will be no genuine Canadian control. Without public ownership there will be no genuine Canadian independence.

What the situation calls for is a fully integrated all-Canadian energy policy based on making energy a public utility with uniform prices and developed to conform with Canadian needs and not with those of U.S. imperialism. The Canadian Petroleum Corporation shies away from this. Its aim appears to be to use public funds for exploration and development and tar sands research and then make the results available to the oil corporations. The Canadian people must reject this approach and press to make energy a public utility. In line with this the Mackenzie Valley pipeline and all other pipelines should be built as needed and be publicly owned, with due regard to the ecology and the rights of the native peoples. They should be built on all-Canadian routes to ensure security of supply. Electric power grids should likewise be built.

The demand for making energy a public utility is receiving ever wider support. The NDP, which tended to equivocate on this issue, has now joined in the demand to make energy a public utility, and for public ownership of the Mackenzie Valley pipeline. This is a welcome development.

Public ownership of all energy resources is an indispensable condition for independent economic development in Canada and for achieving genuine Canadian independence. It is the only way Canadian control can be assured with the benefits of such development accruing to the Canadian people, not to the profits of the multi-national corporations who are responsible for rising prices and for the energy crisis.

The energy crisis has deepened the constitutional crisis over questions of ownership of resources, their control and development. It is precisely provincial ownership of resources that the multi-national corporations have used as a cover through which to fasten control over and ownership of these resources. This must be changed. Federal-provincial agreements and consultations should ensure that these resources are used for the benefit of the Canadian people, not the multi-national corporations.

Such agreements should be combined with measures to ensure balanced economic development of the western provinces, using natural resources for industrialization and building industry near the source of these resources. This should be coupled with measures to equalize freight rates and win guaranteed markets and a guaranteed income for farmers.

CANADA NEEDS A NEW NATIONAL POLICY

Such a new national policy, or new Canadian policy, which the Communist Party has fought for over the years, is long overdue. It cannot and must not be delayed any longer. It should be directly linked to acceptance of energy as an all-Canadian and publicly-owned resource. It should be linked also to nationalization of the multi-national corporations in Canada.

An important part of such a new policy is the strengthening of Canada's ties with other countries. The ability to achieve genuine Canadian independence depends in large measure on the ability of Canada to diversify its economic, political and cultural relations with other countries. As we know, one-sided dependence on the USA in the economic and cultural fields and in every other way can be damaging to Canada's best interests. Our Party has always stood for Canada widening its relations with all countries in the economic, cultural and scientific fields. This is all the more urgent today when trade and jobs are so inextricably bound together. The widening and deepening of Canada's relationships with other countries, particularly with the socialist countries, would strengthen its position and role internationally, and make it a more effective force for peace.

The rising demand for a Canadian identity mirrors the widespread sentiment for Canadian independence throughout the country. For many years monopoly and the mass media generally inculcated an attitude of cosmopolitanism among the Canadian people. This fitted in with their general aims of integration with U.S. imperialism, and still does. All this had an effect on the late emergence of the demand for Canadian identity, a demand which in effect became part of the struggle against U.S. domination and for Canadian independence. This demand has become part of the struggle on the front of education and its content. It has become very much part of the struggle for Canadian culture. In fact, it finds expression in all aspects of life. The struggle for a Canadian identity is one of the general democratic tasks confronting the country, one with which our Party must identify, striving to give it a democratic content and relating it to the overall struggle for genuine Canadian independence and the right to self-determination.

DEFEND AND EXTEND DEMOCRACY

To the struggle for genuine Canadian independence and the right to self-determination the Communist Party must add the struggle in defence of the democratic rights, language, culture, language schools and means of information of the ethnic community. This should be linked to defence of the economic interests of the immigrants, their right to a job, to all democratic rights enjoyed by the Canadian people, and against the discrimination they suffer.

We need a self-critical attitude here. Our correct focus on the struggle for the right to self-determination and the struggle for genuine Canadian independence has often resulted in our overlooking an important part of the working class, in many cases the most exploited section, the most discriminated against, the most unorganized — the immigrant workers. Our struggle must combine two elements: defence of the immigrants as workers, defence of the immigrants as part of an ethnic community. An effective struggle on these two related fronts is a major task that the Party, the working class and democratic movement must undertake. This is an important link in the struggle for a Canadian identity and for democratization of all aspects of Canadian life.

Our Party must stand out as a foremost champion of the democratic rights of immigrant workers, and against all elements of discrimination exercised against them.

Concretely, this means going all-out in the battle to organize, in the struggle to smash the sweatshops, and in all-out efforts to win jobs and equal rights for immigrant men and women alike. This means helping to promote capable leaders and public spokesmen and women from among them.

The Party stands out no less as a foremost opponent of racism in whatever form it expresses itself. In focussing on racism and apartheid in other countries, our Party has sometimes tended to overlook the extent to which racism exists in Canada. The Western Guard in Toronto with its "white power" slogan, which it took over from Enoch Powell of Great Britain, shows how wrong it would be to ignore the need for resolute and united struggle against racism in Canada. The struggle against racism must engage the attention and action of the labor movement and all democratic forces throughout the country. The Communist Party has a special responsibility to see that this is done.

THE FEDERAL ELECTION

All these issues will find expression in the federal election campaign which is now upon us.

The election is being held on the background of a deepening crisis in the capitalist world that finds its expression in Canada also, with monopoly striving to place the burdens of the crisis on the backs of the working people. It is now clear that the central issue of the election will be inflation and rising prices. This issue, together with that of energy, will likely permeate the election campaign. The parties of monopoly may try to side-step the basic issues confronting the Canadian people. However, if one looks underneath the surface of these two issues it is not hard to see how they directly relate to the role of monopoly and the multi-national corporations and to measures of democratic control; to the problems of the farmers; to prices and living standards, excess profits, tax reform, and price controls on essentials such as food, fuel, housing and rent. Nor is it difficult to see the relationship of these questions to the questions of energy and natural resources and the ownership of these resources; to the questions of public ownership and all-Canadian economic development; of environment and ecology; the rights of the Indian and Innuit peoples; and of Canada's relations with other countries, the crucial battle for peace and detente, and the struggle for a new Canadian Constitution.

The growing crisis of capitalist policy, evident everywhere, is giving rise to a growing demand for change. Monopoly interests are striving to sidetrack this demand for change into reactionary channels. The more reactionary forces of this country — those tied to policies of continentalism in one form or another and who continue to opt for the sale of natural resources to other countries rather than processing them in Canada on the basis of industrialization, those who oppose detente and are tied in with the U.S. industrial-military complex — are striving to push politics to the right. These forces are out to impose wage and price controls and to build up a backlash against the working people around the themes of illegal strikes, abuse of unemployment insurance, excessive government spending. They aim to attack the limited gains won by working people. They oppose any extension of social security, including a guaranteed annual income. Their objective is to win a majority government dedicated to those reactionary aims.

There should be no underestimation of the right. Our Party must be in the forefront against the danger from the right, against reactionary policies and in defence of all democratic gains of the people.

In this election our main fire and that of the entire democratic movement should be directed against these more reactionary forces in political life, without foregoing in any way criticism of monopoly-capitalist policies in general, and of right-wing social democracy.

In doing so our aim should be the election to Parliament of an ever larger group of progressives pledged to carry out a program directed against monopoly and the multi-national corporations, and in the interests of the working people. Such a program must include public ownership of energy and of natural resources; the roll back of prices on food, fuel, housing and rent; as well as other essential measures that begin to curb the power of the monopolies. It must include policies placing Canada firmly on the path of detente and independence.

Our policy resolution points out that conditions do not yet exist to advance the slogan of the election of a progressive government centered around a democratic, anti-monopoly and anti-imperialist alliance. The election slogan we advance — "Vote Communist, elect a large progressive group to Parliament" — takes this into account. It corresponds with the present relationship of forces in the country and the interests of the working-class and democratic movements.

When we call for the election of a larger progressive group to Parliament we are opting for the return of minority government. The election of either a Liberal or Conservative majority government would be a step back, not forward. A minority government would in the present circumstances be the best outcome of the election, until conditions mature for the election of a NEW MAJORITY, one based on the working people and directed to chart a new course for Canada.

Our aim in this election is clear and has three aspects to it. Around the demand to CHART A NEW COURSE FOR CANADA we call upon the working-class and democratic forces to DEFEAT THE RIGHT, ELECT A LARGER PROGRESSIVE GROUP TO PARLIAMENT, INCLUDING COMMUNISTS, VOTE COMMUNIST.

Within this framework we will fight for every vote and at the same time work to build our Party, YCL and press.

The federal election campaign will be a good backdrop for the municipal elections this fall and winter. With a correct united front approach, we should make sure that, wherever

Party organizations exist, as many candidates as possible are nominated for the municipal elections, bearing in mind that breakthroughs are possible on this front.

ANTI-IMPERIALIST UNITY

We are part of a great movement throughout the world which battles imperialism on every front. Indeed, it is the unity achieved, as exemplified in the 1969 Conference of Communist and Workers' Parties, that helped to strengthen the battle for peace and compel imperialism to retreat. It shows that the essential analysis made five years ago has stood the test of time. Many changes have taken place in the world since 1969. New conditions, new developments, new tasks, are on the agenda, among them being the fight to make detente irreversible and at the same time create conditions for the forward advance of the peoples everywhere.

The events in Chile and elsewhere show that imperialism is determined to impede democratic advance. Unity of action of all anti-imperialist forces, of Communist and Workers' Parties, is therefore essential to the defeat of imperialism, and to the advance of peace, democracy, independence and socialism. This is why our Party supports the convening of another international consultative meeting of Communist and Workers' Parties.

We are entering a new political situation. This is a challenge for our Party that I am sure this Convention will pick up and act upon. We are confident that the Communist Party will fulfil its reponsibilities to its class and nation, to the unity of the international communist movement and the anti-imperialist forces, to the cause of peace, democracy, independence and socialism.

From the keynote address, 22nd Convention,
Communist Party of Canada.
May 18-20, 1974.

XV

Positive changes in the world and new possibilities in the world revolutionary struggle

The changes coming about in the world before our eyes are all interconnected and condition each other and their totality constitutes an important *objective factor* in international politics today. But they are not alike in character, fundamental causes or international impact. Events and phenomena that add up to detente take place in many parts of the world and involve the masses, governments, social alignments and whole classes.

A mere six years ago the International Meeting of Communist and Workers' Parties set the task of imposing peaceful co-existence on the imperialist powers. Great strides have been made toward accomplishment of this task as a result of the Peace Program of the CPSU and the positive foreign policy of the Soviet Union and the other countries of the socialist community supported by fraternal Marxist-Leninist parties, and due to the efforts of the international working class and the forces of national liberation, peace and democracy.

The past years have seen the adoption of important general declarations and the conclusion of bilateral agreements between the Soviet Union and the United States, Britain, Canada, France, the FRG and Italy, between many socialist and capitalist countries. These documents establish the principles of peaceful co-existence in this nuclear age. They mark a highly important change for the better, for it was not so long ago that many imperialist countries refused to recognize peaceful co-existence as the rule of international relations.

For decades the finest minds of mankind have longed to stop the arms race. All sorts of plans to this end were proposed before both world wars. But it is only today that the removal of the menace of war and the stopping of the arms race have become realistic objectives.

Documents signed by Soviet and United States leaders, first of all the treaty permanently limiting anti-missile defence systems and the provisional agreement on certain measures to limit strategic offensive weapons, show that not even the most complicated disarmament problems are beyond solution. The 1974 meeting at Vladivostok between L.I. Brezhnev and President Ford led to an important agreement regarding the need to conclude a comprehensive and long-term treaty limiting strategic offensive weapons. These and other steps are unquestionable evidence of progress toward detente.

Greater co-operation between socialist and capitalist countries reduces the danger of an armed conflict between the two world systems. The objective necessities of the 70's are to remove the remnants of the cold war; to impart a tangible content to the agreements that have been signed; to carry forward a political dialogue between governments; to expand economic, scientific, technological and cultural contacts and co-operation; and to develop joint efforts in solving environmental problems, combatting diseases, exploring the atom, outer space, the ocean. Detente, which reveals more and more new facets, is *determining the development of international relations on the European continent and throughout the world.*

Detente is becoming the main road that mankind follows in advancing from cold war to a democratic, just and durable peace. This trend is natural as far as the socialist countries are concerned; their system is peace-loving by nature, demonstrating its superiority through constructive labor. As for the rulers of the imperialist world, they are now compelled to accept detente.

This brings us to what we consider the main positive change in the world, the *new alignment of world forces* due to the strengthened economic and defence positions of the Soviet Union and other members of the socialist community, and the increased influence of the world communist movement and the forces of peace, democracy and social progress. It is this that provides the basis for making the present processes of detente irreversible, and for extending them to include military detente.

Even those who clearly do not like the new alignment of forces are compelled to reckon with it. Paul Nietze, former U.S. Deputy Secretary of Defence and Secretary of the Navy, writes that the Soviet Union and other socialist countries "have reason for their stated belief that the net correlation of forces has been changed and is changing in their favor."* Of course, admissions of this nature do not mean that imperialism has resigned itself to its loss of superiority, which it tries to restore. Programs aimed at remedying its situation are put forward. Their purpose is to remove friction in the Western alliance, solve economic and monetary problems of the "free world", and so on. However, even their authors show little optimism about the possibility of putting them into practice. The growing social difficulties of a society in which exploitation, inflation, unemployment and recession are the rule, and increasing inter-imperialist antagonisms are together eroding the capitalist system more than ever.

It is not surprising that in these circumstances the governments and business sectors of bourgeois countries find it harder and harder to reject mutually advantageous economic relations with socialist countries. The economic stability of these countries makes economic relations with them attractive for capitalist companies. Broader trade with the socialist world opens possibilities for greater industrial and business activity in the capitalist countries, thus providing more jobs.

The economic crisis affecting the imperialist states today coincides with the deterioration of their relations with developing countries. The strengthening positions of these

*Foreign Policy, No. 17, Winter 1974-75, p. 147.

countries, especially those that not only have oil but use it as a weapon in their struggle for a new economic order based on equal relations, are a serious factor weakening imperialism and reducing its sphere of influence. The objective character of the new standing of the developing countries on the international scene helps to advance the alignment of forces in favor of peace, democracy, national independence and social progress.

The process of deepening detente will evidently continue for a considerable period of contemporary history. The Communists take this into account in their strategy and tactics. They realize the complexity of this process, which does not proceed smoothly, involving two opposing trends — the growing trend toward detente and the still remaining trend toward going back to cold war and direct military confrontation.

Masses of people are today increasingly aware of the contradictions within the bourgeoisie, between the exponents of realistic views on foreign policy and the advocates of militarist concepts. Imperialist propaganda allegations about the indifference of the "lower" classes to international issues are often manoeuvres of reactionary forces aimed at diverting public attention from the acts of aggression they are planning and, still more often, are attempts to deny the people any influence on foreign policy decisions.

Yet the activity and influence of the public in the sphere of international relations have lately grown to an unprecedented extent. Communist and Workers' Parties have done more than others to stimulate the people's interest in problems of war and peace and in international policies in general. This is very important because at a time when the threat of a nuclear war has not yet been fully extinguished, the life of the people often depends on how foreign-policy problems are solved. It is essential, therefore, to win the masses in capitalist countries for a foreign policy of peace. In carrying out this task, we are guided by the Communist philosophy of peace, which is based on analysis of the real alignment of the forces of war and peace. Its lofty purpose is to find a dependable way to detente, security and co-operation in a complicated world, to prevent disaster.

Communists, including those of Canada, expose the plots of bellicose groups of state-monopoly capitalism. In taking sober stock of progress toward international detente, we do not close our eyes to the fact that it has yet to stop the world arms race, which swallows about $250,000 million a year.* It may well be that in view of the deepened imperialist crisis certain reactionary quarters will try to induce their governments to seek a way out through aggressive policies and sabre-rattling. The threats against Arab countries of the Middle East and other countries made by top U.S. leaders showed the importance of vigilance. It is no secret that in view of the new alignment of world forces these threats failed. They were decisively rebuffed by the countries against whom they were directed, and by all peace-loving countries. In the United States itself, the majority of the population declared against the dispatch of U.S. forces to the Middle East, as a recent poll revealed.

But while imperialism has been weakened and its more aggressive groups find themselves in increasing isolation, it is still a strong, cunning and dangerous enemy. The Communists of Canada are fighting against U.S. imperialism, which interferes in the sovereign affairs of Canada, pressures Canada to step up the arms race and makes threats with regard to its natural resources and energy.

The U.S. imperialists are trying to oppose the tendency to "Canadianization" of our economy; they seek to compel Canada to play the servile role of an instrument of the Pentagon. U.S. interference in the sovereign affairs of Canada is stimulating and widening anti-imperialist sentiment in our country. And this sentiment, in turn, merges with a widening struggle against Canadian monopoly, against multi-national corporations, and in support for measures which would strengthen the real independence of the country through their nationalization.

We do not for one day relax our struggle against U.S. imperialism or our exposure of the dangerous plans of its

*Communist Viewpoint, Vol. 7, No. 1, Jan.-Feb. 1975, p. 13.

reactionary groups. It has become a firm tradition with Canadian Communists to exchange experience in this field with fraternal parties, who also have no illusions about imperialism as a whole or its most powerful contingent, U.S. imperialism.

One is surprised, therefore, by assertions that "a new variety of beautification of U.S. imperialism" has appeared lately in the world communist movement, and that the ability of U.S. imperialism to impose political, military and economic diktat on its "medium" and "small" partners, as well as on some developing countries, is discounted.

We Marxist-Leninists of Canada consider such assertions to be groundless. The Communists have never beautified, and they do not today beautify U.S. imperialism. They are the first to call for vigilance, taking into account that the United States still commands immense military and economic strength that could cause serious misfortunes for the peoples.

At the same time the Communists see the world situation in its entirety: that the socialist countries' united power curbs the urge for aggression shown by the most rabid U.S. reactionaries, and that the growing struggle of the working-class and other democratic forces in capitalist countries increasingly restricts Washington's opportunities to impose its will on even its allies and partners. Anyone who does not see this cannot be considered a realist.

Extremes are always open to question. It is hardly correct to regard U.S. imperialism as absolutely omnipotent, or the imperialism of other countries, for example of Canada, as a "little boy in short pants" running errands for Uncle Sam. This view may cause one to fail to see the sameness of the class nature of both domestic and U.S. monopolies, to lessen blows at the former while concentrating on the latter. Such a tactic is bound to benefit the national big bourgeoisie and strengthen its positions to the working people's detriment.

The Communists of Canada are engaged in struggle against Canadian imperialism, U.S. imperialism, against world imperialism. We maintain that whatever the disguises it uses, imperialism everywhere remains aggressive and reactionary. But we realize that at a time of growing internal political, social and economic difficulties, with inter-imperialist contradictions sharpening and the capitalist strategy in regard to the Third World miscarrying, bourgeois governments cannot now bring themselves to attempt direct attacks against the socialist community and are becoming more receptive to the socialist countries' realistic proposals.

Take, for example, the Canadian government. During the 1974 federal election campaign Prime Minister Trudeau declared repeatedly for detente. Canada is taking part in the Conference on Security and Co-operation in Europe, although we think our government could play a more constructive role in its work.

It is also true that the Western powers, while refraining from frontal attacks on the policy of detente, try to check it. There is no other way of describing the delaying tactics that have marked the second phase of the European Conference. Under pressure from reactionary groups in their countries, the delegations of some Western powers insisted, in particular, on the socialist countries making concessions in the ideological field as the price of detente, specifically, on opening the frontiers of sovereign states to the invasion of bourgeois views, standards and habits.

Bourgeois apologists put forward explicit and implicit, unceremonious and "polite" proposals for an end to the ideological struggle as a prerequisite of peaceful co-existence. The sharp contrast between the stable growth of the socialist economy and economic crisis in the capitalist countries, the moral superiority of socialism and the victorious advance of scientific communism compel the monopoly bourgeoisie to intensify ideological subversion against the Soviet Union and other socialist countries, against Communist and Workers' Parties. The evident purpose of our enemies is to impose the bourgeois concept of life on the forces championing social progress and to disarm them ideologically and theoretically. Hence the importance of the Communists collectively evolving the strategy and tactics of their ideological offensive, to defeat the efforts of anti-communist and anti-Soviet forces.

The ideological struggle between the two systems will inevitably go on. Even bourgeois scholars do not deny the increasing role of ideology in international relations. It is therefore absolutely wrong to think that ideological principles can be a matter for bargaining or that the socialist countries would renounce the principles of Marxism-Leninism in exchange for political and economic concessions.

Reactionary resistance to peace and international detente is backed by the Maoists, who strive for confrontation and greater international tension, because if the cold war were revived it would be easier for them to camouflage their hegemonic policy and their absurd territorial claims against virtually all neighboring countries. Peking's recent forecasts of an "inevitable war" between the Soviet Union and the United States smack of the worst kind of warmongering and give away their authors' intentions.

Genuine revolutionaries have never wanted and never can want war, because war means the greatest misfortunes for the masses and destroys the productive forces. "War is our enemy," the Communists stress. "From now on, let countries with different social systems demonstrate their advantages, not on the battlefield, but in competition for progress and a higher standard of living for the people."

This thesis was contained in the 1957 Peace Manifesto, and the Communist Party of China was one of its signatories. However, the Maoists' present stance, prompted by their undisguised expectation of a "big war" between the two great powers, coincides with the interests of the most reactionary imperialist quarters, which cling to plans for aggression against socialism and its bulwark, the Soviet Union.

The Marxist-Leninist proposition that positive changes in the world, primarily detente, create new opportunities to expand the struggle for social change, is appreciated and supported by broad masses of the people, who are uniting against monopoly and reaction. The foreign policy of individual countries and of whole alliances is an expression and form of class struggle on the international scene. Shifts in international relations to an ever greater degree influence internal developments just as the latter affect the international climate. The struggle for progressive social change, an inalienable part of the daily life of capitalist society, is shaped by the interaction of internal and external conditions.

Peace and detente strengthen the positions of all patriots fighting for an independent Canadian foreign policy; they favor the working-class and the democratic movements. Detente, the turn from cold war and confrontation to negotiation, the reduction of the number of conflict situations that could erupt into local wars, are processes that make it possible to strengthen Canadian control over industry, the economy, natural resources and energy. They enable Canada to extricate itself from the U.S. embrace which increases the economic crisis, inflation and unemployment in Canada and undermines its sovereignty.

Changes in a country's foreign policy, such as opting out of the NATO military structure or simply reducing participation in it or attempting to revise unfavorable agreements with the United States produce repercussions. They stimulate anti-war sentiments and prompt the expansion of the coalition of forces fighting for the immediate demands of society.

Detente creates conditions for accelerating the tempo of social progress. And there are graphic examples of this. About the middle of 1973, fears were voiced in certain quarters, including within the communist movement, that detente would hinder the struggle against imperialism, restrain revolutionary change and result in a world sociopolitical status quo. Less than two years have passed, a very brief historical period. But what do we have on the sociopolitical scene? Substantial changes in Portugal and Greece, where the peoples have cast off the chains of fascist regimes; advances along the road to freedom in Mozambique and Angola, where full independence is soon to be proclaimed; emergence of the state of Guinea-Bissau; successes of the liberation movements in Cambodia, Oman, Rhodesia and

Namibia; powerful blows against the apartheid system in South Africa; an unprecedented upsurge of the democratic movement in Spain. Do all these amount to a socio-political status quo?

At the same time, we are very conscious of reversals. The sorrow and anger bred by the temporary defeat of the revolution in Chile are alive in our hearts. But even such retreats of the revolution have not made imperialism's overall positions any better, all the more so because all fighters for revolutionary change are drawing the necessary conclusions with regard to the plottings of imperialism and local reaction.

The exposure of the role of the CIA and multi-national monopolies in the overthrow of the Allende government hinders imperialism's export of counter-revolution. It is significant that the appointment of Nathaniel Davis — the U.S. Ambassador in Chile at the time when Washington's special services were organizing the Allende overthrow — as a U.S. assistant secretary of state for African affairs was unanimously denounced by the 43 members of the Organization of African Unity. This is testimony of the growing vigilance of peoples and governments.

Imperialism and reaction exploited world tensions to tighten their grip over the masses at home, interfere in civil wars and revolutionary actions abroad, and foster neo-colonialism, this last in the hope of perpetuating their control over the raw material resources of the former colonial peoples.

The changes in the political climate bred by detente make it possible for revolutionary forces to seek and find new ways and means of winning socio-political positions from which to successfully attack monopoly capital. The swiftness and apparent suddenness of the events in Portugal and Greece has alerted imperialist strategists, who continue to eye these countries with apprehension, evidently realizing that the events there were favored and accelerated by international detente as well as by Communist efforts in those countries.

Monopoly suffers defeats in the face of new worker demands. Today the accent is on anti-monopoly, general democratic demands: nationalization in the interests of the working people, curbing the power of banks and corporations, measures to combat unemployment and inflation, worker participation in factory management, the comprehensive development of backward regions. The greater pressure of the working class and its parties in the political, economic and cultural fields, long the preserves of the ruling classes, will continue and expand.

The experiences of Canada and other countries where the positions of monopoly remain very strong, the struggle for basic democratic reforms capable of opening the road to fundamental socio-economic changes and socialism have advanced the unity of anti-imperialist action. Stressing the difference between reforms and reformism, Lenin wrote: "We pursue an independent policy and put forward *only* such reforms as are *undoubtedly* favorable to the interests of the revolutionary struggle, that *undoubtedly* enhance the independence, class-consciousness and fighting efficiency of the proletariat. Only by such tactics and reforms from above, which are always half-hearted, always hypocritical and always conceal some bourgeois or police snare, be made *innocuous*" (*Coll. Works*, Vol. 11, p. 71).

During the election campaigns of the last few years in Canada and other capitalist countries, Communist and Workers' Parties, often jointly with the Socialists, put forward comprehensive programs of reforms that met with a positive response from the people. In their drive for radical change the working class and its allies accumulate experience in political struggle. Looking back over the last few years, we see that they have achieved great new successes in mastering many methods to carry out the dual task bequeathed us by Lenin: to *know how* to fight imperialism, to *know how* to help revolutionary development and the emergence of socialism. (See *Coll. Works*, Vol. 27, p. 65.)

The imperialists are worried by the growth of anti-monopoly sentiment and the new upsurge of class struggle. Nowadays it is not the outworn, so-called "threat of Soviet aggression" that is seen as endangering the security of the "free world" or stability of "Western democracy", but the fact that the working people, the trade unions have "got out of hand" and lost their sense of social loyalty to bourgeois society.

That is why imperialist ideologists have been floating the idea of a summit conference of capitalist countries to discuss the social instabilities of bourgeois society and find a way out of them. One of the exponents of the idea is the notorious anti-communist Zbigniew Brzesinski. If steps are not taken to strengthen "democratic institutions" and reduce internal contradictions, he declares, the Communists are "bound to step in". In fact, fear of the mounting strength and influence of the organized communist movement is the common motive of the most diverse bourgeois political parties, seeking joint action and unhesitatingly discarding the very principles they once proclaimed as sacred. To this trend in the imperialist, anti-communist camp the working class and all democratic forces must respond with the unity and cohesion of their own ranks.

More than ever before it is essential to forge the unity of all anti-monopoly forces within each capitalist country, and of all anti-imperialist forces on an international scale. Of tremendous importance in achieving these objectives is the formulation of correct, rallying slogans and well-thought-out, clear programmatic declarations. The speed of events makes it incumbent on a number of Communist and Workers' Parties to formulate bolder tactical tasks. Of course, every party decides its tactics, strategy and slogans for itself, but the present new situation, of which detente has become the main characteristic, makes it necessary for Communists to pool their efforts to formulate a scientifically based *theoretical and action platform* of the working people for peace, security, co-operation and social progress. The new favorable conditions must be utilized in the anti-monopoly struggle and this, of course, requires revolutionary experience and ability.

In this connection I would like to state my impressions of a recent proposal for West Europe's way out of the present economic crisis. The proposed plan centers on "reconstructing" the "present low-ceiling capitalist edifice in

Europe" which would "enable a progressive way out of the crisis." The "rebuilt Europe" is designed to perform a specific role, to oppose hegemony of any kind. Significantly, however, in their struggle against "North American hegemony" the authors of this plan would push Europe into a special role of its own and seek a special relationship between Europe and the Third World. As far back as 1916, Lenin criticized the "United States of Europe" slogan and warned working-class parties of the dangers of "European chauvinism". To accept such a slogan today would mean to succumb to the virus of chauvinism, disregard the revolutionary energy and potential of the fighters for social progress in all continents, and objectively play into the hands of the enemies of the working class, promoting division rather than unity among anti-monopoly and anti-imperialist forces.

It is an unshakeable rule for Communist and Workers' Parties to check their slogans and tactics against the changing situation. One of those slogans — the fight for peace — is especially important and relevant. It continues to rally people to the fight for democracy and socialism, against reaction and aggressive plans. Its correctness and relevance were reaffirmed by the choice of topic of the Conference of European Communist and Workers' Parties to be held this year in the GDR: "The Fight for Peace, Security, Co-operation and Social Progress in Europe".

The conference will be a major landmark in the peoples' fight for peace, not only in Europe but in other continents as well. It will play an important part in rallying the broad masses to the movement to make international detente irreversible. An essential condition for this is ever greater unity of action of Communist and Workers' Parties on the basis of the principles of Marxism-Leninism and proletarian internationalism.

It is significant that the European Conference of Communist and Workers' Parties will be held in the GDR. The year 1975 is the 30th anniversary of the victory over German fascism. A consequence of that historical accomplishment was the emergence of socialism as a world system of states whose peoples of labor, masters of their lives, look confidently toward the future. The prestige of socialism has risen immeasurably with the formation in the socialist community of the new type of relations between peoples and states based on the principles of proletarian, socialist internationalism, on solidarity, fraternal mutual assistance and mutual support.

There is no denying the importance and significance of regional conferences of Communist and Workers' Parties, of bilateral and multilateral meetings. Greater cohesion in our ranks is an important factor in further tipping the balance of forces in favor of peace, national liberation, democracy and socialism. The Communist Party of Canada, as pointed out at its last convention in May 1974, favors the holding of an international communist conference. It could, we think, discuss the problems generated by international developments since 1969, when the last world forum of Marxist-Leninists was held.

The international meetings of Communist and Workers' Parties held in the 1950's and 1960's were of historical significance for mankind's struggle for peace and social progress. In the 1970's the processes of world development are accelerating and many problems linked with it are becoming more and more complicated. The collective thought of Marxist-Leninist parties, permeated with confidence in the future, should illumine the road of revolutionary struggle and the building of a new life by the peoples. It is the Communists' international duty to consolidate the initiative now in the hands of the fighters for peace, security, detente and social progress, and they will perform it.

World Marxist Review,
June, 1975.

XVI

Canada in a changing world

Summary of a decade of working-class and democratic struggle

In the period of 1966 to 1976 considerable changes have taken place in the world. These find their most vivid expression in two interrelated processes — the growing strength of the socialist countries and the deepening of the general crisis of capitalism. The influence of socialism is growing while the influence of imperialism is declining. These changes in world relationships have had and continue to have a considerable impact on Canada and on the working-class and democratic movements.

Let us look at some of these changes.

The most decisive changes are reflected in the dynamic growth and development of socialism. Despite some temporary difficulties here and there, the general trend of development of socialism has been upward. The stage is being reached when the economic strength of the socialist countries will overtake and surpass that of the imperialist states.

In 1974 the volume of industrial output in the USSR amounted to nearly 80 per cent of that in the USA. The rapid tempo of growth can be seen in the fact that in 1950 Soviet industrial production was less than 30 per cent of U.S. production! Today, the Soviet Union has already surpassed the USA in production of steel, oil, coal, cement, mineral fertilizers, tractors, grain combine-harvesters, diesel and electric locomotives, leather footwear, cotton, woollen fabrics, sugar, milk and butter. And when the current 10th Five-

Year Plan is completed, Soviet industry will equal U.S. industry in volume of production.

As for the socialist community, it has become the most dynamic force in the world economy. Over the past five years the annual average rate of growth of the socialist community has been four times that of the advanced capitalist states. In 1975 alone, industrial output of the socialist countries was more than double that of the European Common Market. The faster pace of growth of the socialist countries is not a flash in the pan for this or that year. It is a consistent trend, seen in the fact that between 1950 and 1975 the growth rate of the socialist countries was 9.6 per cent as against 4.6 per cent for the capitalist countries.

In face of the destruction of the war and the need to undertake vast postwar reconstruction — including the necessity of breaking the atom bomb monopoly of U.S. imperialism, which the USSR accomplished — these advances are nothing short of miraculous. They show what a socialist system can do to develop the productive forces of society, overcome backwardness, and advance within a limited historical period of time to the level of U.S. production. Both in theory and in practice socialism is showing itself to be vastly superior to capitalism in its ability to solve the basic problems of society while systematically raising the living standards of its people and extending socialist democracy.

Economic strength, demonstrated in the continuing and planned growth of the economy, has been buttressed by political and military strength, thereby enabling the Soviet Union and the socialist countries to play an ever more decisive role in world affairs and in the struggle for peace, relaxation of international tensions and in support of the peoples striving for freedom and independence.

The almost complete elimination of colonialism has proceeded side by side with the dynamic upsurge of the USSR and other socialist countries. This was evidenced most recently in the achievement of independence for Mozambique, Guinea-Bissau and Angola. This process is intertwined with the increasing bankruptcy of the policy of neo-colonialism pursued by imperialism. The disintegration of the colonial system of imperialism enabled former colonies to achieve political independence and has helped create conditions for the winning of economic equality as well.

The demand for the establishment of a new international economic order meeting the interests of the peoples reflects this as it reflects at the same time the changing balance of forces in the world, the desire of the peoples of the newly-liberated and underdeveloped countries to become masters in their own house, to own and develop their raw material resources in their own interests. They want equality in economic relations. This gives a new quality, a new dimension to the struggle against imperialism on an international scale. Indeed it is one of the main features of the deepening of the general crisis of capitalism today, and will likely be a major factor in world politics for some time to come.

These developments have made possible a new balance of forces in the United Nations and in international life generally. The majorities the U.S. used to muster in the UN are a thing of the past. Today an alliance of anti-imperialist forces constitutes the majority in the United Nations. This has led to a further growth of progressive trends in world politics and in the balance of forces.

The dynamic upsurge of socialism, the collapse of colonialism, the increasingly strengthened positions of the working-class and other democratic forces in the capitalist world, point up the changing balance of forces in the world.

The change in the balance of forces makes it possible to say that imperialism can now no longer dominate the world. This is the essential change which opens up new prospects of advance in the struggle for peace, democracy and socialism.

It is this change which is the reason for detente. Detente has not resulted simply from good diplomacy. Detente has been achieved because imperialism has had to recognize that the achievements of the socialist system are indestructible and unshakeable, that the socialist system is here to stay.

The struggle against detente by the forces of reaction reveals the nature of the crisis of imperialism. When all is said and done, what it reflects is the fear among the reactionary forces of capitalism — their fear of peace, of peaceful competition with socialism. The various efforts to bring back the cold war illustrate this. They range from the cry that detente aids only the Soviet Union and socialism, to the demand that concessions be made by the Soviet Union as a precondition for detente. These efforts all confirm the one fact — imperialism chokes on peace while socialism thrives on peace.

Of course it is not true to say that detente favors socialism only. Of course it favors it, demonstrating that in conditions of peace the Soviet Union and the other socialist countries can concentrate all their powers on peaceful construction. But detente at the same time favors peace and the peaceful settlement of differences through negotiations, and this is in the interests of all peoples.

This is why the cry advanced today by reaction in the U.S. that the USA must be number one militarily in the world is extremely dangerous. It suggests that a policy of "peace through strength", that is, an arms race, is the road to real peace. This is, of course, nonsense. For this was exactly the road U.S. imperialism took after the Second World War that led it into a cul-de-sac. After all, the USA was number one militarily for a whole period following the war. It tried to use that situation to force its will on the world through atom diplomacy, a policy of containment, a war of aggression against the peoples of Vietnam and Indochina, as well as against other peoples. The policy that the USA must be number one militarily has led to no successes for U.S. imperialism. On the contrary, it has brought it humiliating defeats.

Mr. Kissinger has learned some of the lessons of this misadventure, to use a kind term. In a March 22, 1976 speech at Dallas, Texas, on foreign policy and national security, he stated:

"No responsible leader should encourage the illusion that America can ever again recapture the strategic superiority of the early postwar period. In the 1940's we had a nuclear monopoly. In the 1950's and early 1960's we had an overwhelming preponderance. As late as the Cuban missile crisis of 1962 the Soviet Union possessed less than 100 strategic systems while we had thousands.

But today, when each side has thousands of launchers and many more warheads, a decisive or politically significant margin of superiority is out of reach. ... No net advantage can be long preserved by either side."

Clearly peace cannot be achieved through military strength or through being number one militarily. Peace can only be achieved through detente and disarmament based on equality of security. In today's world there is no alternative to nuclear war other than peace and peaceful co-existence. This is the starting point for any realistic foreign policy today.

Because this is so there is need to overcome opposition to detente by all those reactionary forces that still wield a considerable influence in the capitalist world. To return to the cold war means to return to a policy of confrontation and possible hot war. This is why attitudes to detente constitute a dividing line in world politics today.

While detente has to do directly with state relations, it also influences class relations. Detente has opened up new prospects in the fight for social progress, exercising a growing favorable influence on the class struggle. It pushes aside impediments thrown up by the cold war, impediments calculated to freeze the status quo. Detente creates better conditions for advancing the struggle for working-class and democratic unity against monopoly and the multi-national corporations. It creates more favorable conditions to advance the fight for Canadian independence, for trade with the socialist countries and away from one-sided dependence on the USA.

A further profound feature of the changing world is the deepening of the general crisis of capitalism. This finds its reflection in the growing contradictions between imperialism and the newly-liberated and underdeveloped countries, in the crises of raw materials and energy, in the monetary crisis, with all of which capitalism's general crisis is bound up. These in turn have a bearing on the course and development of the economic crisis which has afflicted the capitalist world.

The pretence that capitalism has finally found a cure to

economic crisis — that capitalism has licked unemployment and inflation and overcome economic and political instability — has been rudely shattered by the reality of a continuing and prolonged economic crisis, and by a "recovery" that is accompanied by mass unemployment.

It is therefore not so easy these days for the apologists of capitalism to deny the crisis afflicting capitalism. The *International Herald Tribune* was compelled to admit there is a crisis in the industrialized nations. In a rather lengthy editorial entitled "A Dual Crisis" it went on to say "that it was doubtless with great pleasure that Premier Kosygin delivered his address at the Congress (25th CPSU Congress. *Ed.*) in Moscow outlining the progress that the Soviet Union had made industrially, and contrasting it with the 'crisis of capitalism' that afflicts the West. Nor can it be denied that the industrialized nations are in a crisis although it is rather hard to accept Mr. Kosygin's strictures on the militarization of the capitalist economy."

However, in order to soften the impact of the admission the same editorial went on to say that "what may be more significant was what the Premier did not say about the crisis of Communism."

Before dealing with this "crisis" it is important to note two things. The media are compelled to admit there is a crisis in capitalism but no crisis in the Soviet Union. This is a rather important admission to make, the significance of which may not be fully understood by the selfsame media. In the past the media kept on telling the people about a "crisis of socialism". They are now forced to move away from such fables. In the past they wrote about the strength and permanence of capitalism. Now they are compelled to admit it is in crisis.

It is in this context that one has to see the "crisis of Communism". What the apologists of capitalism are here referring to are the views advanced by some Communist Parties about their independence. This, according to them, is an expression of the "crisis of Communism".

But the facts belie their contention. All Communist and Workers' Parties are independent and sovereign. That was established a long time ago. The real question at issue is a correct understanding and application of proletarian internationalism.

Proletarian internationalism is not only a question of international solidarity. Proletarian internationalism is above all agreement on the general laws of revolutionary change. These have to do with the relationship of the general and universal to the national and the specific. The creative approach to the specific of one's own country is one thing. This needs to be developed to the maximum, but not by foregoing general and universal principles that are valid for all countries aspiring to achieve and build a socialist system of society.

On the basis of exchanges of views, negative tendencies which can do great harm to the cause of the revolution can undoubtedly be overcome, and the process of unity given a new impetus.

There is, therefore, no "dual crisis" — of capitalism and of communism. There is only the deepening general crisis of capitalism.

The confusion and pessimism afflicting the capitalist world are underlined by the fact that the present economic crisis is the first capitalist-wide crisis in the postwar period, and the deepest. Unemployment of 15 million in the advanced capitalist countries contrasts vividly with shortages of labor in the socialist world. Inflation which continues at high levels in the capitalist world stands in marked contrast to stable prices of essential goods, rents and housing in the socialist world. While in the capitalist world attacks mount on health services, on education and pensions, in the socialist countries pensions and health services are non-contributory, and stipends are made available to students in higher educational establishments.

It should be noted that over the past decade unemployment has been a chronic feature of contemporary life in Canada. It has not only become chronic but risen with every passing year. In 1967 there were 315,000 unemployed in Canada; in 1974 there were 520,000. In 1975 there were close to 800,000 unemployed in Canada; in 1976 unemployment may rise again.

What is apparent is that irrespective of the movement of the economic cycle, full employment has gone by the board.

The dignity of the individual in the socialist world, his or her security, contrasts sharply with spreading and worsening poverty in the capitalist world. Indeed in Canada, despite the expenditure of billions of dollars these last 20 years no change in income has taken place in favor of the working people. The poor remain poor and the rich become richer. Statistics Canada figures show that the lowest 20 per cent of the population received only four per cent of the total income in 1974, a decline from about 4.3 per cent in the late 1960's. On the other hand the top 20 per cent received 42.4 per cent of total income.

Poverty, inflation, unemployment, inequality — these are all built into the capitalist system. To eliminate them will require more than tokenism. It will require a real attack on monopoly power and the multi-national corporations, the source of these evils.

Some conclusions can be drawn from the growing crisis of capitalism.

The crisis has undermined the theory of "planned capitalism" which tried to depict government regulation of the economy in the interests of monopoly as being in the interests of the people. Events have clearly demonstrated that attempts at state regulation of the economy under state-monopoly capitalism cannot ensure a planned economic development of society as a whole. This is so because capitalist ownership and exploitation of wage labor remain the basis of production.

The Keynesian theories of a regulated capitalism, of a "new capitalism", the "affluent society", the "welfare state", have all ended up on the rubbish heap of history.

Despite the efforts of imperialism to adapt to new conditions and its striving to mitigate the most acute contradictions of capitalist society, it is unable to do so. What is increasingly apparent is the inability of imperialism to contend with the productive forces it has developed. The sharpened contradiction between productive forces and production relations emphasizes anew the inevitability of the collapse of capitalism.

Events in Canada are increasingly moving in a direction where the capitalist system is being questioned and challenged by more and more people. This brings home the truth that Canada is not separated from the tremendous changes presently underway in the world. The fact is that the growing strength of socialism and changes in the balance of forces in the world are also helping to change the balance of forces in Canada in favor of the working-class and democratic movements.

This is seen in the vigorous way the working class is fighting the crisis policies of monopoly and its government.

In seeking a way out of the crisis, monopoly tries to unload the burden on the backs of the working people. The wage restraint program of the Trudeau government is an expression of this.

Sections of monopoly, in light of the bankruptcy of Keynesian economics, are looking for new gods, new solutions to the crisis. Galbraith and Rostow of the USA have become apostles of "New Economics". The sum total of these "new" economics is the claim that *big business* and *big labor* are jointly responsible for the inflation and recession that afflict the capitalist world today. The solution to the crisis offered by these gentlemen is that controls be established over both big business and labor through greater measures of centralized management and some form of planning. The essence of this, in effect, is increased state intervention in the interests of monopoly.

Prime Minister Trudeau has embellished this proposed frontal attack on the trade union movement with the name of "New Society". The essential thrust of the "New Society" is to permanently restrict the rights of the trade union movement, undermine collective bargaining and the right to strike, all in the name of the "collective good".

The government's proposals to increase state intervention in the economy in order to cope with inflation fail to tackle a rather basic question, the role of the multi-national corporations in Canada as factors breeding inflation. Regulating the trade union movement will not resolve inflation or the economic crisis. Regulation and control of the multi-national corporations is a way of getting at inflation, the economic crisis and not least, the independence of Canada. A government policy geared to tackle inflation cannot possibly succeed if it fails to come to grips with the multi-national corporations, fails to regulate them and place them under democratic control.

Despite the harmful line of the government with respect to wage restraint, other voices are being raised for an even tougher stance against the working class. This finds expression in proposals for measures to bring about a "better balance of power between management and labor". One of the advocates of these proposals says that "Even if achieving this balance means a short-term labor strife and the resulting problems, it will be worth it for the long term. We may have to take some strikes and lockouts to achieve this goal. When we let things go for too long the way we have, perhaps the only way to turn things around is to have a bit of suffering."*

It is obvious what these reactionary forces of monopoly have in mind. Their assumption is that they can ride roughshod over the working people and find a way out of the crisis on their backs by shifting politics to the right.

The working class and working people are fighting for a different way out of the crisis. The Marcusian theories about a declining working class, about a bourgeoisified working class are being smashed to smithereens by the ever growing upsurge of the working-class struggle. This struggle, while limited by and large to the economic field, is by the logic of circumstances being widened to take on the character of a political struggle against state-monopoly capitalism.

Mr. Joe Morris, president of the Canadian Labor Congress, and others of its spokesmen are increasingly impelled to draw attention to the alliance between the state and the employers. The 10-point program of the CLC goes beyond the field of collective bargaining and advances an economic and social program as an alternative to the crisis policies of

*Donald Lanskail, president of the Council of Forest Industries of B.C., *Globe and Mail*, April 10, 1976.

the government. Leaders of the trade union movement who earlier spoke of a general strike as being "subversive" now declare themselves to be in favor of a general strike that is by its very nature a political act whose aim is to compel changes in government policies — in this case the wage restraint program and government policies of high unemployment.

The sharpening struggle must find its "logic" in the battle to change the composition of Parliament, to change the balance of forces there so that it increasingly reflects the views of the working class and its democratic allies.

In the course of the struggle the CLC is being compelled to criticize NDP policies of support to wage restraints, its policy of retreat and compromise rather than of principled support to the struggles of the working class. Increasingly the trade union movement is being impelled to move to the left to defend its standards, its rights and jobs, while the NDP, under right-wing leadership, keeps on sliding to the right.

The crisis is not only leading to an upsurge of working-class action; it is also resulting in a broadening of the struggle against monopoly. The growing offensive by monopoly and federal and provincial governments on the social gains of the working people, whether in regard to education, health or social legislation, is widening the people's struggle against monopoly. What is shaping up is a merging of the struggle of the working class against wage restraints and a people's struggle against cutbacks in social legislation. Inevitably this must lead in the direction of uniting all these movements against monopoly in a broad anti-monopoly alliance, with the working class at its center.

This means that the coming period of time will be a period of great challenge.

Truly can it be said that Canada is at the crossroads. The working class and working people are not only faced with the necessity of uniting their ranks to defeat the monopoly offensive; the Canadian people are also faced with the necessity of checking and defeating the growing pressures of U.S. imperialism on Canada, and winning a new direction in Canadian policy. This is a crucial task today.

In the postwar period Canadian monopoly pursued a

course of economic and cultural integration with the USA. This course found expression in the Abbott Plan on one hand and subordination of Canadian foreign policy to the needs of U.S. imperialism on the other. Indeed, both aspects went together, showing that economic policy and foreign policy are inextricably bound together.

On the economic front, this course of Canadian monopoly took the form of support for policies of continentalism, the opening of Canada's doors to U.S. economic penetration, particularly in the field of natural resources and energy. It took the form of a Canada-U.S. auto pact that was to be the opening shot for similar measures of integration in other industries.

In the field of culture, it led to the further undermining of the small shoots of Canadianism, as they became engulfed in the wave of U.S. culture, magazines and the U.S. mass media generally.

In foreign trade policy, this course found expression in acquiescence in the U.S. policy of "no truck or trade" with the socialist countries, while U.S. imperialism used its levers, the multi-national corporations, to prevent such trade developing.

The course of economic and cultural integration of Canada with the USA was expressed in foreign policy through Canada's full support to the cold war, NATO, the arms program with billions of dollars going down the drain which could have been used for constructive projects to build Canada. It found expression in Canada's covering up for U.S. aggression in Vietnam.

These imperialist policies came up against the growing resistance of the peoples of the world. Above all, they came up against the changing balance of forces in the world — of which the dynamic growth of the socialist countries was a decisive part.

This compelled imperialism to move over from politics of confrontation to policies of peaceful co-existence with the socialist countries. At the same time, it compelled Canadian monopoly interests to modify Canada's relations with the

USA as well as with the socialist countries, and to try to strengthen its independent role and image in the world.

The Trudeau government gave expression to this shift in policy. This was reflected in the advancement of policies of diversification and Canadianization which monopoly considered would best advance its interests.

Diversification took the form of efforts to overcome Canada's one-sided relationship with the USA and to develop trade and closer ties with the socialist countries, Latin America, the Pacific Rim countries and Western Europe.

Canadianization took the form of measures to limit the entry of foreign capital, including U.S. capital, into Canada and to strengthen Canadian control over the economy. The Foreign Investment Review Act was one such measure, however limited in scope.

Canadianization also found expression in efforts to strengthen Canadian culture through greater measures of support to the arts and literature; in steps to control the distribution of literature and to limit U.S. control over TV.

Not least, Canadianization took the form of efforts to patriate the BNA Act and transform it into a Canadian constitution. These efforts have been accompanied by continued attempts to deny the national rights of the French-Canadian people.

In foreign policy, Canadianization and diversification found expression in more energetic and active measures to strengthen the role of Canadian monopoly in the developing countries.

These significant shifts in policy are not accidental. They reflect the efforts of government and of monopoly to accommodate state-monopoly capitalism in Canada to the significant changes in the world and the necessity for changed relations with the USA. Canadian monopoly is trying to find a place for itself in a changing world.

It would be illusory, however, to think Canadian imperialism can be relied on to lead the struggle for genuine Canadian independence or to achieve it. Canadian imperialism is part of the whole imperialist system and beset by imperialism's contradictions. It is under constant pressure from U.S.

imperialism to adopt a policy of continentalism and to open wide Canada's doors to U.S. takeover of its natural resources and energy. Only a powerful people's movement headed by the working class can lead that struggle for independence and a new direction in Canadian policy — a decisive component of which is the struggle against a policy of continentalism and its carriers, the multi-national corporations.

The struggle for a new direction in Canadian policy is underscored by the need for a truly national energy policy, an economic policy of growth based on public ownership of energy and natural resources and the resultant industrialization of the country; a truly all-Canadian transportation system; an end to foreign takeovers; Canadianization of the economy based on democratic control and public ownership of the multi-national corporations; the adoption of a new made-in-Canada constitution; and achievement of a truly independent, sovereign and united trade union movement.

More favorable opportunities now exist to achieve these objectives. They arise from a changing balance of forces in the world, the defeats suffered by U.S. imperialism and the possibility of expanding trade with the socialist and newly-liberated countries on the basis of mutual advantage.

These more favorable opportunities are inextricably tied in with the struggle for a truly independent foreign policy for Canada. Canada's security and its future are dependent on consistent support by Canada of peaceful co-existence and detente, of the struggle to implement detente and extend it to military detente, and on Canada's support of measures to eliminate hotbeds of war and check reaction.

The deepening crisis, which is also a crisis of bourgeois ideology, has stimulated a demand for change in Canada. This demand for change is growing. The reactionary forces of monopoly know and fear this. They therefore strive to divert the desire for change into reactionary channels. Despite their efforts, however, they cannot hide the new currents shaping up in Canada. For these have an objective base, demonstrated in the growing desire to develop good relations with the USSR and other socialist countries, in the

growing number of delegations that visit the Soviet Union —
delegations ranging from the NDP to the Liberal Party, the
trade union movement, youth movement, farm movement
and others.

All this reflects the changes shaping up today, changes that
stand in sharp contrast to the dark days of the cold war.

Clearly Canada is not separated from the warm waves of
detente and peaceful co-existence characterizing present-day
international relations. These "waves" are of great importance for Canada. They constitute the best conditions for
strengthening Canadian independence. They constitute the
best conditions for democratic advance and social progress.

The past 10 years of struggle have demonstrated that the
minimum and maximum programs of the Communist Party
are both soundly based and firmly grounded in the reality of
Canadian political life, in the growing struggle of the
working-class and other democratic forces. This is a credit to
the powers of scientific socialism, of Marxism-Leninism.

The past 10 years have been years of consistent effort by
Communists to bring the policies of the Communist Party to
the people — of Communist effort to be seen and to be
heard, to break through the blackout of the monopoly mass
media and defeat the attempts of monopoly and its
hangers-on to cut our Party off from the working class.

The past 10 years have been years of consistent effort by
Communists to expose currents from the right and the "left"
that would either swamp the working class in opportunism
and reformism, or lead it into the blind alley of ultra-
revolutionism.

A relatively new situation has opened up in Canada, one
that offers possibilities for the strengthening of the
working-class and other democratic movements, for the extension of the fight for democracy and independence and
for merging that fight with the struggle for socialism.

New possibilities are correspondingly opening up to unite
the working-class and democratic movement around the
struggle against monopoly and the multi-national corporations. Conditions are ripening to build the united front of

the working class, to achieve a democratic alliance against monopoly and to link up this alliance — led by the Canadian working class — with the demand for radical reform, to open the pathway to socialism.

A new chapter of struggle opens up.

June, 1976

Submission to the
Special Joint Committee on the
Constitution of Canada
from the
Communist Party of Canada

May 12, 1971

INTRODUCTION

We shall set forth in this submission our opinions as to how the building of the unity of Canada can best be advanced in a new Confederal Pact based on the complete equality of two national communities and on their right to self-determination, and as to why separation of them would not be in the best interests of either.

Only a united Canada creates the best conditions for a successful struggle by the Canadian people, led by a united working class, for Canadian independence from the growing pressures of U.S. imperialism. It is this which the Communist Party advocates.

As long as the existence of the French-Canadian nation is unrecognized, as long as its right to self-determination up to and including separation is denied, as long as Quebec is oppressed under draconic police-state laws, and stands under the shadow of military occupation, the crisis of the Canadian confederation and in the relationships between our two national communities will rapidly deepen.

And this, of course, is not only because of today but because of over 200 years of yesterdays back to the Conquest. Those who find it fashionable now to talk of violence in Quebec would do well to reflect on *that* act of violence — akin to the kidnapping of a whole population by a foreign army.

I. THE PRESENT CRISIS

But let us focus briefly on much more recent history.

Last October there took place in Montreal two political kidnappings. Other states have dealt with such problems either through negotiations, or through the due process of criminal law. The Canadian state proved incapable of pursuing either course with consistency.

Instead there took place a massive onslaught on the democratic rights of *all* Canadians, with its sharp edge turned against the people of Quebec. Quebec was occupied by military forces. The War Measures Act which allows for an impermissible overriding of the Canadian Bill of Rights was proclaimed — to be followed by the passage of an equally anti-democratic law, the Public Order (Temporary Measures) Act.

The police forces were unleashed to make over 3,000 raids, and to detain without bail nearly 500 people active in the labor and people's movements of Quebec. Finally only 62 people were charged with any offence whatever. Already major criminal charges have been quashed because they could not be made to stand up. Two-thirds of those charged are not even alleged to have had a direct connection with the specific crimes. On the other hand, for many weeks the police proved incapable of finding the persons actually alleged to have perpetrated the crimes of kidnapping and murder. Tom Hazlitt of the *Toronto Star* wrote on January 16: "The vast powers granted the police had no impact whatsoever on the all-important kidnapping investigations ... informed sources close to Canada's biggest manhunt now admit privately that the usefulness of the emergency powers had another purpose altogether."

The Central Committee of the Communist Party of Canada at its meeting last November 14-16 approved the report by our leader, William Kashtan, which declared that "the direct cause of this crisis is the refusal of the Trudeau government and of monopoly to recognize the existence of the French-Canadian nation and its right to self-determination. It is this non-recognition of the French-Canadian nation and the consequences arising therefrom which have aggravated and continue to aggravate the crisis of confederation."

It will be recalled that on October 14 a statement was issued jointly by the presidents of the two Quebec trade union centers, the president of the Corporation of Quebec Teachers, the leader of the Parti Québecois, the editor of *Le Devoir*, and other responsible leaders in Quebec society. They said:

"The fate of these two lives, the reputation and collective honor of our society, the evident danger that it faces at the present time of social and political degradation — all of this makes obvious for us the fact that it is first of all in Quebec that the responsibility to find a solution remains and should remain."

There is evidence of a direct connection between this appeal for the right of self-determination and the denial of that right represented by the proclamation two days later of the War Measures Act.

For example: The *Toronto Star* on October 21 in a Canadian Press Special dispatch from Calgary quoted Patrick Mahoney, Liberal MP for Calgary South as saying, "The cabinet was undecided on implementing the (War Measures) Act, but the statement from the ten Quebeckers 'tipped the scales' and prompted fast action." Significantly, this assertion has never been explicitly denied by anyone in authority either in Ottawa or Quebec.

In the absence of such denials, important sections of responsible Canadian public opinion are justified in concluding that this statement of leading Quebec citizens constituted in the mind of Prime Minister Trudeau a major factor in that so-called "apprehended insurrection" by means of which the War Measures Act was justified.

In making the point that the massive reaction of the federal government was directed in the first place at the demands of the people of Quebec for their democratic rights, we do not suggest that the government of Quebec was a helpless victim. We agree with the widespread opinion in Quebec that their government abdicated its responsibility, and turned the *major* decisions over to Ottawa.

With excellent foresight, the executives of the Quebec Federation of Labor, the Confederation of National Trade Unions, and the Quebec Teachers' Corporation meeting on October 17 summed up the situation:

"The three union organizations must denounce the regime of force imposed by the Trudeau government, supported by the surrender of the Bourassa government in panic, oppressing the civil liberties of Quebec's citizens and instituting a rigid sort of military rule by military junta.

"As union representatives and as citizens of Quebec, we deplore what seems to us a conspiracy between the Quebec and Ottawa governments to make people in the rest of the country believe Quebec is ruled by anarchy, chaos and insurrection, just when Quebec citizens were starting to prove democracy viable in Quebec.

"We indeed wonder if this conspiracy does not aim to make this nascent democracy impossible in Quebec."

When the leaders of organized labor can thus assert that both senior governments are conspiring to make the development of democracy impossible, and when they can subsequently win to this point of view their memberships, then it should be obvious that the original actions of those governments have been irresponsible.

THE THREAT OF MORE VIOLENCE

But of course irresponsibility in government leads to irresponsibility elsewhere.

For example:

— on November 3, Douglas Fisher writing in the Toronto *Telegram* asked, "Why has no federal minister ever declared that our Confederation shall not be peaceably sundered? . . . If separation should come on strong in spite of Mr. Trudeau's lead, perhaps even because of it, it would be useful to know where he would stand on a much more powerful federal intervention."

— on January 3, Peter C. Newman, then editor-in-chief of the *Toronto Star* wrote: "It is still possible that the French-English partnership will survive, through some kind of semantic juggling. This might involve Quebec staying as part of Canada on terms which its government believes will grant it most of the prerogatives of a nation-state, while Ottawa will stoutly continue to maintain that Quebec remains a territory with some special privileges, but a province nevertheless. Still, the alternative of armed intervention by the federal government to keep Quebec from breaking away can no longer be discounted."

When prominent journalists like these feel impelled to write this way, it is safe to assume that the ideas of all too many English-Canadians, poisoned by decades of Anglo-Saxon chauvinism, are being expressed in an even more bloodthirsty fashion. This in turn can only lead ever more Québecois to the conclusion that the only future lies in complete separation — and through armed struggle if that is necessary.

It is time for all responsible Canadians to reject out of hand any conception that the Canadian confederation can be preserved by force. It is time to cast off all illusions that some solution can be found in the "semantic juggling" referred to by Peter Newman and quoted above, which has been all too evident in the unreal abstractions that have marked so much of the discussion to date about a new constitution for Canada, or worse still about the possibilities of amending the BNA Act.

It is for this reason that the Communist Party of Canada submits to this Joint Special Committee that it should at once recommend:

1. that the Parliament of Canada declare by joint resolution that it recognizes the existence within the borders of this country of two nations, each of which possesses the right to self-determination, which includes the right to freely separate from the other if its people so desire.

2. that the Parliament of Canada should declare it has no intention of adopting other legislation of a similar oppressive, anti-democratic character as the Public Order (Temporary Measures) Act which was allowed to lapse primarily as a result of united widespread opposition by democratic forces, including the trade union movement in English as well as in French Canada; that the Ministers of Justice of Canada and of Quebec should act to drop all charges and quash all convictions arising out of the present crisis which are not directly related to the kidnappings and to the murder of Pierre Laporte; and that all persons now in custody under such charges and convictions be liberated and compensated.

Such action would create the atmosphere for negotiation without coercion which is essential for frank discussion of a new constitution for Canada, at the heart of which must be the affirmation of the sovereignty and equality of the two nations in Canada.

II. THE RIGHT TO SELF-DETERMINATION

The Communist Party is dedicated to the establishment in Canada of a socialist and ultimately a Communist society.

We see the road ahead for the Canadian peoples as one of struggle led by the working class, for the extension of democracy and for the curbing and ultimate elimination of the great corporations — the most profoundly undemocratic institutions in our society.

We are convinced that in the course of this struggle the peoples of this country will come to see the necessity of establishing a socialist society.

We do not believe that socialism can be achieved or built without the support of the majority of the people We reject any idea that socialism can be won through putsches, conspiracy or individual acts of terrorism.

Because we work always for the unity of the working class, we fight against every form of national privilege, of small nation exclusiveness, and against national oppression and discrimination of every kind.

It is this which determines our fundamental position on the relationships between Quebec and English-speaking Canada. As we said at our Central Committee last November: "The Communist Party thus stands for the unity of the working class of the two nations in a united struggle against our common enemy — Canadian monopoly and U.S. imperialism, both to regain Canadian independence and in the struggle for a socialist Canada."

In his report to the Central Committee meeting of last November cited above, William Kashtan reaffirmed our Party's position in the following words: "Separatism would not be in the interests of the national aspirations of the French-Canadian people, nor of the working class because it would divide its forces in the struggle against monopoly and for fundamental social change. As internationalists, Communists support the progressive and democratic content of the national question, while opposing its reactionary aspects."

But before coming to an elaboration of this position, we must address ourselves to that obstacle which is blocking the way to the achievement of any meaningful new relationship between the two national communities.

The Communist Party of Canada, many years ago, recognized that the French-Canadians in Quebec constitute a nation and have the right to self-determination, that is, to choose the form of sovereignty for Quebec which they, in their majority, desire.

This position is embodied in our Party's program, and we argued for it before the Royal Commission on Bilingualism and Biculturalism (hereinafter referred to as the Royal Commission) some seven years ago.

Our most recent reiteration and updating of this position took place at our 20th Convention in April 1969, at which time we adopted a policy statement, entitled "A New Constitution for Canada". We shall refer to this document throughout this brief as our Policy Statement.

We said in this statement:

"Recent federal-provincial conferences have served only to underline how hopelessly the relations between the two nations of Canada have sunk into the constitutional quicksands of the British North America Act.

"It had been hoped by the establishment that the election of

Pierre Elliott Trudeau, their favorite French-Canadian, as Prime Minister of Canada with the main slogan — 'One Canada, One Nation' — would 'put Quebec in its place' and thus bring about 'better relations' between English Canada and Quebec; but experience has shown that the relations have worsened.

"Those who glibly speak of making some amendments to the BNA Act which would clarify federal and provincial responsibilities as the basis for solving this fundamental problem of Canada are simply trying to conceal the fact that the profound inequity and national oppression to which the French-Canadian nation is subjected are embedded in the very nature of this colonialist Act which serves as Canada's constitution.

"In life the oppression finds expression in the refusal to recognize the right of the French-Canadian nation to self-determination, to recognition of its rights to a national state, or even of its existence as a nation; in constantly lower incomes and more unemployment than the average for English Canada; in the imposition of English as the language of work in the main centers of Quebec and in numerous other ways. No efforts to introduce French-language instruction in English Canada can wipe out these grave inequities to the people of Quebec.

"Nor can the introduction of certain civil rights for individuals in English and French Canada substitute for the undemocratic refusal to recognize in the Constitution of Canada the collective rights of the French-Canadian nation."

WHAT IS A NATION?

It is impossible for anyone to deny the fact stated by Dr. Eugene Forsey in his presidential address to the Canadian Political Science Association in 1962: "Canada is both two nations and one; two nations in the ethnic, cultural, sociological sense; one nation in the political, legal, constitutional sense."

The deepening dilemma of Canada arises out of the fact that Senator Forsey, Prime Minister Trudeau and many others in positions of authority believe or pretend to believe that by some kind of fiat it is possible to decide that only the political, legal, and constitutional definition of "nation" has meaning for Canada, and that the sociological definition can be denied or ignored.

The truth of the matter of course is that laws and constitutions which do not correspond to historically evolved social facts are doomed inevitably in the end to collapse.

All the legalistic pronouncements and election promises, all the pious speeches and dire threats that we have heard in this land from the times of Lord Durham onward have not succeeded in disposing of the fact of the existence of the French-Canadian nation.

There it stands — a historically constituted, stable community of people formed on the basis of its common French language, its territory in Quebec, an economic life based on its developed agriculture and industry, with its distinctive psychological make-up manifested in a common culture.

By the same standards, there also stands the English-Canadian nation.

Nor is there anything unique about the existence of two nations within one state. There are, for example, two nations in Belgium, and three in Switzerland. We have not met many Welshmen or Scotsmen who would take kindly to the suggestion that they are part of the English nation. As for the Irish, we find that the source of their problems is the opposite of ours — the existence of two states within one nation.

Even when the proponents of the "One Canada, One Nation" view are finally compelled to concede the self-evident existence of the French-Canadian nation as a sociological fact, they promptly seek to rob that fact of its profound significance with respect to legal and constitutional relationships.

They deny that the people of a nation or at least the people of this particular nation possess *collective* rights as distinct from their rights as individual citizens.

Yet the recognition of collective as well as individual rights is a fundamental concept of democracy. '

In this connection, the Royal Commission made an important and so far too-little heeded contribution to the thinking of Canadians, when in the General Introduction to its report it said:

"Finally, let us consider another dimension of equality between the two communities — the political dimension. This covers the possibilities for each society to choose its own institutions or, at least, to have the opportunity to participate fully in making political decisions within a framework shared with the other community.

"The collective aspect of equality is here still more evident; it is not cultural growth and development at the individual level which is at stake, but the degree of *self-determination* (emphasis in original) which one society can exercise in relation to another. We have in mind the power of decision of each group and its freedom to act, not only in its cultural life but in all aspects of its collective life. We are no longer concerned with the characteristics which distinguish the two communities qualitatively, or even with their respective social and economic positions, but with the extent of the control each has over its government or governments. This is the basis for the discussion of the constitutional framework in which two societies can live or aspire to live; a unitary or a federal; special status for the province in which the minority group is concentrated; or again, for the same part of the country, the status of an associate state; or finally, the status of an independent state."

The Commission seems to have written these paragraphs with a cautious eye to its own extremely narrow terms of reference. Hence the avoidance of the word "nation". We would suggest with respect, however, that they could serve as a starting point for any examination of the "constitutional framework in which two societies can live or aspire to live."

For here is indicated the fundamental principle of the right of nations to self-determination — a principle which is enshrined in Article One of the Charter of the United Nations.

It is a reflection of the profound problems in which this country finds itself that this concept which is so ignored and denied in English-speaking Canada, is so widely understood and accepted in French Canada by people holding political views over a wide spectrum.

For example, Claude Castonguay, a prominent and respected member of the present Quebec government, is quoted in the *Montreal Star* report of January 17: " 'If we arrive at a new constitution that places Quebec in exactly the same basis as the other provinces or if it does not clearly recognize our sociological reality from a cultural and social point of view we will have gained little.

" 'We won't have attained the goal that has to be attained and this fairly rapidly if we can judge from what has been going on in the province of Quebec.'

"Mr. Castonguay continued his theme that unrest in Quebec won't be cured through simple economics.

" 'The approach must be more global,' he said, 'and must keep the concept of identity in mind.

" 'French-speaking people in Quebec clearly constitute a sociological entity.' "

The Quebec New Democratic Party in its February 1971 convention went further in declaring "that Quebec has the right to determine the appropriate degree of its sovereignty in all fields"; and as two of its officers elected in the convention wrote to the *Montreal Star* of March 3rd, this recognizes "that the Quebec people has the right to determine for itself if there should be a partnership at all and, if so, to the extent it should enter that partnership."

The right of a nation to self-determination cannot in any way be qualified. To say, for example, that a nation which is part of a larger country in which another nation exists cannot separate from that country if its people so decide is to deny the right to self-determination altogether.

It is this non-recognition of the right to self-determination up to and including separation for the French-Canadian nation, and indeed the non-recognition of the very existence of that nation, which lies at the heart of the oppression of French Canada within the Canadian confederation.

This oppression has been, and continues to be, only too tangible to those who are oppressed.

TWO CENTURIES OF NATIONAL OPPRESSION

From the time of the British conquest, French-Canadians have not been in control of their national destiny. Decisions which vitally affected them were imposed first of all by the British colonial authorities, and from the middle of the 19th century by an Anglo-Canadian majority within Canada.

The chief tensions which have affected the Canadian confederation over the last century have been directly related to this fact. We have discussed the present, and we need only cite further here: the execution of Louis Riel, the issue of Canadian participation in the Boer War, and the conscription crises during both world wars. In each instance, the will of the Anglo-Canadian majority was imposed upon the French-Canadian minority. It may be argued with some justice that in fact politicians manipulated the Anglo-Canadian majority to achieve the particular results they sought. But the distinction between the political leaders in Ottawa and the Anglo-Canadians as a whole is not easy for the people of the oppressed nation to make.

From the development of the dominant English-speaking fur trade and commercial interests in the late 18th century, down to the present day, the commanding heights of the economy of Quebec have been in the hands of English-speaking business leaders.

It is indisputable that today, the principal manufacturing and resources industries of Quebec are owned by great U.S. and Anglo-Canadian corporations. The Royal Commission points out in the third volume of its report (paragraph 127): "(Francophone Canadian manufacturers) employed only 22 per cent of those working in manufacturing industry ... these same establishments accounted for a still smaller proportion — only 15 per cent — of total value added in the manufacturing industry in Quebec. In the establishments owned by Anglophone Canadians, 47 per cent of the labor force produced only 43 per cent of the value added. In contrast, establishments under foreign ownership employed only 31 per cent of the manufacturing labor force but produced 42 per cent of the value added."

It will be recalled that John Porter's survey of the economic elite, some years ago, showed that only seven per cent were Francophones.

This fact of economic domination has had far-reaching consequences in terms of inequality of wage levels and living standards as between Quebec and Ontario — the other most industrialized province in the country — and as between the Francophone and Anglophone communities within Quebec.

There is, we are sure, no need to recapitulate the studies of these deep-going problems contained in the third volume of the report of the Royal Commission.

By no means the least significant of these problems is that of the language of work — the stubborn and continuing resistance to the use of French by the Anglophone owners and managers of the dominating corporations.

All these manifestations of economic domination and inequality are expressions of the fundamental problem of national oppression. We would submit further that it is the desire to maintain these relationships for their own profits which stands at the center of resistance of the Anglo-Canadian establishment and their French-Canadian junior partners to the recognition of the right of the French-Canadian nation to self-determination.

THE BNA ACT — FRAMEWORK OF OPPRESSION

The British North America Act is the constitutional framework for the national oppression of French Canada.

The essence of the BNA Act was the granting to the French-Canadian people in Quebec of certain limited aspects of those rights which should pertain to a nation — control of education including guarantees of the preservation of the confessional school system; the right to the use of French in the Parliament of Canada, in the Legislature of Quebec and before the federal courts — while at the same time in effect denying that the French-Canadian people in Quebec constitute a nation and are entitled to all the sovereign rights of a nation.

Furthermore, the fact that the use of English was established as a guaranteed right in the Quebec Legislature and before Quebec provincial courts, *without any provision for French in English-speaking Canada,* was intended as a privilege for Anglophones deriving from the British Conquest, but in the light of attitudes to national minority rights today rather constitutes blatant discrimination against Francophones in English Canada.

These results were achieved by establishing Quebec as a province, possessing a "local government" (as Sir John A MacDonald described it) in the same relation to the central Canadian government as those provinces which are part of the English-Canadian nation. Instead of establishing a pact of confederation between the two nations, the BNA Act led ultimately to the establishment of 10 provinces of which Quebec was but one — a province "like the others".

This constitutional structure, which was always fragile, has been rapidly crumbling in recent years, especially over the past decade. This had been the result of the rapid industrialization of Quebec, accompanied by the breakdown of the rural society which was formerly the dominant characteristic of Quebec life. As industrialization has placed an increasing emphasis on education in modern science and technology, so has grown the increasing indignation of French-Canadians, and especially the young, over the occupation of the main posts in industry and commerce by Anglophones.

It has become increasingly apparent that French Canada does not have at its disposal the state machinery to carry through the far-reaching measures of economic reform which are necessary to the full flowering of its national life. Indeed, it has become clear that without such a state at its disposal, the nation will not even be able to preserve the limited cultural and linguistic rights established in 1867.

This in turn places the working class of that nation in a position of grave disadvantage adding especially grave additional burdens to the exploitation to which it is already subjected, in common with all workers everywhere in capitalist society.

The French language which could be preserved in a relatively isolated rural community will not be preserved in the industrial centers if it does not become the language of work. But this in turn poses sharply the fact of Canadian and U.S. monopoly control of industry.

An illuminating illustration of this problem is provided by the Royal Commission in its discussion of the question of the working language in volume three of its report. It says with respect to Hydro-Quebec:

"What impresses us most forcibly is the striking change in attitudes to language since the nationalization of 1963.

"The Brazeau-Dofny study noted the scepticism prevailing at Hydro-Quebec at the time with regard to the official adoption of French as the language of work at all levels of the company. The preponderance of English in the technical, commercial and administrative sectors in North America seemed to present an insurmountable obstacle. Particular concern was voiced over the necessity of communicating with the surrounding Anglophone world. In such a contest, the adoption of French as the language of work seemed unrealistic, and there was fear that this might turn Hydro-Quebec into an enclave.

"But the use of French as the language of work has succeeded, and the early fears have proved unfounded. We have reason, therefore, to wonder whether the real needs of the situation had simply been overshadowed by the sheer weight of traditional and historical circumstances."

Here surely is a valid example of the need for far-reaching nationalization of industry as an essential act in defence of the linguistic and cultural rights of the nation. This constitutes an additional reason for a program of nationalization, which we see as imperative to the maintenance of the independence of both Canadian nations, and to the development of their economies in the interests of their working people.

The point we would emphasize here is that Quebec is not now in possession of the state structure which is necessary for a widespread program of nationalization. Even granting that a province under the British North America Act possesses the controls over fiscal and monetary policy, the ability to mobilize the entire financial resources of the nation to carry through successfully a program of extensive nationalization is still missing.

It is because of these limitations imposed on Quebec as a province "like the others" that the demand for the right of self-determination arises and will continue to arise ever more insistently. This factor we see as central to the course of political developments in Quebec and as cutting across differences of opinion as to the way in which self-determination would be exercised. No government in Quebec City, no matter what its political complexion, can for long ignore this irrepressible tendency. In Quebec, the national struggle inevitably enters into every social struggle. For example, the sharply deflationary policies pursued last year by the federal government with their inevitable consequences in unemployment were criticized and opposed by the labor movement across the country. This was true in Quebec also, but there all the forces concerned about the development of the nation came into play as well.

It is the uneasy recognition of this truth which in January led Robert Stanfield to speak of the special character of the unemployment crisis in Quebec, and the Quebec Minister of Labor to talk about the danger of "revolution". Ministers in the English-Canadian provinces would hardly put it that way.

THE INTERESTS OF ENGLISH CANADA

The framework of the British North America Act is also profoundly inimical to the interests of the people of the English-Canadian nation.

The treatment of Quebec as one of 10 provinces, rather than as the homeland of a nation, in the context of the mounting French-Canadian demand for the right to self-determination, has given rise to a tendency on the part of the English-Canadian provinces to push their own jurisdictional and fiscal claims to the uttermost limits. We have no doubt that this tendency reflects in part the "empire building" aspirations of certain provincial politicians, who are also only too eager to secure a free hand for the sell-out of more provincial resources to U.S. corporations. But irrespective of the motivation, the justified demands of Quebec provide at least the pretext for these demands from provinces which are part of the English-Canadian nation.

The result is at best the constant manoeuvring and "buck passing" which has characterized federal-provincial conferences, and at worst the fragmentation of English Canada.

But all this runs counter to the basic social and economic needs of the people of English Canada. Those needs demand effective central taxation of the large corporations located in Ontario, and the establishment of equal and steadily improving access to the best educational and health facilities, as well as the institution of other necessary social reforms. This must be achieved without infringing in any way on the rights of French Canada to self-determination.

But reforms in this direction which are necessary to the proper social development of a modern state are rendered impossible by the failure to recognize that Quebec is the homeland of a nation, and not simply one of 10 like provinces.

In other words, the whole complex of relationships between Ottawa, the English-Canadian provinces and the municipalities are capable of adjustment in the interests of the people only when it is recognized that there exists an English-Canadian nation distinct from the French-Canadian nation. Otherwise the problems of regional disparity, of totally inadequate financial resources in the great urban centers will remain and deepen.

THE PROPOSED AMENDING FORMULA

We cannot emphasize too strongly that there is no way that the British North America Act can be amended or patched up. While we of course consider it to be an absurd and possibly dangerous anachronism that any Canadian constitution should continue to exist in the form of an act of the British Parliament, there is no solution to be found to the problems of Canada in "repatriating" this instrument of inequality. And the search for an amending formula will in the long run only compound the problem.

The formula which was advanced by the federal-provincial conference last February is presented as one which would give Quebec a veto over constitutional changes — that is, as long as it continues to embrace 25 per cent of the Canadian population. (The continued non-recognition in this of its special position as the homeland of a nation should be carefully noted.) But the real truth of the matter is that under this formula Quebec, with respect to any extension of its legislative powers, is in fact subjected to the veto of Ontario, to that of any two of the western provinces, providing that 50 per cent of the population of these provinces is represented (which in effect also gives British Columbia the power of veto), and to that of any two of the four Atlantic provinces. Thus under this formula the French-Canadian nation would be bound even more tightly into a constitutional strait jacket, and left under the complete domination of the governments of English-speaking Canada.

Over much of the last decade wide currency has been given to the so-called "bilingual and bicultural" approach to the solution of the problems facing Canada.

We should say that we are in favor of the establishment within English Canada, in areas with a significant French-speaking minority, of schools using French as the language of instruction.

The position of the Communist Party of Quebec, fully endorsed by the Communist Party of Canada, is:

"To support every effort to encourage the strengthening and flowering of the French language in Quebec, to remove every fetter imposed by Anglo-Canadian and American domination as well as by the confessional system of education;

"Precisely as the result of the Anglo-Canadian domination rooted in the British Conquest, we declare ourselves against the preservation of all privilege imposed in favor of the English language, for example, the use of English as the language of work."

To this end the Communist Party of Quebec advocates:

"that the French language be recognized as the principal and general language in Quebec, and that the policy of bilingualism be rejected;

"that every collective agreement, every directive and information bulletin, every training program, etc., in commercial and industrial establishments be in French and where necessary also in English;

"that every child have the opportunity and be obliged to learn French adequately as a requirement for all diplomas granted by the Department of Education;

"that where 10 per cent of the parents in a school area request a school or classes where the principal language of education be English, that this right be granted and financially supported by the government of Quebec."

We agree with the policy now being implemented by the government of Canada under which subsidies are provided for instruction in the second language in both national communities.

We are also in broad general agreement with the recommendations of the Royal Commission on Bilingualism and Biculturalism with respect to the preservation of the cultural heritage of Canadians of national origins other than French or English.

But we must make clear that we take these positions because they represent a just and democratic approach, which would be appropriate no matter what the future relations between the two nations may be. We do not believe that the fundamental problems of relationships between French and English Canada can be in any way resolved by such measures.

The rights of nations are not reducible to questions of language and culture. They pertain to the full gamut of political, economic and social relations.

A French-Canadian should be able to live in English Canada with the knowledge that he will have the opportunity to educate his children in the French language if he wishes, to listen to radio and television in his own language. But he should not be made to feel that his only opportunities for economic advancement lie in emigration from Quebec. He should be able to live within the homeland of his nation, and enjoy the full benefits that derive from its unfettered national development.

Similarly, an English-speaking Canadian should be able to live in Quebec without suffering discrimination against his language, and without the Anglophone ruling class continuing to enjoy the special privileges which have been their prerogative since the British Conquest.

All this is important if the peoples of the two nations are to live together, work together, and struggle together for a better life in a binational, democratic and sovereign state. What is most fundamental, we repeat, is the establishment of the complete equality of the two national communities based on the recognition of the right of each to self-determination.

III. OUR OPTION — A NEW CONFEDERAL PACT

The right to self-determination for a nation, while it must include the right to separation if it is to be meaningful, does not necessarily have to be exercised in the form of separation, any more than does the existence of the right to divorce have to necessarily lead to the dissolution of all marriages.

Our Policy Statement said:

"The sovereignty of a national state may be expressed in the free national choice of one of three forms: a separate state; a confederation of equal states; autonomy. Providing the nation in question freely chooses, any one of these forms is a genuine expression of sovereignty. Separation is only one expression of genuine sovereignty and by no means always the expression that is in the best interest of the working people involved."

The attitude of the Communist Party of Canada toward this matter of options of self-determination was most recently defined at our 20th Convention in April 1969 in the following terms:

"A just and democratic solution of the present crisis requires full and unconditional recognition of the right of the French-Canadian people to decide for themselves the course of their national development, the form of their national state, and the nature of their relationship with English Canada. This right means that the French-Canadian nation shall be free to choose between separation from Canada and some form of political union with English Canada.

"Our view is that, of the various options, the most advantageous solution for both peoples would be the working out of a new confederal relationship. But our expression of this opinion is in no way to be construed as an effort either to curtail Quebec's freedom of choice or to cling to any element of that Anglo-Canadian ascendancy that has made the federal union of 1867 unworkable in practice and unacceptable in principle.

"A working-class policy in the circumstances of Canada today can only be one of combatting U.S. domination, Anglo-Canadian monopoly and the national oppression of French Canada. The Communist Party of Canada stands pledged to work for the unity of the forces of labor and democracy in both our nations, in the struggle for the right to national self-determination. We see in the national movement of French Canada a vitally important potential ally of the working class in its struggle against monopoly rule, imperialism and war."

We have recognized as the above statement indicates that "work for the unity of the forces of labor and democracy in both our nations", if it is to be successful, must be imbued with the clear understanding that the decision as to which option of self-determination will be chosen must be freely made by the people of the oppressed nation. That this is the case, with respect to the Communist Party of Canada, is made clear in the statement of the Communist Party of Quebec which is submitted as an addendum to this brief. For the information of members of the Committee we are also filing with this submission copies of the constitutions of the Communist Party of Canada and the Communist Party of Quebec in which is defined the position of the latter as "a distinct entity, within the Communist Party of Canada, having complete control of its own policies and structures in Quebec."

AUTONOMY

With respect to the option of *autonomy*, our policy statement says: "We believe that the autonomy proposal ('special status' under the amended BNA Act) in the circumstances of Canada would continue the non-recognition of the French-Canadian nation. This preferred solution of the French-Canadian bourgeoisie, expressed in different words by the Quebec Liberal Party and Union Nationale, would maintain national discrimination." It would not break out of the strait jacket imposed by the BNA Act. It does not establish the full equality of two sovereign nations each possessing the right to self-determination.

In its usually presented form, the "autonomy" option, as our Policy Statement says, "seeks to gain more sovereignty for Quebec only by increasing that of all ten provinces, in the expectation that only Quebec would use its new powers, thus achieving 'special status'. It is unworkable and would increase the fragmentation of English Canada."

SEPARATION

With respect to the option of *separation,* the Policy Statement embodies the standpoint of the Communist Party of Quebec, and endorsed by the Communist Party of Canada in these terms:

"The separatist solution, preferred by a section of the French-Canadian petty bourgeoisie, would entail severe additional economic hardships to the working people of both nations and would weaken their political unity against their common enemies: monopoly capital, Canadian and U.S. imperialism. In so far as Quebec separatists fight for national and democratic rights of the French-Canadian nation, Communists will fight at their side, while criticizing their separatist solution as one which contradicts the real national interests of Quebec and particularly of the French-Canadian working people.

"In so far as Quebec separatists and nationalists try to substitute discrimination against the English-Canadian minority or against immigrants for the present discrimination against the French-Canadian nation, or practise and preach national exclusiveness and egoism, Communists will reject such efforts and approaches. The democratic national forces of French Canada are a powerful potential ally of the labor movement in common struggle against Canadian and U.S. imperialism. That is why every effort should be exerted to combat and defeat these dangerous tendencies."

Inherent in the above position is a rejection of the view put forward by some sections of the *indépendantistes* in Quebec, especially on the left, that Quebec is a colony of English Canada.

The characteristic relationship between a colony and its metropolitan imperialist master reduces the economy of the colony to a producer of raw materials for the metropolitan country while the latter compels the colony to serve as a protected market for its finished products.

The colonial state is either directly or indirectly (in the case of a neo-colony) controlled by the metropolitan imperialist country in order to perpetuate and secure this outright robbery.

But this is not the economic relationship between English and French Canada. Indeed, French Canada is highly industrialized. Its urban concentration compares favorably not only with English Canada, but with any advanced capitalist country in the world. Quebec is not reduced to producing raw materials for the secondary industry of English Canada, and to buying its finished products.

What is true is that the most powerful sections of finance capital in both English and French Canada have deliberately chosen to subordinate the economy of Canada to that of the United States, to serve as auxiliaries for U.S. imperialism in its economic, political and military drive for world supremacy. Despite tortuous manoeuvres to carve out for itself a somewhat better, but nevertheless subordinate, niche in the imperialist camp, this policy of deliberate subordination to U.S. economic control has remained the dominant feature of the policy of both English-Canadian and French-Canadian monopoly capital.

The facts show that the decidedly inferior status of French-Canadian capital to Anglo-Canadian capital, and even more so to U.S. capital, in no way has converted the French-Canadian capitalists into a real or potential genuine leader of a national-liberation movement. This is abundantly clear from the declarations in favor of U.S. investment in Quebec not only from the spokesmen from the traditional parties — Liberal and Union Nationale — but from René Lévesque and his colleagues in the leadership of the Parti Québecois.

One can only conclude from these incontestable facts that those who put forward the thesis that Quebec is a colony of English Canada, whatever their motive, succeed only in denigrating the leading role of the working class in the struggle for national and social emancipation, and the overriding necessity of unity of the working class of English and French Canada.

If Quebec were a colony, all democrats would be obliged to demand not only the right to self-determination for the French-Canadian nation, but its independence, its separation from English Canada. This is indeed the underlying motive of many of those on the left in the *indépendantiste* movement for putting forward this superficial and erroneous thesis. This thesis furthermore ascribes a revolutionary role, actual or potential, to the French-Canadian capitalist class akin to that of the capitalists in other colonial countries, which is very far from reality and dangerously illusory.

But although Quebec is not a colony of English Canada, the French-Canadian nation is an oppressed nation.

The struggle to free the French-Canadian nation from its position of an oppressed nation is the task of all democratic, patriotic, anti-monopoly forces, *led by the working class.* The working class of both nations thus face a common enemy, and we constantly stress, therefore, the necessity of working-class unity against the enemy, the unity of both Anglophone and Francophone workers within Quebec and the unity of the working class of both English-speaking and French Canada.

CONFEDERATION OF EQUAL STATES

The option which we advocate is that of a New Confederal Pact based on a voluntary equal partnership of the nations in a democratic sovereign and binational state and their right to self-determination up to and including separation. This has been the consistent position of the Communist Party of Canada.

In support of this option, the Communist Party of Quebec has developed the following line of argumentation as contained in an article by its president, Samuel Walsh, in the magazine *Communist Viewpoint:*

"Quebec forms part of the continental territory of Canada. It is not separated by sea or by color of skin from the metropolitan imperialist country, as is Angola from Portugal or as was Algeria from France. The intensity of exploitation and discrimination is therefore not as extreme. *But the French-Canadians are an oppressed nation* within the metropolitan territory of the advanced, imperialist Anglo-Canadian bourgeoisie, which itself is delivering, for a price, big chunks of Canada and its resources to the vastly more powerful and voracious U.S. imperialism. Hence when French Canadians hear the galling slogan of 'one Canada, One Nation', the reaction is different only in degree of intensity and in solutions proposed to the reactions and solutions of the Algerians when they heard the slogan, 'Algeria is France', or when the Angolans hear the slogan, 'Angola is Portugal'.

"Although *the problem is fundamentally the same,* i.e., the refusal to recognize the right to self-determination, the solution to the problem in the interests of the working people is in practice different in form and to some extent in content precisely because Quebec is part of the continental, metropolitan territory of Canadian imperialism, and because U.S. imperialism, the main enemy of all nations, of all humanity, lies along the entire length of our southern border, and seriously undermines the independence of *both* Canadian nations — the oppressed and the oppressor.

"These are the underlying reasons why the Communist Party of Canada fights for the unqualified right of the French-Canadian nation to self-determination up to and including separation. This is a principled, Leninist, position from which the Communist Party will not deviate, will not waver, or even appear to waver, lest we lose all chance of winning the confidence of the working people of French Canada, who will then have no reason to distinguish Anglo-Canadian Communists from run-of-the-mill Anglo-Canadian chauvinists.

"But while consistently and publicly upholding their *right* to separate, are we obliged to *advocate* that the French-Canadian people use their unquestioned right to decide their own future precisely in the way the Algerian people have done, even if this does not conform to the real circumstances in French Canada and to the interests of the working class?

"Decidedly not! For separation of Quebec under the present circumstances would do very grave harm to the economic and political interests of the working people, and *could* throw both nations into the suffocating embrace of different sectors of U.S. imperialism."

IV. FOR A RELATIONSHIP OF EQUALITY

Having established the option which we advocate for the exercise of the right of self-determination for French Canada, we have considered how this option might best be achieved in the complicated political situation which we have described earlier in this presentation.

As our Policy Statement says, "Experience has shown that the present federal-provincial framework makes negotiations on an equal basis between the two nations impossible."

A NEW CONSTITUTION FOR QUEBEC

The Statement continues, "Hence the 20th Convention of the Communist Party of Canada reaffirms the party's support for the demand of the Communist Party of Quebec advanced in September 1967 for the adoption of a Quebec Constitution which will establish Quebec as the sovereign national state of the French-Canadian nation and will assert control by the government of Quebec of all the political, economic, social and cultural powers necessary for the flourishing of the French-Canadian nation, wiping out of all special privileges for the English-speaking minority, but prohibiting any discrimination against it or against immigrants who choose to become part of it."

The Communist Party of Quebec has not been alone in the advocacy of such an approach, and we are pleased to see that it is again being taken up by public men in other parties. For example, Marcel Masse, a former minister in the Union Nationale government is quoted by the *Montreal Star* for Jan. 19 as stating to the Richelieu Club in Montreal that "Quebec's position within the Canadian community can best be determined by Quebeckers themselves. This can be achieved by giving Quebec its own constitution ... 'Quebec must affirm the conditions of its participation within the Canadian community, and with its own constitution', declared Mr. Masse." Although we have many differences with Mr. Masse, we welcome this statement.

The proposition for a new Quebec constitution, as advanced by the Communist Party of Quebec, is neither a proposal for some variation on the outworn theme of "special status", nor is it a proposal for the establishment of an independent state.

Our Policy Statement makes this clear. It says: "Having thus established sovereign control over their own state in the matters of vital national interest, the people of Quebec will be in a position to compel negotiations as equals with representatives of English Canada to work out a new Confederal Pact, a new Constitution for Canada.

"Such a Constitution can achieve unity only it if recognizes that

Canada is composed basically of two nations each having the right to self-determination, to political sovereignty, up to and including the right to separate if the majority of one or the other nation so desires. The representatives of the two nations will have to decide voluntarily what aspects of foreign relations, defence, customs, immigration, money and postal matters should be turned over to a confederal government together with the tax resources to sustain them."

Clearly, the representatives of the two nations would have to reach mutual agreement not only on the jurisdiction but also on the structures of such a new confederal government. It is difficult to foresee at this stage the exact form of such structures, but certainly they would have to eliminate forever the possibility that on any question the Anglo-Canadian majority could impose its will on the French-Canadian minority.

POSSIBLE NEW STRUCTURES

We did suggest in our Policy Statement the following possibility:

"We propose a confederal republic with a government consisting of two chambers: one, such as the House of Commons today, based on representation by population; the other, to replace the present Senate, to be composed of an equal number of elected representatives from each of the two national states. Each chamber should have the equal right to initiate legislation, but both must adopt the legislation before it becomes law. This structure will protect both democratic principles: equality of rights of nations whatever their size, and majority rule."

Our Policy Statement said:

"For English Canada a new Constitution such as we propose will make it possible to mitigate the regional inequalities which result from the inability of the Atlantic and Prairie provinces to tax the big corporations centered in Ontario which draw their profits from the exploitation of the country as a whole. It will make it possible to unify and centralize social legislation in all of English Canada without transgressing on the sovereignty of Quebec and on the national sentiments of the French-Canadian people. It will reassure all provinces that the great corporations will not be able to escape responsibility for establishing equal opportunities throughout English Canada in education, living standards, social welfare legislation. It will become possible to achieve high uniform standards of education with due regard for needed regional emphasis in all of

344

English Canada. Above all, it will strengthen the bonds of solidarity of the working people of both nations."

To sum up this argument in support of the course of action which we advocate, in the words of our Policy Statement:

"The growing disunity between English and French Canada can only be reversed if its causes are removed. These lie not in cultural, language or religious differences, but in the national oppression and inequality practised in daily life for centuries and enshrined in the British North America Act.

"A new Constitution such as suggested will lay a solid foundation for united resistance to the domination by U.S. imperialism of our economy, our political life and our foreign policy and the consequent erosion of our Canadian identity."

IT IS NOT YET TOO LATE

But then in our Statement, which was written two years ago, we sounded a note of warning:

"Time is running out. If the Canadian people of both nations permit the establishment's Trudeau government to continue very much longer with its hard-faced policy of non-recognition of the French-Canadian nation, there will inevitably be very serious consequences, the forms of struggle being impossible to foretell at this time."

The truth of that warning has been fully borne out by subsequent events, and we must repeat it now again in the same terms, but with even greater urgency.

Have the actions of the federal and Quebec governments during and since October now made the separation of Quebec inevitable? Is it now too late to think in terms of any other outcome? This is a question which must in all honesty be asked.

Our reply, which takes into account the thinking of many public spokesmen in the democratic movements of Quebec, which takes into account especially the viewpoint of the labor movement, is "No. It is not yet too late." It is still possible to repair the grave damage that has been done. The labor and democratic movements of French Canada are uniting with forward-looking Anglo-Canadian Québecois to seek to repair it.

But if the federal government and its sycophants in Quebec continue stubbornly along their present line, and if the people of English Canada do not reject this line, we will reach the point of no return — that point where the very real disadvantages of separation will be outweighed by a relationship that has become finally and completely intolerable.

We again commend to your Committee the recommendations we have made in this submission, as measures which could make a profoundly significant contribution toward opening the way for the negotiation of a new confederal pact on the basis of complete equality between our two nations.

V. CONCLUSION

In conclusion:

We are quite well aware that there are deep differences between our party and yourselves with respect to the long-term goals which we advocate.

But we are primarily dealing here with the search for solutions to a great democratic problem upon which agreements can be reached between socialists and non-socialists providing they are consistent democrats.

We are convinced that it is possible, given a truly democratic outlook, for the people of this country on both sides of the Ottawa River to join in common efforts for the realization of their aspirations.

We have been compelled to stress in this submission the difficulties, the problems of national oppression and inequality which have weighed so heavily on Canada's past. But there are brighter pages in our history suffused with the spirit of democracy and of solidarity of the peoples of two nations.

We would recall from our past, as challenges to all of us today, these two statements:

A letter from Louis Joseph Papineau sent March 15, 1836 in the name of the Lower Canada Assembly to that of Upper Canada in which he wrote of "the earnestness with which we are endeavoring to secure the establishment and recognition of the political rights of our colonial fellow-subjects as well as of our own. To whatever extent the blessings of a just, cheap, and responsible system of government are obtained by us, to that extent and amount will the people of the British North American colonies participate in the same blessings."

And the Declaration of Toronto Reformers in July of 1837:

"That the Reformers of Upper Canada are called upon by every tie of feeling, interest and duty, to make common cause with their fellow citizens of Lower Canada, whose successful coercion would doubtless be in time visited upon us, and the redress of whose grievances would be the best guarantee for the redress of our own."

ADDENDA

DECLARATION DU PARTI COMMUNISTE DU QUEBEC SUR LE MEMOIRE DU PCC A PRESENTER AU Comité spécial mixte du Sénat et de la Chambre des Communes sur la constitution.

Le Parti Communiste du Québec est un organisme distinct ayant le contrôle complet, au Québec, de sa politique et de ses structures. Reflétant le caractère binational de la classe ouvrière du Canada, le PCQ fait partie du Parti Communiste Canadien.

Nous sommes pleinement d'accord avec la politique du PCC vis-à-vis une nouvelle constitution pour le Canada, car cette politique se base sur les propositions suivantes:

1. L'AABN ne peut pas servir de base pour une nouvelle constitution, car il sert de cadre constitutionnel pour l'oppression de la nation canadienne-française.

2. Une nouvelle constitution canadienne doit avoir à sa base le droit à l'autodétermination et l'égalité des deux nations.

3. Le rejet de l'option séparatiste comme étant nuisible à la situation économique et sociale des Québecois et à l'indépendance canadienne de l'impérialsme américain.

4. Affirme que l'unité canadienne offre les meilleures conditions pour la lutte conjointe des deux nations pour une meilleure vie, pourvu que cette unité soit librement consentie.

5. Accepte la proposition du PCQ pour une constitution pour le Québec servant de base pour la négociation, sur un pied d'égalité avec le Canada Anglais, d'une nouvelle constitution canadienne.

Samuel J. Walsh, président

10 mai 1971

Submission to the Standing Committee on Finance, Trade and Economic Affairs, House of Commons, Ottawa from the Communist Party of Canada

June, 14, 1973

The issue of foreign investment and of foreign ownership and control, has plagued this country for many years.

We have been told time and again, that without foreign investments the economy would collapse, unemployment would rise, living standards would decline. Behind these myths foreign investments, in particular U.S. investments, have grown to fantastic proportions. Sixty-one per cent or more of Canadian industry is foreign owned, and in some sectors of the economy, there is 80 to 100 per cent foreign investment and ownership. Not satisfied with achieving control over decisive sectors of the Canadian economy, U.S. interests, and others too, are now encroaching more and more on Canadian land. Foreign investment and ownership have never prevented unemployment and stagnancy in the economy.

Rather than diminishing, foreign investments, ownership and control, are growing. They have been growing not only through direct investments but increasingly through the use of Canadian capital through profits accumulated in Canada out of the hides of Canada's working people. *Foreign Direct Investment,* which has been published by the Government of Canada, states on page 26 that "over 60 per cent of the financing for the expansion of foreign-controlled firms in the 1960-1967 period came from sources in Canada." The fact is that 94 per cent of investment by U.S. subsidiaries in Canada is carried out by using profits, dividends, retained earnings and tax reserves, all acquired in Canada.

The implications are self-evident. The foreign-controlled sectors of the Canadian economy will continue to grow, even if new outside capital is cut off or comes to an end. It exposes the false claims of those who say foreign investment is essential for Canada's economic growth and employment. Canadian capital is being used to strengthen foreign ownership and control. What growth there is, is growth of foreign ownership and profits.

A second feature which should be noted is that foreign investments have led not to gains but to losses for Canada.

In the period of 1960 to 1969 new U.S. investment in Canada totalled $5 billion. But the corporations received $6.25 billion back in the form of interest and dividends, plus $1.75 billion in royalties and fees. This resulted in a net loss to Canada of $2.5 billion.

One of the conclusions which can be drawn from this one-sided benefit to the U.S. corporations is that U.S. imperialism pursues an imperialist and neo-colonialist policy toward Canada somewhat similar to that which it pursues toward the Latin American, Asian and African countries, despite the claim to the contrary of Prime Minister Trudeau. This can be seen from the *Globe and Mail* report (March 23, 1973) of a press conference statement made by Mr. Peter Flanagan, executive director of the President's Council:

"Confirming the concern of Canada and other major U.S. trading partners, Mr. Flanagan said the United States wants to turn its worldwide merchandise trade deficit — estimated to be $6.8 billion in 1972 — into a surplus. He said the United States requires a $9 billion trade balance swing that would give it a surplus of about $2.4 billion in order to balance the outflow of U.S. dollars for military and foreign aid."

Moreover, foreign investment has brought with it interference in Canada's trade with other countries, a decline in technological development, cultural domination, and infringements of Canada's sovereignty. The structure of our economy and the priorities of our industrial development are in large part determined by corporate decisions taken in another country which reflect the needs and interests of these trans-national corporations and the economic, political and foreign policy positions of the particular foreign government. Canadian economic development is determined, not by what is good for Canada, but by foreign investors. By their enormous economic and political power, which often supersedes that of the country in which it is situated, trans-national corporations constitute a direct menace to the sovereignty and independence of Canada. They are able to switch exports from country to country, close down plants at will, shift production from one country to another, thereby arbitrarily creating unemployment. Canadian working people have already felt the full effects of this arbitrariness in plant close-downs and unemployment.

It is inevitable that foreign ownership and control over the economy or segments of the economy, carries with them intervention by foreign-owned firms into the policies and politics of the host country, both directly and indirectly. The authors of the Government of Canada's publication *Foreign Direct Investment in Canada* were sufficiently concerned about this that they listed six different degrees of possible intervention [see pages 300 to 305, under sub-head *The Behavior of Foreign Controlled Firms (Inputs)*].

That the issue of foreign investment and of foreign ownership, is thus of crucial importance for the Canadian people is further emphasized in light of the growing pressures by the U.S. administration on Canada's energy reserves, the proposed James Bay development and MacKenzie River Valley Pipeline, and Canada-U.S. trade negotiations. The U.S. government not only wants Canadian oil and gas, uranium, coal and water and power resources. It wants Canadians to give up their sovereignty and to subordinate Canada and its resources to the interests of the giant U.S. corporations and U.S. foreign policy.

This is why the overriding issue of strengthening sovereignty and achieving true economic independence is of major urgency in Canada today.

Does the proposed Foreign Investment Act come to grips with this question? In our view it does not.

It is of course true to say that under pressure of public opinion the Act has been extended to include not only the screening of foreign takeovers of Canadian firms but also the review of new foreign enterprises in Canada, and the expansion of existing foreign companies into "unrelated fields". From this standpoint only it is a step forward.

However, on the essential question of foreign ownership and control and its implications for Canada, the Act is totally inadequate. The screening device will do absolutely nothing to end U.S. control or that of trans-national corporations over the Canadian economy. Indeed, the Act fails to come to grips with foreign control. There is nothing in the proposed legislation which relates to foreign control over Canada's basic resources, or which proposes to restrict or end foreign control. And yet this issue is of greater urgency than that of takeovers, important as this question is.

The main thrust of the Foreign Investment Act appears to be to direct foreign investments to certain areas deemed important by

350

the government. Indeed the Act is not intended to put a stop to foreign takeovers of Canadian firms; its aim, rather, is to create a mechanism with which and through which the government hopes to strike a bargain with the trans-national corporations regarding the terms of sale of natural resources and takeovers.

Clearly, what is intended is that the "benefits from foreign investment be increased". This is the sum and substance of the proposed Foreign Investment Act. In short the "fast buck technique" to organize a better sale of Canada is to be improved upon.

Even if foreign takeovers of Canadian firms were stopped, this would not change the situation in any fundamental way. This is so because foreign control of domestic industry would continue due to foreign reinvestment in Canada. Thus, to halt the growth of the foreign-controlled sector of the Canadian economy requires not only that takeovers be stopped but that effective measures be taken to deal with foreign investment and foreign ownership. This again, the proposed Act does not do.

For these reasons the Communist Party of Canada sees no value for the Canadian people in the Act as presently formulated.

It should be pointed out that the Communist Party is not against foreign investments per se, providing they can be proved useful to the Canadian people and do not impinge on the sovereignty and independence of Canada and its people. Foreign investment in the form of loans is one thing, and equity capital is another. What we oppose is foreign ownership and control of any part of the Canadian economy, including the land. This applies not only to U.S. ownership which is dominant but to British, Japanese, West German and any other foreign ownership and control as well.

The argument will be advanced, as it has in the past, that Canada needs foreign investment and that without it the economy will falter. This appears to be the positon of Messrs. Bourassa, Davis and Barrett (an interesting political trio, to say the least).

How true is that argument which was used for many years to open the door to the "sell-out" of Canada? It is not true at all. There are enormous sums of Canadian capital invested in the USA and in other countries, not to speak of huge sums of monies in Canada itself, all of which must be made use of for all-sided and balanced economic development of the country. Moreover there are the enormous assets at the disposal of the government.

This is being emphasized by more and more spokesmen for business and government. Mr. Gillespie, Minister of Industry,

Trade and Commerce, told this Committee that "Canada, as a measure of increasing maturity, is much less dependent upon long term capital flows." The *Gray Report,* on page 12, makes the same point when it states that "Canada's anticipated savings rate will be entirely or almost entirely adequate to meet Canadian capital needs." These views are further emphasized by Mr. John E. Toten, vice-president for planning and economics of the Bank of Montreal who stated he did not think Canada would require a large inflow of capital from abroad.

We can already draw some conclusions from what has been said above:

1. Foreign control is growing in Canada. Moreover, to the picture of massive U.S. domination there is now added growing Japanese and West German control.

2. The growth of foreign control comes largely from Canadian capital. Canadian capital is being increasingly used to fasten the noose over Canadian sovereignty and independence.

3. Foreign investments, rather than assisting Canadian development, are creating a lopsided situation, aggravate regional disparity, impinge on Canadian sovereignty and, not least, lead to net losses for Canada.

4. There is no lack of Canadian capital for development.

5. The proposed Foreign Investment Act will not end U.S. control or limit it in any way.

Clearly, the central issue is that of Canadian control — this is the heart of the question before the country. Foreign control can only be eliminated by establishing Canadian control.

How can this be achieved? In our view there is no other way except through public ownership, whether in the form of Crown Corporations or in some related way.

There are others, like the Committee for an Independent Canada, which also opt for Canadian control. Their conception of Canadian control is that ownership be placed in the hands of Canadian monopoly interests rather than in the hands of U.S. or other foreign corporations.

However, the record of the past and of the present, makes unmistakably clear that monopoly interests in Canada will never defend the true national interest and genuine Canadian independence. Their motive, first, last and always, is profit, come where it may. It is with this in mind that they sold and continue to sell the natural resources of our country and consummate takeovers by foreign interests. Their record today with regard to natural resources and energy suggests they will continue to make deals and bargains at the expense of Canada's true interests. Canadian control for them means increased profits through increased exploitation of the Canadian people.

Furthermore, genuine Canadian control will not be achieved through Canadian directors on U.S. and other foreign-owned corporations. The principal beneficiaries of such "control" will be a handful of directors with fancy titles and increased incomes.

For Canada it changes nothing. Foreign ownership remains, foreign control remains, decisions contrary to the real Canadian interest remain. Further concentration of wealth and power in the hands of a small minority of Canadian monopolists will not benefit the Canadian people. Rather, such a concentration of power and wealth will constitute a threat to democracy.

Mr. Kimber, president of the Toronto Stock Exchange, addressing the American Society of Corporate Secretaries in Vancouver, June 17th, 1972, put it on the line when he stated:

"American capital did not steal into Canada, behind our backs. We sought it largely and it is hardly appropriate for us to now scream 'rape'. If we are to call off the relationship we can expect some resentment from the other party. While we have the right to change the name of the game, we have no right to arbitrarily demand to be restored to our original position of uncompromised virtue."

It would of course have been useful were Mr. Kimber to say that the "we" he speaks about is the economic and political establishment in Canada, not the Canadian people, or political organizations such as the Communist Party of Canada that since 1947, when the fatal policy of integration was embarked upon, warned of the dangers it would hold for Canada. The Abbott Plan and integration was not imposed on a reluctant bride, on the contrary, influential circles of Canadian capital supported it based on the concept of cold and hot war which was at the heart of U.S. foreign policy. The Canadian people have paid dearly for this fatal policy. Canada has not been taken over by foreign arms, but with the eager compliance of the establishment for a fast buck. This policy is now in crisis, as is the cold and hot war pursued by U.S. governments.

Events have borne out the claim of the Communist Party that what is needed are new national policies of balanced and all-sided economic development, with the natural resources of our country being used as a basis for vast industrial development. All questions of foreign investment must be related to this central issue.

Any serious approach to the question of foreign investment must come to the conclusion that the way to end foreign ownership, control and domination, is by public ownership. Only public ownership under democratic control can assure that the benefits of Canadian resources will remain under the sovereign control of the Canadian people. Until this is acted upon the sell-out of Canada will continue and affect the jobs and living standards of the Canadian people, as well as Canada's ability to make its own decisions.

In light of the foregoing, the Communist Party of Canada proposes the following immediate steps:

(a) that the Act spell out fully and clearly the prevention of further takeovers of Canadian firms, the elimination of U.S. controls regarding Canadian foreign trade, the prevention of the close down of plants and layoffs of workers by the trans-national corporations in Canada, the mandatory development of technology in Canada.

(b) that the Act state clearly and categorically its intention to achieve Canadian control through public control and ownership of the key natural resources of the country and industries related thereto, including energy resources.

(c) that the government in consultation with provincial governments state unequivocally that foreign investments will from now on be restricted to loan capital only and secondly, that no foreign corporation or individual, who are non-resident of Canada, can purchase land in Canada.

While pressing for these immediate measures, we emphasize that the Communist Party's long-term aim is public ownership of the key industries, banks and credit system, communications and transportation system, which taken together provide the economic basis upon which to achieve a fully independent Canada.

All of which is respectfully submitted on behalf of the Communist Party of Canada.

Put the multi-nationals under democratic nationalization

Submission of the Communist Party of Canada to the Royal Commission on Corporate Concentration

November 11, 1975

The ramifications of the concentration of corporate power, both economic and political, are complex and varied. However, one basic factor is abundantly clear, namely, a veritable handful of huge corporations controls the Canadian economy from the extraction of natural resources, energy, manufacturing, transportation, distribution and, finally but not least, finance capital. Some examples, chosen at random, follow.

International Nickel (INCO) and Falconbridge produce 99 per cent of Canada's nickel. Four companies produce 88 per cent of Canada's copper. All of Canada's mining and smelting is carried out by nine corporate complexes.[1] The petroleum industry is concentrated in the hands of a few huge oil monopolies like Imperial Oil and Gulf Oil; they are so few they can be counted on the fingers of one hand.

Monopoly control extends into manufacturing. Three electrical firms, General Electric, Westinghouse and Northern Electric accounted for 44 per cent of the industry's sales.[2] Three huge American automobile companies have an almost unchallenged grip on auto production, while six or fewer companies produce 90 per cent of all farm machinery bought in Canada. The steel industry is virtually the preserve of Canada's three giant steel firms.

Transportation and communication is equally in the hands of the few. Canadian Pacific Investments and Power Corporation own virtually all of Canada's transportation industry, not including Air Canada and the Canadian National which are crown corporations.

The news media is highly monopolized. K.C. Irving owns all of New Brunswick's English language newspapers; Power Corporation owns most of Quebec's French language newspapers; Southam and Thomson are household names not only in the newspaper business but in the television and radio world as well.

Meat packing and food processing corporations such as General Foods, Burns Foods and Canada Packers through monopolization of the market are able to dictate the price of products they buy from the farmer and the price to the consumer. The marketing of food is another important source of high profit-taking. Loblaws, Dominion Stores, Steinberg's, Safeway and the Oshawa Group account for the great majority of the food sold in Canada.

Monopoly in production and the market place goes hand in hand with the existence of conglomerates. As already mentioned, nine important mining corporations control almost all of Canada's mineral production. Some of these mining conglomerates have diversified into fields unrelated to mining. Falconbridge is the mining nucleus for American-owned Superior Oil Co., Cominco is a subsidiary of Canadian Pacific Ltd. which has interests in all modes of transportation from airlines to railways (CPR), as well as steel, pulp and paper, hotels, oil and gas, pipelines, real estate, etc. Dominion Stores is a subsidiary of Argus Corporation which has extensive interests in iron ore production, farm machinery, pulp and paper and broadcasting.

Monopoly is growing at a rapid rate in Canada. Capital in Canada is becoming ever more concentrated. This can be seen even over such a short period of time as four years. In 1968 corporations with over $100 million in assets inçreased their total assets from 53.3 per cent to 57.7 per cent in 1971. Their share of sales increased from 24.3 per cent to 27.5 per cent during the same period of time.[3]

In 1974 the Abitibi Paper Company outbid Power Corporation's Consolidated Bathurst for control of the Price Company. Price is now being merged with Abitibi to make the newly enlarged company the largest pulp and paper company in the world. As a consequence of the takeover, Abitibi Paper's sales increased by 37 per cent from $403.5 million to $551.9 million. Its assets doubled from $425.1 million to $846.9 million and its profits increased from $55.32 million to $91.98 million.[4]

Last year three real estate developers merged into one huge monopoly now known as Cadillac-Fairview. This new monopoly is the second largest company in assets, and the largest in sales, in the real estate industry.

The period since 1971 has seen Canadian Pacific substantially increase its oil and gas interests; it has taken control of MacMillan-Bloedel, the second largest pulp and paper company and Trans-Canada Pipelines, the largest gas line operator in Canada.[5] And in June 1974 this huge conglomerate took over Canada's third largest steel company, Algoma Steel, and all its subsidiaries.[6]

In fact, it is the tendency of concentration of finance capital into fewer and fewer hands that is responsible for the creation of this Royal Commission. Had Power Corporation succeeded in taking over Argus Corporation it would have become a conglomerate rivalling Canadian Pacific in size and diversification.

Monopolization, diversification and the concentration of corporate economic power have certainly paid off. According to the *Toronto Star*, corporate profits reached an all-time high in 1973, amounting to a whopping $15 billion.[7] The bigger the corporation, the bigger the profits. In 1971 Canadian Pacific reported a net income of $63.7 million. Three years later it had *tripled* to $181.3 million.[8]

No serious examination of corporate power can be complete without examining the financial institutions. The holdings and power of Canada's financial institutions are more than comparable to Canada's largest corporations. For example, Sun Life Assurance Co. of Canada with assets of over $4.3 billion is Canada's largest life insurance company.[9] It is larger than all of Canada's mortgage and trust companies, yet smaller than the five major banks to which it ranks a poor sixth. Nevertheless it is larger than all of Canada's corporations with two exceptions — Bell Canada and Canadián Pacific Ltd. It has more assets than Imperial Oil and Ford Motor Co. of Canada combined. Its assets are greater than the combined assets of International Nickel and Stelco.

The concentration of capital can be viewed in another way. Canada has 18 corporate companies with assets of more than a billion and 23 financial institutions in the same category. The top five financial institutions are all chartered banks, namely, Royal Bank of Canada, Canadian Imperial Bank of Commerce, Bank of Montreal, Bank of Nova Scotia and the Toronto-Dominion Bank in descending order. The Royal Bank is the largest corporation of any kind in Canada with assets of almost $217 billion. *It is therefore five times bigger than the Sun Life Assurance Co. of Canada* which, as we have just noted, has more assets than any non-financial company in

Canada with two exceptions. In fact the Royal Bank is four times bigger in assets than Canadian Pacific Ltd. and three and a half times bigger than Bell Canada.

The concentration of corporate wealth and power becomes even more menacing to the public good when we combine the assets of the five largest banks and discover that they are two times greater than the combined assets of the next 25 largest financial institutions and two times greater than the combined assets of Canada's 30 largest companies. Huge as they are, Algoma Steel Corporation and Simpson's-Sears, Canada's largest merchandising company according to assets, are the smallest of the top 30 firms.

Financial power is concentrated in other ways as well, particularly through interlocking directorships. Both the Royal Bank of Canada and the Canadian Imperial Bank of Commerce have four directors each on Sun Life's board, while the Bank of Montreal has three. On the other hand no bank has a representative on the board of directors of the General Motors Acceptance Corporation. However, two representatives of this corporation are on the board of directors of the Canada Permanent Mortgage Corporation which is owned by the Toronto-Dominion Bank.

Most monopoly corporations have direct or indirect ties (often both) with Canada's five major banks. Canadian Pacific Ltd. and companies which it controls have very strong representation in Canada's three largest banks. It also has members on the boards of the other two. Power Corporation wields influence on all the banks but one — the Toronto-Dominion Bank. Its chief connections are with the Royal Bank and the Bank of Montreal.

U.S. corporations have their representatives on Canada's banks as well. For example, Falconbridge has four members on the board of directors of the Canadian Imperial Bank of Commerce, International Nickel sits on the boards of all the banks except the Royal Bank, Gulf Oil has three representatives on the Canadian Imperial Bank of Commerce, two on the Toronto-Dominion and one on the Bank of Montreal.[10]

As providers of huge amounts of credit, Canada's financial institutions, especially the banks, are the linchpins of corporate wealth and power in Canada. In the banks and financial institutions, finance capital and industrial capital merge as one. Through the banks vast quantities of Canadian wealth are concentrated in the hands of a closely-knit clique of the corporate elite.

An examination of inter-corporate ownership and inter-corporate directorships establishes a dangerously high degree of foreign, mostly U.S., ownership of the commanding heights of the Canadian economy. Representatives of U.S. corporations sit on the boards of Canada's banks. Interconnections exist between Canadian and U.S. monopolies as well. The president of Argus Corporation heads a conglomerate which collaborates with U.S. steel companies in the extraction of iron ore. In return a Canadian sat as a director of Avco Corporation, a huge U.S. conglomerate whose subsidiaries include large defence plants, radio and TV stations, a credit card system, land development, consumer finance and insurance operations. Indeed, Argus Corporation's preparedness to act as a middleman to ensure a supply of Canadian iron ore to steel plants in the United States represents a general agreement which exists between Canadian and U.S. monopoly. It conforms to what has been government policy since the implementation of the Abbott Plan in 1947.

In 1947 the book value of foreign direct investment in Canada was $2,986 million. American investment constituted 85 per cent of the total amount, or $2,548 million.[11] In 1973 foreign direct investment totalled $32,783 million, of which 79.4 per cent or $26,225 million was American.[12] In other words, in the last 26 years, foreign direct investment increased 11 times while U.S. direct investment increased just over 10 times. The decline in the U.S. share of foreign direct investment does not of course signify a decline in U.S. corporate influence. It is still decisive. What it does signify is that Japanese and European monopoly capitalists have improved their financial and political positions in Canada.

United States direct investment is also decisive in terms of where it is invested. In 1968, 58 per cent of all of Canada's manufacturing assets were owned by foreigners, mostly Americans. Foreign-owned firms accounted for 63.4 per cent of the profits, 55 per cent of the sales and 62.4 per cent of taxable income. The greatest amount of foreign ownership was in natural resources (almost 100 per cent of oil and gas, 55 per cent of primary metals, 52 per cent of non-metallic minerals) and manufacturing (93 per cent of rubber products, 87 per cent of transport equipment and 81 per cent of chemicals and chemical products).[13] When other industries are taken into account, foreign interests constitute 61 per cent of the ownership of Canadian corporate assets.

It is important to note that since 1945 there has been a remarkable shift in the relative industrial distribution of U.S. direct investment in Canada. In 1945, 51.7 per cent of U.S. direct investment was directed to manufacturing, 6.1 per cent to petroleum and natural gas, and 9.3 per cent to mining and smelting. In 1967, the proportions were 43.5 per cent for manufacturing, 25.2 per cent for petroleum and natural gas and 13.5 per cent for mining and smelting.[14] In 1945 natural resources accounted for 15.4 per cent of U.S. direct investment; in 1967, the proportion was 38.7 per cent. The fact that 65 per cent of the 1971 capital inflows from the United States was directed to this sector would suggest that the percentage of direct investment has increased since then.[15] All of the foregoing indicates that U.S. imperialism, with the help of Canadian monopoly, is reducing Canada to an industrial backwater of the United States.

An examination of U.S. financial activity in Canada shows that Canadians actually finance the loss of their own economy. During the 1960-1967 period, $3,361 million of direct capital investment and $373 million portfolio investment entered Canada. In addition these same corporations between them remitted profit income to the United States to the tune of $5,869 million[16] for a capital loss of $1,865 million for that period. U.S. monopolies are buying Canada up with Canadian funds and making a profit besides.

Ownership of the commanding heights of the economy by U.S. monopolies creates distortions in the structure of the Canadian economy. Foreign ownership of Canada's natural resources has meant underdevelopment of the processing and manufacturing industries associated with them. This means fewer jobs for Canadian workers. The natural resource industry is not a good job-creating sector of the economy. It is capital intensive. In 1970 mineral production accounted for seven per cent of the GNP, but only 1.4 per cent of the labor force was employed in mining.[17] Clearly foreign ownership of the economy is detrimental to the creation of jobs in Canada.

The Canadian state is used as a vehicle for the implementation of the policies of monopoly capital. The state collaborates with the corporate elite in its efforts to maximize its control over the political, economic and social life of the country for the purpose of assuring maximum monopoly profits at the expense of the working people.

Monopoly dominates the state and the state is run for its purposes. The government's advisory boards, such as the Economic Council of Canada, consist mainly of the representatives of the monopoly corporations. Even the boards of the universities, hospitals and charity organizations are controlled by monopoly.[18] Government policy and monopoly policy are closely meshed. Both strive to create the necessary conditions for the making of maximum monopoly profits. In fact the make-up of this very Commission and of its legal advisors reflects the close affinity of the government and the corporate community.

In Canada, the monopoly corporations raise prices at will. They enjoy what amounts to an unrestricted right to make maximum profits. In this they receive government assistance in the form of subsidies, orders, contracts, tax allowances for depreciation, for the introduction of new production techniques, exploration and so on.

The federal government's present anti-inflation program is the latest example of the subservience of government to the interests of the monopoly corporations. While hypocritically presented as an attack on inflation, it will neither beat inflation, restrain price increases, nor stop monopoly profiteering. For it is not designed to do so. It is designed in the first place to guarantee monopoly profits and corporation dividends, at a time of deep economic crisis, through what in effect is an actual wage-cutting program.

We draw the attention of the Commission to the inflationary aspects of the expansionist drive for ever greater accumulations of capital by the industrial and financial corporations. The search for ever mounting cash flows to finance investment outlays on the latest technology has caused monopolistic price raising. This in turn has been financed by an expansion in the credit, provided at a rate far exceeding the growth in real output, which has unleashed an almost runaway pace of inflation. In general the speeding up of the scientific and technological revolution calls for such an increase in capital investment as to strengthen the tendency for finance capital to expand the whole credit structure in an inflationary way. This is one of the chief sources of the present inflationary spiral.

In examining the economic, political and social impact of the corporations, mainly U.S.-owned or controlled, on the Canadian community as a whole it is necessary to acknowledge the decisive role of the multi-nationals. It is well known that the multi-nationals, conglomerates, branch plants and subsidiaries are well entrenched in the commending heights of the Canadian economy. Consequently the corporations exert a decisive role in shaping the Canadian economy, decision-making and on the very lives of Canadian citizens. Indeed, the multi-national corporations are instruments through which U.S. imperialism exercises its domination over the Canadian economy. They are the Trojan horse of U.S. imperialism in Canada.

The power and spread of the multi-nationals make it possible for them to influence, directly or indirectly, the policies and actions of their "host" countries, even to the extent of placing these countries in dependent positions in their "home" countries. Canada is one of such "host" countries. This is one of the major questions which the Commission needs to face up to. For the impact of the multi-national corporations in Canada has placed in jeopardy the sovereignty of Canada. In addition, the multi-nationals interfere with our national priorities, distort consumption patterns, income distribution and redistribution of national income. They have the capability of affecting governmental monetary, fiscal and trade policies. They are able to develop into commercially viable products and processes the technological knowledge generated through government-financed research — finances taken from the public treasury raised through taxation of the people.

Taxation of the multi-national corporations creates many difficult problems such as: inter-country differences in tax rates, definition of taxable incomes and taxation principles, to mention only a few such problems. The decisive role of the multi-nationals involves equally wide problems for Canada's foreign trade. The same is true in respect to energy and the resources industry in general.

The corporations use their extensive power to attack the living standards, democratic rights and interests of the people. They raise prices at will, close plants and lay off workers at will, and generally pursue policies inimical to the public interest and the all-sided development of the Canadian economy. As a consequence the anti-monopoly classes and groups, in defence of their own economic and political interests, are compelled to fight back against the power of the monopolies much of which is wielded through state channels.

The small business and industrial enterprises are likewise victimized by the corporations as the concentration of capital proceeds apace. The economic viability of small and medium business and industrial enterprises, indeed their very existence, is threatened by the policy of accumulation followed by the big industrial and banking corporations. The increasing closures and bankruptcies of enterprises where concentration is relatively low are manifestations of a definite trend existing in the economy to oust small and medium ownership as a factor of reproduction.

Monopoly operates in agriculture as it does in industry. Financial and industrial monopolies control and exploit the agricultural economy. Land and capital tend to become concentrated in ever fewer hands. This tendency operates as well in the large urban centers where large corporations or their subsidiaries amass land banks large enough to influence land and housing prices in a scandalously inflationary way.

As a concession to broad public opinion and the pressure of certain Canadian financial interests, the federal government established the Foreign Investments Review Board to screen foreign takeover bids and mergers for the stated purpose of increasing the Canadian content of capital investment in the country. Unfortunately, the Review Board has not been able to check in any appreciable way the process of foreign mergers and takeovers.

There have been proposals advanced that the best way to combat the foreign-based multi-nationals and conglomerates is to build Canadian multi-nationals and conglomerates. While this road would undoubtedly be favored by certain circles of Canadian finance capital and monopolies, it would not serve the interests of the working people, farmers, professionals or the small and medium businessmen and industrialists. It would be like jumping from the frying pan into the fire. For this proposal begs the main question: whose interests are these huge concentrations of Canadian capital and property going to serve? Are they going to serve only the profit interests of the corporate elite? Or are they going to serve the interests of the Canadian community as a whole? This is the sixty-four dollar question.

Whether the big corporations are U.S.- or Canadian-owned and controlled, there are at present no adequate safeguards to protect the public interest from corporate concentration and avid profit-taking. The state must intervene to bring an end to this situation and assert sovereign ownership of these corporations and conglomerates. This is the way to uphold the public interest and the independence of Canada.

We propose that the recommendations of the Commission include measures that will begin the process of breaking up the multi-national corporations and to prohibit the operation of conglomerates in Canada. As a first step in this direction we propose that the Combines Act be amended to include measures to forbid mergers and takeovers which undermine (a) Canadian sovereignty, and (b) the public interest; failure to comply with such measures to be met by nationalization of the holdings in Canada of the participating parties.

We further propose that the Canada Development Corporation be authorized as a vehicle through which public ownership of those monopoly corporations which transgress Canadian sovereignty or the public interest are carried through.

We consider the foregoing proposals as only first steps toward the breaking up of the giants and super-giants of the corporate community. Government policy should be directed toward placing the monopoly corporations under strict Canadian ownership and democratic control, i.e., control bodies fully representative of the Canadian community, backed up with the appropriate government regulatory measures to protect the public interest. Failure to comply with such measures to be severely dealt with, up to and including nationalization of the property of the offending corporation.

We advocate nationalization of all multi-national corporations in Canada as a first step toward the nationalization of the banks, trusts, insurance companies and the credit system — to secure the necessary capital for the planned, balanced development of the economy under public ownership and control serving the public interest.

The Communist Party is not opposed to bigness as such. What we are concerned with is: who owns the bigness and whose interests does it serve? Centralization and concentration of capital into the hands of a small group of huge corporations, which in reality constitute a government within government, is an objective process under capitalism. The history of capitalism in Canada is development from laissez-faire capitalism and the free market, to monopoly and its control of the market, to state-monopoly capitalism. As Lenin correctly said: there is no going back to free-competition capitalism. From modern capitalism there is only one path and it leads toward socialism. Lenin had good reason to emphasize that "State-monopoly capitalism is a complete *material* preparation for socialism, the threshold of socialism, a rung in the ladder of history between which and the rung called socialism there are no intermediate rungs."[19]

The Communist Party urges the Commission to give serious consideration to the above proposals which we believe are vital to the process of Canadianization of the economy, and essential to Canada's independence, Canadian sovereignty and the well-being of the Canadian people.

REFERENCES

1. The big nine (9) mining monopolies are International Nickel, Falconbridge, Noranda Mines, Cominco, Teck Corp., Texasgulf, Anglo-American Corp., Rio

Algom Mines, Bethlehem. Abitibi Paper Co., the Sullivan Group, Argus Corp., Dome Mines, Johns-Manville and Denison Mines have substantial but considerably smaller interests.

2. *Report on Current Economic Conditions and the Electrical Manufacturing Industry in Canada*, Biennial Conference of the United Electrical, Radio and Machine Workers of America (UE), April 17-20, 1975, p. 34.

3. *Corporation Financial Statistics 1968-1971*, Statistics Canada, p. 11, Ottawa, 1973.

4. "Summary Review Service", April 8, 1975, published by *Canadian Business*.

5. *The CPR; A Century of Corporate Welfare*, Robert Chodos, pp. 122-123, James, Lewis and Samuel, Toronto 1973.

6. *Financial Post*, June 15, 1974.

7. *Toronto Star*, April 30, 1975.

8. "Summary Review Service", July 8, 1975, published by *Canadian Business*.

9. "The Top 200: Canada's Largest Companies", in *Canadian Business*, July 1975.

10. *The Directory of Directors*, 1975, MacLean-Hunter, Toronto.

11. *Canada's International Investment Position, 1926-1967*, Statistics Canada, September 12, 1975.

12. *Infomat*, Statistics Canada, September 12, 1975.

13. *A Citizen's Guide to the Gray Report*, prepared by the editors of *Canadian Forum*, p. 31. New Press, Toronto 1971.

14. *Direct Investment — Inflows and Outflows to Fourth Quarter 1971*, Foreign Investment Division, Department of Industry, Trade and Commerce, p. 1.

15. *A Citizen's Guide to the Gray Report*, p. 34.

16. *Silent Surrender*, Kari Levitt, p. 168. Macmillan Co., Toronto 1974.

17. *A Citizen's Guide to the Gray Report*, p. 19.

18. All derived from *The Directory of Directors*.

19. V.I. Lenin, *Collected Works*, Vol. 25, p. 359.

Submission to the Mackenzie Valley Pipeline Inquiry from the Communist Party of Canada

May 26, 1976

The Communist Party of Canada has given careful consideration to the questions your Commission is called upon to deal with on the basis of its terms of reference. As we understand it, it is one of determining the effects of a Mackenzie Gas Pipeline on the Native peoples, the environment and the ecology.

Underneath these questions is a more fundamental one, that of the future of the North. This includes the question of energy supplies for Canada in the foreseeable future, questions of ownership and control of these resources, the role the Native peoples should and must play in decisions affecting their rights, their livelihood and their way of life. It is with this in mind that the Communist Party of Canada advances its views on the pipeline.

1. The North, as has been said more than once, is Canada's last frontier. We need to made sure it does not become Canada's *lost* frontier by virtue of being taken over — lock, stock and barrel — by the U.S. multi-national corporations, in the same way they have taken over other parts of the Canadian economy, with the complicity of federal and provincial governments. If a similar "sell-out" takes place today, if U.S. imperialism through these multi-national corporations is allowed to control the energy and natural resources of the North, it will in fact control the whole of the Canadian economy.

The North, as we know, is rich in oil and gas. It also has tremendous resources of iron ore, copper and other precious minerals. These constitute important reserves for the further and future development of Canada. To deplete them now, apart from the major question of the rights of the Native peoples, problems of ecology and the environment, means to deplete them in the interests of the U.S. multi-national corporations, in the interests of industry in the USA, and not in the interests of Canada. Canada has other sources of energy at this time which can and should be used for its development and further industrialization. The present reserves of gas and oil can be left in the ground for future use *at a time and pace* that coincides with the best interests of Canada, her people and the peoples of the North.

2. It is this which determines our basic approach to the construction of a Mackenzie Gas Pipeline at this time.

Construction of such a pipeline should be held up until there is assurance of Canadian control and ownership of the pipeline and energy resources, and their use for Canadian development. Construction of the pipeline at this time would not serve the Canadian interest. It would serve the U.S. interest primarily. This is so because its main purpose would be to guarantee the wholesale export of Canadian resources to the USA. In this sense the construction of the pipeline by the Canadian people, at great cost to themselves, would be a form of subsidization of the USA. Alberta would become a corridor, like the Panama Canal, for the shipment of natural gas and oil to the USA, and all this guaranteed by Canada. The pretence that Canada could "shut the tap" later on if it wished to is so much nonsense. We have the experience of the Columbia River steal, and other sell-outs, to show this will not be the course of development. Once ownership lies in the hands of U.S. multi-national corporations, once the energy is used mainly to satisfy the U.S. market and becomes indispensable to the USA, it will mark the end of a Canadian resource and a Canadian asset.

3. What is involved here is not only the construction of a pipeline. The core of the problem is the development of the North and its resources — by whom, for whom, and under what conditions.

The myth is being spread that building a pipeline *constitutes* Northern Development. This is not so. A pipeline may constitute a part of Northern Development, but it is not basic to it.

The claim is being made that a Mackenzie Gas Pipeline would have an impact on Canada similar to the building of the trans-Canada railway system many years ago. This is manifestly false. The railways helped to unite Canada from the Atlantic to the Pacific. That was part of the concept of a "national policy" advanced by the then prime minister of Canada, John A. MacDonald, the aim of which was to build one market in Canada, help stimulate industrial development and protect it.

This is not the concept of the Mackenzie Gas Pipeline. Its primary purpose is to serve the USA, not Canada. It will move Alaskan gas to the USA and sell Canadian gas to the USA, and at a pace which will deplete this resource and prevent its use for Canadian development. Its aim is not the "national interest" but maximum profits for the multi-national corporations and their subsidiaries in Canada. The pipeline will not bring wealth to the North; it will siphon it away from the North and leave ugly scars in its place. No solid economic base is being proposed which will have permanent value to the North and its people. The North is looked upon as a hinterland, a supplier of raw materials such as gas, oil and minerals, a kind of colony — and not an area which ought to be developed in a way that will serve the North and its people and at the same time serve the interests of Canada and her people.

Where then is the comparison between a national policy which served to unify Canada, and a policy presently proposed which is geared primarily to serve the USA, not Canadian development? There is no comparison and those who try to make it so are guilty of hoodwinking the Canadian people.

4. Northern Development cannot be separated from recognition of the justness of the land claims of the Native peoples. The Native peoples have made it clear in their representation to your Committee, and in statements to the press and mass media generally, that they are not opposed to the development of the North. They want to establish their land claims first. They want to have a say over development of the North. They want to be the beneficiaries of such development, not its victims. They want to protect their culture, their identity as a people, their fishing and hunting rights.

All these are just demands which cannot and must not be ignored. Tokenism here cannot and must not substitute for recognition of these basic rights.

What must be established is the recognition by the federal government, and by provincial governments also, of the national identity of the Native peoples as distinct peoples. The government ward status must be abolished where it exists and full political equality established for the Native peoples, including their right to decide on all matters pertaining to their distinctive development.

The Dene Declaration which Mr. Judd Buchanan so cavalierly rejected, must not be ignored by the Canadian people. Mr. Buchanan sees it as a "separatist document" when in fact it is the expression of a distinct people who, due to historical circumstances, have not yet emerged to full nationhood. The task of the Canadian government, and certainly of all democratic Canadians, is to recognize this and draw conclusions from it.

The colonialist mentality toward the Native peoples was most crudely expressed by Mr. David Searle, Speaker of the House in the Northwest Territories, when he undertook a wholesale attack on them as a people. One is reminded of other Mr. Searles who tell us that "some of my best friends are . . ." What is evident from Mr. Searle's proposals is that he is prepared to do almost anything except get off the backs of the Native peoples.

Mr. Searle is quoted as saying "we are a sick, sick, society." How true. Only such a "sick society" and such a sick person could advance such a sick point of view.

It seems to us that with such an attitude Mr. Searle ought to retire as Speaker of the House in the Northwest Territories. He is unfit to hold that high office.

Unfortunately for the Northwest Territories there are other red necks around, holding similar views.

Is Mr. Buchanan so much better when he refuses to face up to the basic rights of the Native peoples?

The time is long past when the rights of a people can be ignored, set upon or spat upon.

In our Program, *The Road to Socialism in Canada,* a program we adopted November 27-29, 1971 we state:

"A socialist Canada will take meaningful measures to compensate the Native peoples for the historic injustices perpetrated upon them by the British and French colonizers in Canada and continued under the rule of monopoly capital. Such measures will include full recognition of their national identity and development of their native cultures; full power of decision making on all questions pertaining to their affairs as Native peoples; the rooting out of all vestiges of racism and discrimination, full equality before the law and in society; a massive economic and social program to bring their living, health, housing and education standards, training and job opportunities up to acceptable Canadian standards. The Indian and Inuit peoples will enjoy regional self-government and full rights to their language and culture" (page 62, *The Road to Socialism in Canada).*

We are convinced that only on such a basis can the national rights of the Native peoples, their identity, language and culture be guaranteed within the framework of a "True North Strong and Free."

We call upon the other political parties to end their evasiveness and ambiguity and clearly enunciate their positions with regard to the basic rights of the Native peoples.

(a) *The core of the problem is the necessity of a treaty with the Native peoples of the Northwest Territories* which clearly defines the question of development of the North, the role of the Native peoples in decision making, and all other questions pertaining thereto.

(b) The federal government which has complete control over Northern Development from the Yukon to the Northwest Territories must first of all come to a principled agreement with the Northern and Native peoples with respect to their national rights and land claims, as well as with due regard to ecology and environmental control, before in any way proceeding with a Mackenzie Gas Pipeline, a railway or other developments of a like kind.

(c) Such a principled agreement should include the recognition of the necessity of preferential treatment of the Native peoples. *Indeed it is only through preferential treatment that the Native peoples can be assured of equal treatment.* Any other approach would be discriminatory and downright harmful to the immediate and long-term interests of the Native peoples. Such preferential treatment should find its reflection in housing, education, medical services and in training programs. Such treatment must go alongside the guarantee of their rights as a people with respect to language and culture, including their right to have an effective voice on all questions having to do with Northern Development, and the protection of their vital interests. Moreover, nothing done by way of development must interfere with their hunting and fishing grounds. What must be established in principle as well is that the Native peoples receive priority in jobs and the right to highly skilled jobs based on adequate training.

As can be seen the debate around the Mackenzie Gas Pipeline raises questions much larger than the pipeline. The underlying issue involved is whether Canada shall continue the role of supplier and reserve of raw materials and energy for the USA, with its attendant regional inequalities under monopoly control, or strike out in a direction assuring Canadian development and control through public ownership.

The challenge before Canada is to reverse the trend of building up the industries of the USA with Canadian resources, and embarking instead on a course which could transform Canada into a great independent industrial state, pursuing an independent foreign policy and developing extensive and mutually satisfactory two-way trade with the socialist and newly-developing countries, including the countries of Latin America.

Canada needs an all-inclusive energy policy based on an inventory of energy resources. Such an inventory is essential before questions of exports of gas and oil can be considered.

Such an inventory is absolutely essential now when statements are made about an alleged shortage of energy. The National Energy Board blows hot and cold about shortages whenever it is deemed necessary to carry out certain objectives. Today we are informed of a shortage of energy so as to compel agreement by Canadians that prices should be raised with the benefits accruing to the multi-national corporations in the way of additional profits. Is there a shortage? No one really knows. But it seems more than coincidental that the alleged shortage has been announced just recently, precisely when decisions have to be made about a Mackenzie Gas Pipeline. Canadians should ask who is behind this claim of an alleged shortage and for what reasons.

In any case, be there a shortage or no, an inventory is required of all energy resources in Canada and the prospects of their utilization, so that Canadians know the scope of the problem and how to solve it. In point of fact Canada has no shortage of energy. It is one of those fortunate countries in the world which has an ample stock. It is also one of those unfortunate countries in the world in which this irreplaceable resource is in the hands of others, due to short-sightedness, due to the effort to make a fast buck at the expense of independent economic development of the country. Energy is too precious a commodity to be left in the hands of the multi-national corporations or under the sole control and ownership of this or that province. Energy is an all-Canadian resource which ought to be used for all parts of the country, for the benefit of all Canadians irrespective of where they live, and at a cost which would ensure continuing long-term development and growth.

To ensure this, these invaluable resources and assets must be taken out of the hands of the multi-national corporations and made public property. This is the only way to ensure they will be developed in the national interest.

A fully integrated all-Canadian energy policy based on public ownership under democratic control is therefore essential to the achievement of these aims and to balanced economic development, job opportunities, rising standards and Canadian independence.

In summary, the Communist Party of Canada proposes:

1. The land claims of the Native peoples must be resolved to

their satisfaction. This must be incorporated in a treaty with the Native peoples of the Northwest Territories;

2. Economic development in the Northwest Territories must be based on agreement with the Native peoples. This should include the question of a pipeline, railway system, protection of the environment and ecology of the North;

3. As part of any agreement, the principle of preferential treatment for the Native peoples must be clearly established.

4. It follows from the above that the Mackenzie Gas Pipeline should not be built at this time.